LEGAL TERMINOLOGY

ASPEN PUBLISHERS

LEGAL TERMINOLOGY

Robert J. Glidewell, J.D.

AUSTIN BOSTON CHICAGO NEW YORK THE NETHERLANDS

http://paralegal.aspenpublishers.com

Aspen Publishers
Attn: Permissions Department
76 Ninth Avenue, 7th Floor
New York, NY 10011-5201

To contact Customer Care, e-mail customer.care@aspenpublishers.com, call 1-800-234-1660, fax 1-800-901-9075, or mail correspondence to:

Aspen Publishers
Attn: Order Department
PO Box 990
Frederick, MD 21705

Printed in the United States of America.

1 2 3 4 5 6 7 8 9 0

ISBN 978-0-7355-7697-1

Library of Congress Cataloging-in-Publication Data

Glidewell, Robert J.
Legal terminology / Robert J. Glidewell.
p. cm.
Includes index.
ISBN 978-0-7355-7697-1
1. Law—United States—Terminology. 2. Law—Study and teaching—United States. I. Title

KF156.G58 2009
349.7301'4—dc22

2008038693

About Wolters Kluwer Law & Business

Wolters Kluwer Law & Business is a leading provider of research information and workflow solutions in key specialty areas. The strengths of the individual brands of Aspen Publishers, CCH, Kluwer Law International and Loislaw are aligned within Wolters Kluwer Law & Business to provide comprehensive, in-depth solutions and expert-authored content for the legal, professional and education markets.

CCH was founded in 1913 and has served more than four generations of business professionals and their clients. The CCH products in the Wolters Kluwer Law & Business group are highly regarded electronic and print resources for legal, securities, antitrust and trade regulation, government contracting, banking, pension, payroll, employment and labor, and healthcare reimbursement and compliance professionals.

Aspen Publishers is a leading information provider for attorneys, business professionals and law students. Written by preeminent authorities, Aspen products offer analytical and practical information in a range of specialty practice areas from securities law and intellectual property to mergers and acquisitions and pension/benefits. Aspen's trusted legal education resources provide professors and students with high-quality, up-to-date and effective resources for successful instruction and study in all areas of the law.

Kluwer Law International supplies the global business community with comprehensive English-language international legal information. Legal practitioners, corporate counsel and business executives around the world rely on the Kluwer Law International journals, looseleafs, books and electronic products for authoritative information in many areas of international legal practice.

Loislaw is a premier provider of digitized legal content to small law firm practitioners of various specializations. Loislaw provides attorneys with the ability to quickly and efficiently find the necessary legal information they need, when and where they need it, by facilitating access to primary law as well as state-specific law, records, forms and treatises.

Wolters Kluwer Law & Business, a unit of Wolters Kluwer, is headquartered in New York and Riverwoods, Illinois. Wolters Kluwer is a leading multinational publisher and information services company.

To Students

Summary
Table Of Contents

Contents

Preface

Striking a balance

As I pondered the idea of writing a textbook my first thoughts centered around creating a learning tool for my students. I began listening to their critiques about the textbooks we had been and were using and realized that I needed to strike a balance between text and exercises as well as a balance between technical language and a more informal, conversational style of writing. It was shortly after my text was accepted for publication I realized that I also needed to strike a balance between a textbook as a learning tool for students and also as a marketable product to instructors.

My overriding desire was still to achieve a more informal type of text, but doing so without losing the technical necessities that law requires would be a challenge. Some instructors will find the style of the text a little too informal and possibly incomplete or imprecise as to a definition or the context in which a term is used. In further discussing the text style with some gracious students who agreed to read some sample chapters and work the exercises I learned even more that convinced me to stay with a slightly informal style. A legal secretarial student and one court reporter who had enrolled in paralegal courses said something that should have been obvious: Enrollees in legal secretary and court reporter programs, who are the most common Legal Terminology students, don't need to dissect the nuances or technical definitions of legal terms. (S)He just needs to recognize the term and the context in which it is used, and be able to spell it correctly. A paralegal student will have the opportunity to analyze the technical nuances of a term in the upper level courses. "Just keep it a little on the lighter side" was the overall suggestion. "Don't scare off a good potential paralegal student by trying to teach them everything in the first course" was another comment. "The examples and the similar, different, and unusual 'cases' break up the dull flow of technical material" came from other students. I was somewhat surprised when several students nodded their head when one student said "the more exercises the better." I decided to stay with the informal style. They loved the summaries at the end of each topic.

The Flow

Students wanted to study criminal law first but I felt that the more accepted course of action was that civil litigation was the heart and therefore the starting point for learning law. Criminal law would come immediately after civil litigation to keep the interest of the students. It was necessary to transition to traditional civil law quickly to present the more common topics of common law that would be seen most frequently in civil litigation. By this point half of the text flow was decided upon. Business law, family law, and law and the government fell easily into place to complete the substantive topics to be covered. The last chapter was almost an afterthought as I simply consolidated the major aspects of a law office into one chapter as an insight for the student as to their future life.

Then came the problems. Evidence was a necessary topic to cover, as was bankruptcy, and constitutional law had to be covered specifically in criminal law and as a separate topic. I did not wish to dwell so much on each topic as to award each with a full chapter but they had to be included. The idea of the chapter appendix was adopted. Evidence would fit smartly in connection with civil litigation at the end of Chapter 3 and constitutional law in connection with criminal prosecutions fit at the end of Chapter 4. The appendices at the end of Chapters 10 and 12 require a little more rationale. I have always contended that corporations create more legal work than sole proprietorships and partnerships and should be the primary topic in Business Organizations but I knew that I could not forsake the other forms of business organizations. The appendix came to the rescue again. I was totally unsure as to what to do with Bankruptcy. The only slight connection to any other topic came from Secured Transactions, so there it fell.

I was tempted to put Wills, Trusts, and Estates in its usual place next to property. But that left Domestic Relations all by itself and a one chapter section seemed inappropriate. Having worked as a personal trust officer and trust counsel I knew full well that the easiest part of that job was handling the property disposition issues while the hardest part was dealing with the family members. The two chapters had their connection.

That left Administrative Law and Constitutional Law, which matched perfectly. All I needed was a title for that section. I simply succumbed to the one chapter section with Chapter 16 by process of elimination of all other chapters.

The Case Analysis

I found this case while researching legal issues in connection with the rewriting our college's Academic Integrity policy when I sat on the committee of the same name. I began using it as a class project in all law classes including Legal Terminology and Legal Environment of Business. I would read the facts to the students and allow them to serve as the jury informing me of their decision and rationale. Then I would read the appropriate parts of the appellate court decision to them. They were fascinated. They wanted to dissect the terms and clauses of the decision as they related to the facts (not to mention disagree with the decision). I now had my term project for my textbook. Reading an actual case that has over 60 terms found in the textbook that come from over half of the chapters would be an excellent exercise for the paralegal students to learn why so many different topics and terms of law must be learned in order to excel in a law office.

The Exhibits

A Summary Proceeding – This was chosen as more of a study guide for the student to quickly wrap up a topic. One student even referred to is as a "big flashcard."

Examples – Examples are used to offer the term in context and application. Almost all examples are either actual cases or closely patterned from actual cases.

The Latin Language – I rejected the idea of phonetically pronouncing every legal term at the suggestion of the students. They stated that they rarely, if ever, even look at the pronunciation. The students almost uniformly agreed, though, that Latin terms did need pronunciation assistance.

An Unusual Case – Some of these involve legal cases but many do not. These are situations where some aspect of the legal topic being discussed is an "exception to the rule;" something slightly "out of the ordinary;" and sometimes present a lighter look at the subject.

A Different Case – These exhibits usually present situations that are contrary to the rule being discussed or have a similar term with a completely different meaning.

A Similar Case – These are few but they present terms and concepts that are used in two different context but retain the same meaning.

The Exercises

I was surprised when my group of test students did not clamor for multiple choice questions. When asked they explained that fill in the blank questions require them to look up the term rather than guess the correct answer and that they learned more by looking up the term and the context in which it was used. They found the Word Association/Matching to be challenging but both analytical and fun (especially when they got all the right answers). They also explained at this point that a glossary was mostly used as a shortcut to find the correct answer and that a lack of a glossary forced them to review more chapter content. Hence, there is no glossary.

Robert J. Glidewell

September 2008

LEGAL TERMINOLOGY

Section I

Practice and Procedure

Chapter 1

Introduction to Law and the Legal Process

Opening Statements

Our legal system exists to resolve disputes, which frequently arise between two individuals. This makes our system **adversarial** in that these two people are **adversaries**, or opponents represented by **advocates**, or attorneys. Legal disputes are not limited to two people, however. It is better said that there are "two *sides* to every story," but sometimes many more than two opponents. Take, for instance, a **class-action** lawsuit in which there are hundreds, and maybe thousands, of **plaintiffs** who have been injured by a product, and three **defendant** firms involved with the manufacture and sale of that product. When two sides need a dispute resolved there must be some basis – a set of rules and guidelines – for resolving that dispute. That is where the **law** comes in. The first question is, where does law come from?

Sources of Law

Common Law

Common law is a body of law developed over hundreds of years in England, even during the time England was part of the Roman Empire (hence, the use of Latin in the field of law). As cases were resolved, the judges, magistrates, and chancellors deciding a particular case would record basic information such as the facts, decisions, and reasoning and keep that information in written form. This collection of information produced **case law** or **precedent,** or in its simplest terms, a similar case that preceded the case you now have. Applying the precedent to the current case is the concept of **stare decisis,** which gives us continuity to the law. Case law, or precedent, continues to be a main source of law today.

Statutory Law

Statutory law is a body of law developed, or **enacted,** by the legislatures of both federal and state governments. Statutory law "codifies and modifies" common law. To *codify* simply means to put the law into **code** form. *Modify* means altering the common law principle of law, or adding new principles of law, according to the actions of elected representatives to the state and federal government. The results are called **statutes.**

An Unusual Case

Most states adopted common law as their first statute and stated in the statute that common law would be in effect unless otherwise modified by the code. Such a statute would serve as a "backstop," so to speak; if, as an example, a murder statute was declared invalid by a state court, there would still be common law murder concepts under which to prosecute the defendant. If a state no longer adopts common law and relies solely on legislative law, however, then that state might not have a way to prosecute for murder.

Constitutional Law

The federal government and each state government have one supreme concept of law, and that is a **constitution.** As the United States has a federalist form of government, the U.S. Constitution becomes the **supreme law of the land,** outranking all other forms of law.

Administrative Law

Administrative law is the procedural part of regulatory law. Here, we find the **regulations** of governmental agencies. It may be the fastest growing field of law that currently exists.

Executive Orders

Executive orders are directives from the **chief executive** of a state (i.e., the governor), or the nation (i.e., the President). These orders apply only to the governmental agencies and employees of the respective state or nation.

Treaties

Treaties are signed by two countries and control how the laws of each country will apply to each respective set of businesses and citizens. Treaties cover such things as international trade, for example, imports and exports, taxation of citizens of one country living in another, and **extradition** (i.e., when a criminal flees from one country to another).

A Summary Proceeding (1.1) – Primary Sources of Law

Common Law – Case law developed into precedent and applied by stare decisis

Statutory Law – Created by legislatures who codify and modify common law

Constitutional Law – The supreme law of the land

Administrative Law – The rules and regulations of government agency

Executive Orders – Directives of a chief executive of a state or nation

Treaties – An agreement between two countries as to the application of law

The student should realize that in addition to the previously discussed **primary sources of law**, there are also many **secondary sources of law.** These secondary sources include **legal dictionaries** and **encyclopedias**, as well as **Law Reviews** and **Law Journals,** which contain legal essays written by law students, law professors, and attorneys. A more thorough discussion of these sources of law will occur in Chapter 16 and in your Legal Research and Writing classes.

Classifications of Law

Civil Law vs. Criminal Law

Civil law involves individuals who have suffered an injury due to one or the other's wrongful actions, and both of whom have retained attorneys to resolve their disputes as to **fault** and **liability** through a lawsuit. This is known as the **litigation** process. **Criminal law** involves an individual who has committed a wrong against society and a **prosecutor,** a representative of the government, who seeks to **prosecute** and **punish** the individual for his/her wrongs. Civil law is a form of private law, whereas criminal law is a form of public law.

Substantive Law vs. Procedural Law

Substantive law is the law that decides who, or what, is right or wrong (i.e., guilt or innocence in a criminal matter or liability in a civil matter). **Procedural law** is the law defining the process of deciding who is actually right, wrong, guilty, innocent, or liable. It includes such actions as **notice** of the charges and the **opportunity to be heard** (i.e., having your "day in court"), as well as the rules for the hearing activities such as the presentation of evidence against you.

The Courts

Winding through the maze of courts in our country that comprises the **judiciary** or the **judicial branch** of the government can be perplexing, but regardless one must find the correct court in which to resolve the dispute for the resolution to be binding on all parties. Our court system is determined by one of the two basic forms of government that exist in the United States: the federal government and the state government. As you will see, there are similarities within each system but it must be recognized that each state establishes its own unique system of courts, with dramatic differences among them.

The Federal Court System

At the initial level is the **U.S. District Court**. In this court, trials are conducted to determine who wins or loses a lawsuit or prosecution based on the facts and law governing a case. Each state has at least one District court *within* the state. Larger, more populated states may have two, three, or even four federal District Courts, each defined by geographical area. A federal judge presides over a District Court.

The second level of courts in the federal system is the **U.S. Circuit Court of Appeals**. It is here that the losing party at the **lower court** level, except prosecutors, may appeal for a redetermination of the case based on the laws applied at the lower court level. Appeals courts do not retry the case as to **questions of fact**, evidence, and witnesses, but rather they conduct **appellate review** of any **errors of law** made by the lower court judge. The burden is usually on the **appellant** to provide **clear and convincing evidence** of an error, as the review of the case will be in a light most favorable to the **appellee**. Appeals courts usually use three-judge panels, but occasionally all appeals court judges in the circuit will sit to hear an appeal. In these instances, the court is said to sit **en banc**. The appeals court level is the primary level of written **opinions** for precedent, but in some instances a District Court may report the case for precedent. There are currently 11 territorial circuits, the District of Columbia Circuit, and the United States Court of Appeals for the Federal Circuit. Each state falls under one of the 11 circuits *for* that state's cases, but not necessarily *within* that state's borders.

Example 1.1:

Arkansas has two U.S. District Courts, the Eastern District and the Western District. Arkansas is in the Eighth Circuit Court of Appeals, which is in St. Louis, MO with a branch in Minneapolis, MN.

The highest court in the federal system, as well as in the nation, is the **U.S. Supreme Court**. Many cases are submitted to the Supreme Court but few are heard. This court is authorized by the **U.S. Constitution** and is impaneled with nine sitting **Justices** who sit en banc for all cases. The U.S. Supreme Court is the ultimate interpreter of the U.S. Constitution.

Finally, there is a level of **Specialized Courts** in the federal court system. These courts hear only specific types of cases. Two of these courts are the **Bankruptcy Court**, the other

Constitutionally derived court, which hears only bankruptcy cases, and the **U.S. Tax Court**, which limits its cases to tax matters under the Internal Revenue Code.

The State Court Systems

One of the two initial levels of state courts is the **Inferior Court** level. Some states call this the **Municipal Court** level, whereas others call it the **District Court** level. *Inferior* means that the court is not a **court of record.** This also means that the court does not keep an official **transcript** and has no **jury**. There may be separate court divisions such as Traffic, Criminal, and Environmental in larger metropolitan areas. If one loses at this level, the appeal, usually to a Circuit Court level, will be a **trial de novo**, which is a complete new trial. The appeal will be to a court of record, and your trial will start from the beginning as to evidence and witnesses. The higher court in this instance will not review the lower court's actions, as there is no record.

The other initial level of courts in most states is the **Circuit Court** level. Some states call this the **Superior Court** level. This is a court of record, and is the most frequent trial court level. Juries may or may not be used depending on the case presented. Most states have eliminated the old dual court system of Circuit Courts for **actions at law** and **Chancery Courts** for **actions in equity** by merging those courts into one system with varying divisions.

Next is the **Appeals Court** level, at which three-judge panels review the errors of law that may have been committed by the **lower court**. At this level opinions are issued that become precedent for lawyers within the state.

Reaching the top of the average state court system we find the **State Supreme Court**. Paralleling the federal system once again, most state Supreme Courts have seven to nine **Justices** who review cases while sitting en banc. This level provides the most important precedent as to that state's law.

A Different Case

The state of New York refers to trial courts as Supreme Courts and refers to appeals courts as either Appellate Courts or Courts of Appeal.

States also have a level of **Specialized Courts**. Included will be a **Juvenile Court** system to handle the legal matters of minors; a **Small Claims Court** system that allows for the adjudication of specified legal matters in **summary proceedings**, involving smaller sums of money without the formalities of higher courts; and a separate **Probate Court** for handling decedents' estates, guardianships for minors and elderly, and administration of trusts. Some states simply include the probate court with the Circuit Court level in a separate division.

A SUMMARY PROCEEDING (1.2) – THE COURTS

FEDERAL

U.S. District Court – Federal trial court level; at least one in each state

U.S. Circuit Court of Appeals – Initial appeals court level; one for each state; sits three-judge panels or en banc

U.S. Supreme Court – The highest court in the land; interpreter of the U.S. Constitution; sits en banc

Specialized Courts – Includes Bankruptcy and Tax Courts, which hear specific legal matters

STATE

Inferior Courts – District and Municipal level; not courts of record

Circuit Courts – Initial trial court level; hears de novo appeals from inferior courts

Appeals Courts – Hear appeals from Circuit Courts on errors of law; three-judge panels

State Supreme Courts – Highest court in most states; most important state law precedent

Specialized Courts – Small Claims and Juvenile courts; hear limited legal issues

Jurisdiction

Once you have familiarized yourself with the court system you must choose a court that has **jurisdiction,** or the authority to hear a case. If you choose the correct court, you have a **court of competent jurisdiction.** There are ten types of jurisdiction with which the legal professional should be familiar.

Subject Matter Jurisdiction

Subject matter jurisdiction can be discussed by separating the law into two major divisions: **law** and **equity**. Law matters include criminal prosecutions and civil litigation that involves monetary damages. Juries are available in actions at law. Civil litigation of equitable matters does not normally involve **monetary damages,** and these trials do not have juries. Actions in equity are for wrongs that cause **irreparable harm** that will not be satisfied by money award. This distinction is not as important for choosing a court as it used to be, however, because most states and the federal court system do not maintain separate courts for **actions at law** and **actions in equity**.

Example 1.2:

If you are involved in an automobile accident and sustain property damage and personal injury, you would file an action at law to recover monetary damages to reimburse you for your losses and costs. If your neighbor plays loud music that causes you to lose sleep, however, you are suffering irreparable harm for which money cannot compensate you. You would instead file an action in equity, which could provide you with the remedy of an injunction, or a court order for your neighbor to stop playing loud music.

General Jurisdiction

A court with **general jurisdiction** can hear many types of cases, whether they be law or equity matters. They can also hear all types of criminal and civil cases including, but not limited to, property disputes, statutory cases, regulatory cases, domestic relation cases, and contract disputes.

Original Jurisdiction

Courts with **original jurisdiction** will be the first to hear your case. Often, this is the trial court level that corresponds to the District Court in the federal system and the Circuit Court in most state systems.

Limited Jurisdiction

Courts with **limited jurisdiction** can hear only specific types of cases, such as bankruptcy, tax, small claims, and probate. In general, specialized courts have limited jurisdiction.

Exclusive Jurisdiction

Exclusive jurisdiction means that only one specific court can hear your case. Again, you can refer to bankruptcy, tax, and probate courts, because specialized courts also generally have exclusive jurisdiction. A federal court will have exclusive jurisdiction over federal cases brought under federal statutes or regulations and will have exclusive jurisdiction over issues under the U.S. Constitution.

Concurrent Jurisdiction

Concurrent jurisdiction means that two courts may have jurisdiction at the same time. For example, if a person murders a federal employee, the U.S. District Court could have jurisdiction and a State Circuit Court could assert **concurrent jurisdiction** under state murder statutes.

Amount in Controversy Jurisdiction

Amount in controversy jurisdiction means that there is a minimum or maximum amount involved in a case that the court may hear. Examples are the maximum amount, say $5,000, that a Small Claims court can hear, or a minimum amount, $75,000, which must be present before a U.S. District Court will assume jurisdiction under certain types of cases.

Appellate Jurisdiction

Courts of Appeals have **appellate jurisdiction** to review appeals. Lower courts normally do not have the authority to hear appeals except in the case of appeals from state specialized courts.

U.S. District Court Jurisdiction

U.S. District Courts have two basic types of jurisdiction:

1. **Federal Question Jurisdiction** – Legal cases arising from federal statutes, regulations, and the U.S. Constitution are federal questions and must go to the federal courts.
2. **Diversity of Citizenship Jurisdiction** – When citizens of two states are involved in a dispute and the amount is over $75,000, the U.S. District Court may assume jurisdiction. If such a case is filed in a state court, the defendant may petition to **remove** the case to federal court and it will automatically be removed. The plaintiff may petition the federal court to **remand** the case back to state court, but that will be done only at the discretion of the federal court.

A Summary Proceeding (1.3) – Courts and Jurisdiction

FEDERAL COURTS

District Courts – Original, general, subject matter, exclusive, concurrent, federal question, diversity of citizenship, and amount in controversy jurisdiction

Circuit Courts – Appellate and limited original jurisdiction (patent cases)

U.S. Supreme Court – Appellate and limited original jurisdiction over disputes between two or more states

Specialized Courts – Bankruptcy and Tax Courts – Limited and exclusive jurisdiction

STATE COURTS

Inferior courts – Original, limited subject matter, and exclusive jurisdiction

Circuit Courts – Original, general, subject matter, and concurrent jurisdiction

Appeals Courts – Appellate jurisdiction

State Supreme Courts – Appellate jurisdiction

Specialized Courts – Small Claims: Limited original, subject matter, and amount in controversy jurisdiction

Juvenile and Probate Courts – Limited and exclusive jurisdiction

Court Personnel

Judges and Justices

The figure with the most authority in a courtroom is a **judge**. A judge is said to **preside** over a court and is referred to as the **presiding judge**. It is his or her courtroom, and the judge makes the rules. Violating a judge's rule, whether you are an attorney, a witness, a spectator, or a party subjects the violator to a **contempt citation**. Citations for contempt are usually in the form of monetary fines but can also include being incarcerated. A judge is addressed as "your honor."

Federal judges obtain their position through an appointment process. The President nominates individuals for all federal judgeships, District, Circuit, and Supreme Courts, and the U.S. Senate has the power to confirm or deny each nomination. All federal judges serve for life. The only way to remove a federal judge from his or her position is by **impeachment**. State judges are usually elected for a term and consequently serve at the pleasure of the voting public.

Judges who sit on a Supreme Court, whether for a state or for the United States, are referred to as **Justices**. Each Supreme Court will have a **Chief Justice**, and the remaining Justices are referred to as **Associate Justices**. Supreme Court justices are addressed with the title "Justice."

A Different Case

The word "justice" is used in two different ways in the world of law. Justice is the title generally reserved for Supreme Court Judges; Justice is also the process by which the law resolves disputes.

Magistrates and Masters

Many judges and court systems maintain other figures who have judicial authority. Two such figures are **Magistrates** and **Masters**. Federal courts generally maintain magistrates for such matters as pretrial motions, hearings, and execution of warrants and subpoenas. Masters are generally considered "experts" or "fact finders" in some field of judicial activity. Frequently, a Master in Chancery hears uncontested divorce cases before directing the petitioner and documents to the judge. Masters can also be investigative in nature for complex litigation.

Clerks

The **court clerk** is the administrative manager of the court. He or she is responsible for managing the filings of the case, the records and transcripts, and service of process documents, and sometimes assists in managing the jury pool/jury selection information. The **county** or **circuit clerk** is an elected individual who is responsible for filing and recording functions of the judicial system. A **law clerk** is a recent law school graduate who researches law for a judge, usually an appeals court judge or justice.

Bailiff and Court Reporter

The **bailiff** is the law enforcement official of the courtroom and is responsible for maintaining order in the court. A **court reporter** is a licensed professional. His or her job is to record the courtroom proceedings to compile the **record.** Court reporters prepare **transcripts** of the courtroom proceedings for appeals.

A SUMMARY PROCEEDING (1.4) – COURT PERSONNEL

Judge – The presiding officer of a court
Justice – A Supreme Court judge
  Chief Justice – The presiding justice of a Supreme Court
  Associate Justice – An additional justice of a Supreme Court
Clerks of the court
  Court clerk – The administrative manager of a court for records and transcripts
  County/circuit clerk – An elected official for administration of the court system
  Law clerk – A recent law school graduate who researches for a judge or justice
Bailiff – The law enforcement official of a court who maintains order in the court
Reporter – A licensed professional who prepares transcripts of court proceedings
Master – A court "expert" or "fact finder" for expediting and investigation complex cases
Magistrate – A federal judicial official who conducts pretrial matters, hearings, and motions

Alternative Dispute Resolution

Before we proceed to civil litigation, it is imperative that the student understand that alternatives exist to filing a lawsuit to have the courts resolve a dispute. Lawsuits are time consuming and expensive; generally one party has to be the loser, and frequently the winner is less than excited over the award. Without **Alternative Dispute Resolution (ADR)** the court system would be even more clogged. Two forms of **ADR** are arbitration and mediation.

Arbitration

Arbitration is **final dispute resolution** that is considerably quicker and less expensive than litigation. A brief listing of the differences between arbitration and litigation follows.

In arbitration, the aggrieved or injured party submits a grievance or claim known as a **submission.** The party has approximately 30-90 days to file the claim after the injury occurs. Compare this to the concept of the **Statute of Limitations,** which gives plaintiffs 1-3 years to file many lawsuits. No lawyer is necessary to file an arbitration claim, lawyers are becoming involved in the process more frequently.

Once the party being claimed on is notified of the claims, each party will mutually agree on a panel of three **arbiters** or **arbitrators.** These three panelists will be experts in the field in which the arbitration is filed, and one may very well be an attorney.

The first "**hearing**" can frequently be a telephone conference call during which all parties discuss the timing and process that will be conducted. Each party may put in their request for documents, and time will be allowed for exchange of information. A follow-up phone call can be arranged to discuss the documents and issues for the formal hearing. Finally, a formal hearing takes place in front of the three arbiters, with evidence presented by both sides. The arbiters take the matter under advisement and usually issue an opinion within 30-90 days.

Arbitration can be **binding** in that appeals are very, very limited. Many industries are now requiring arbitration to avoid costly litigation. The Securities industry has **compulsory arbitration** for all matters involving brokers, clients, and employees.

Mediation

Mediation differs from arbitration in that it is not final dispute resolution, but instead is more **conciliatory** in nature. The mediator is a **neutral third party** who is versed in **conciliation**. Mediators are frequently used in employee–employer disputes; in labor negotiations to get unions and management talking at the contract bargaining table; and in domestic relations cases involving divorce, property settlements, and child custody issues. Many Attorney General offices throughout the United States offer consumer complaint divisions that attempt to mediate disputes between businesses and customers.

A Summary Proceeding (1.5) – Alternative Dispute Resolution

Arbitration – An alternative to a lawsuit that uses an expedited time frame and a panel of arbitrators who are experts in the field of the claim filed; a final dispute resolution method that may be compulsory and binding on the parties

Mediation – A conciliatory effort by a neutral third party who assists the parties in resolving their dispute; not a final dispute resolution method

Conclusions of Law

More important than just introducing the student to law and the legal system is the fact that learning about the law, as well as the law itself, is a process. First, we have to define the reason for law, and that is to finally resolve disputes so order can be maintained in our day-to-day lives. Next, we must study how law was developed and evolved; here, we discussed sources and classifications of law. Third we discussed where, or by whom, the law is applied, and that is the court system. Because the law itself is complex, however, the court system has become complex. We must therefore make sure we have the right court with jurisdiction, or the authority to hear and decide a case. We also learned that there are individuals within the courts that cause the process to occur. Finally, we saw that a lawsuit is not the only way to formally resolve a dispute, as there are ADR methods.

The Latin Language

Below are the phonetics of the Latin terms and phrases used in Chapter 1.

Stare Decisis – *stair*-ee dee-*sayh*-sis

En Banc – ahn bonk

Trial de novo – trial duh no-vo

Exercises – Chapter 1

True/False Correction Determine if the statement is true or false; if false, insert the correct term in the blank below the question for the term in bold to make the statement true.

_____ 1. A U.S. District Court has **limited** jurisdiction.

_____ 2. Stare decisis is the application of **precedent**.

_____ 3. Administrative law consists of **statutes**.

_____ 4. Executive orders apply to the **general public**.

_____ 5. In civil cases defendants are found **guilty**.

_____ 6. A **prosecutor** represents the government and society.

_____ 7. **Substantive** law includes notice and opportunity to be heard.

_____ 8. **Inferior** courts are courts of record.

_____ 9. A **small claims court** has amount in controversy jurisdiction.

_____ 10. The law enforcement official in a courtroom is a **master**.

Definitions Insert the correct legal term in the blank above the definition.

1. ______________________________

   A neutral third party who assists in the resolution of a dispute

2. ______________________________

   Alternative dispute resolution that is required within an industry

3. ______________________________

   The period in which a plaintiff must file a lawsuit

4. ______________________________

   The person within a court that prepares a transcript

5. ______________________________

   The penalty for violation of a judge's rules

6. ______________________________

   The term for a U.S. District Court sending a case to a state court

7. ______________________________

   The court that hears legal issues of minors

8. ______________________________

   The type of jurisdiction in which two courts may hear the same case

9. ______________________________

   A legal action to recover monetary damages

10. ______________________________

    The supreme law of the land

11. ______________________________

    The result when found guilty of a crime

12. ______________________________

    A secondary source of law for definitions of legal terms

13. ______________________________

    The type of law made by legislatures

14. ______________________________

    Two opposing parties in litigation

Word Association/Matching Match the term in the left column with the most appropriate term in the right column.

_____	1. regulations	A. lawsuit
_____	2. chief executive	B. federal statute
_____	3. law review	C. administrative manager
_____	4. civil litigation	D. new trial
_____	5. class action	E. supreme court judge
_____	6. specialized court	F. law journal
_____	7. federal question	G. supreme law of the land
_____	8. magistrate	H. injunction
_____	9. court clerk	I. return of criminal
_____	10. submission	J. U.S. Tax Court
_____	11. trial de novo	K. decedents' estates
_____	12. U.S. Constitution	L. legal encyclopedia
_____	13. probate court	M. administrative law
_____	14. equitable remedy	N. case law
_____	15. compulsory	O. court expert
_____	16. justice	P. federal judicial officer
_____	17. extradition	Q. multiple plaintiffs
_____	18. precedent	R. required
_____	19. secondary source	S. arbitration claim
_____	20. master	T. governor

List/Fill in the Blank List the six sources of law:

1. ______________________________

2. ______________________________

3. ______________________________

4. ______________________________

5. ______________________________

6. ______________________________

List five types of jurisdiction of a federal district court:

1. ______________________________

2. ______________________________

3. ______________________________

4. ______________________________

5. ______________________________

List two additional terms for precedent:

1. ______________________________

2. ______________________________

List three types of clerks in the court system:

1. ______________________________

2. ______________________________

3. ______________________________

Chapter 2

Civil Litigation – Pleadings and Pre-Trial

Opening Statements

Although many attorneys never appear in court for **litigation** reasons, the perception is that the practice of law consists of suing people and going to court for trials. Litigation can be considered the ultimate application of the law, so it will be discussed first. A brief look at the process in advance of the discussion will help the student maneuver through the activities of this topic.

A Summary Proceeding (2.1) – Pleadings and Pre-Trial

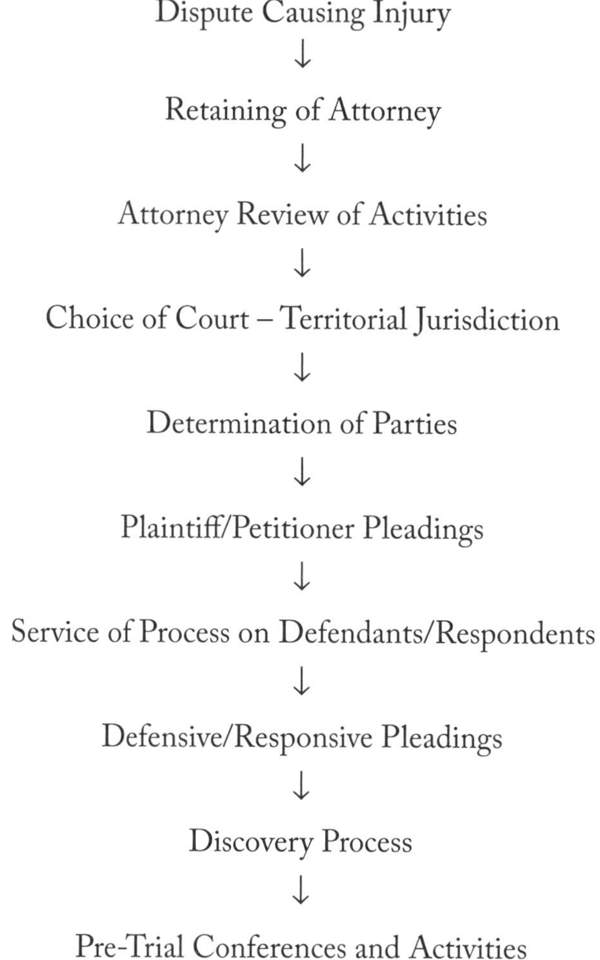

Initial Activities

In a typical dispute, one or both parties feel they have been wronged by the other and that the other should pay for that wrong; they usually end up in a lawyer's office, wishing to sue. These parties seek to **retain** an attorney for the purposes of **litigation**. Frequently, the injured party will first talk to a paralegal. It will be the paralegal's job to obtain sufficient information for the attorney to determine if an injury has occurred and whether or not there is a **cause of action** after discussion of the dispute. A cause of action is a legal reason to sue or **file suit**. It is a reason that the law has recognized as a grievance, which can be redressed by a court. Note that small amounts of damages may not be appropriate for suit.

Initial Interview

The initial interview must obtain the **facts** of the case. An important fact is when the injury occurred, because an **aggrieved party has** only so long after the injury to institute litigation. This concept is known as the **statute of limitations**, and the length of time one has to sue depends very much on the cause of action. Statutes of limitation may also **toll,** or not **run**, depending on certain facts such as concealment of a wrong by the defendant or the absence from the state of a criminal defendant. In actions in equity, the period of time in which filing must occur is called **laches** and is not as specifically defined in terms of length of time.

Conflict of Interest Check

Before agreeing to take a case, the attorney must investigate a few other things, based on the information obtained from the paralegal and the client. First would be a **conflict of interest** search or check. Has the attorney or the firm possibly represented the other party at some time in the past? If so, does the attorney have in his/her possession material and adverse information about the other party that could affect representation of the new client? If either is true, the attorney must decline the case.

Example 2.1:

You visit Attorney Adams with the desire to sue Mr. D for damaging your car in an accident. Attorney Barnes, Adams' partner, previously represented Mr. D in a divorce action and has details about Mr. D's driving record. Attorney Adams should refuse to take the case because of a conflict of interest.

Fees

If the attorney feels the case is an appropriate one to take, and does not feel that Alternative Dispute Resolution is an appropriate option, he or she should have the client execute a **fee or engagement letter.** This letter will establish the attorney as the agent for the client for litigation purposes and further establish the attorney's fees. Attorneys' fees can be of three basic types:

1. **Flat fee** or a single amount for the entire representation.
2. **Contingent Fee** or a percentage of the amount received for the client.
3. **Hourly fee** usually with a **retainer** for several hours collected up front and a monthly billing thereafter.

Settlements

The attorney may decide to delay filing a lawsuit in favor of a negotiated **settlement in lieu of litigation.** These settlements are sometimes offered by insurance companies to avoid **nuisance lawsuits** having damage amounts that are too small to warrant a lawsuit.

Case in Controversy

Next, the lawyer should review the facts and parties of the case to see if the case is **justiciable.** This means the case must be a **case in controversy**, where the party suing has **standing** and the issue is **ripe.** *Standing* means the party bringing the lawsuit is the aggrieved party or else can legally represent the aggrieved party.

Example 2.2:

Mr. P, the natural father of Amy, wants to sue the local school district for making Amy say the Pledge of Allegiance with the words "under God." Amy's mother, who is divorced from Mr. P, has legal custody of Amy. Mr. P does not have standing, only Mrs. P does.

The **ripeness doctrine** requires the act or event that injures you to be final and actually create harm. This doctrine frequently surfaces with decisions by government agencies that deny benefits, but the decisions have not been appealed within the government agency first. The decision to deny benefits is not final until appealed within the agency.

Territorial Jurisdiction

In Personam Jurisdiction

The lawyer must now choose a court based on certain geographic considerations. If you want a **judgment at law** or **decree in equity** for something an individual, or person, has done to you, the court must have **in personam** jurisdiction over the individual. This usually means the defendant resides within the geographic area of the court's authority and can be personally served with a notice to appear and defend him or herself.

In Rem Jurisdiction

Other matters could be within **in rem** jurisdiction, or jurisdiction over the matter. Matters usually concern such things as marriage, land, and decedents' estates. A court could exercise jurisdiction over each of these matters respectively if one of the spouses resides in the state, the land is located in the state, or the decedent died while residing in the state.

Quasi In Rem Jurisdiction

Another form of territorial jurisdiction is **quasi in rem** jurisdiction. This is where a court has jurisdiction over a person's interest in a matter, usually property, but the property is not the matter of the litigation. For instance, a court may execute against a piece of land that someone from out of state owns for purposes of satisfying a debt that was subject to suit.

Long Arm Jurisdiction

One important issue about territorial jurisdiction is the problem of the defendant not being a resident of the state in which the injury occurred. States can exercise **long arm jurisdiction** to obtain personal jurisdiction over nonresidents if the nonresidents have had some **minimum contacts** with the state.

Example 2.3:

Mr. D is from Illinois and drives through Tennessee on a vacation. Mr. D causes an automobile accident in Tennessee but returns to Illinois before the injured party can serve Mr. D with a lawsuit in Tennessee. By driving through Tennessee, Mr. D had minimum contacts with that state and is now subject to the authority of the courts of Tennessee. Mr. D can be served while in Illinois.

Venue

Finally, we must talk about **venue,** which is the geographic location of the judicial district. A judicial district may serve more than one defined area, such as two counties. Each county could have its own separate court and courthouse. Choosing the proper judicial district would be an issue of venue; choosing the proper county would be an issue of **forum conveniens**, or most convenient forum. If a defendant is not satisfied with the convenience of the forum, the defendant must make a motion for **forum non conveniens** to move the trial to another court. A **change of venue** occurs most frequently in a criminal case when the location of the court precludes the defendant from receiving a fair trial.

A Summary Proceeding (2.2) – Initial Activities – Civil Litigation

Injury sustained by plaintiff
Consultation with paralegal/attorney
Determination of cause of action
Review of statute of limitations
Conflict of interest check
Retain attorney with fee or engagement letter
Verify case in controversy for standing of party and ripeness of issue
Determination of jurisdiction, venue, and forum

Parties

A party who sues for an action at law is called a **plaintiff.** A party who sues for an action in equity is called a **petitioner.** A party being sued for an action at law is called a **defendant,** whereas a party being sued for an action in equity is called a **respondent.** A generic term for all parties is **litigants.**

Some actions, especially probate actions, do not expect, nor do they always have, an adversarial party. This type of action would be an **ex parte** action, or an action without another party. Other actions such as **class action** suits must have a large number of plaintiffs certified as having the same cause of action.

Pleadings

The initial pleading by the plaintiff is a **complaint**, whereas the initial pleading by a petitioner is a **petition**. (Unless otherwise stated, the text discussion will assume a complaint at law has been filed seeking monetary damages.)

Injunctions and Restraining Orders

Filed with some actions may be a **preliminary injunction** or **temporary restraining order (TRO)**. Frequently these are used to temporarily remedy a wrong involved with the action. In a nuisance suit, such as an attempt to get your neighbor to stop playing loud music, a preliminary injunction could be issued and served with notice of the suit. Your neighbor must stop the music until the court can hear the matter. In divorce cases, it is not uncommon for one spouse to seek a TRO to stop the other spouse from harassing them.

Captions

Each pleading document must have a **caption** at the top of the document to identify the court, the case, and its parties. A typical caption is shown here.

IN THE CIRCUIT COURT OF PULASKI COUNTY, ARKANSAS
SIXTH JUDICIAL DISTRICT

PETER PAULSON, PLAINTIFF

VS. CASE NO: CV 08-______

DANIEL DODSON, DEFENDANT

COMPLAINT

The Circuit or County clerk with whom the pleading is filed will assign the case a chronological number for future reference as well as a judge for the case.

Allegations

Listed next in the complaint will be the **allegations** of **jurisdiction** and **cause of action**. The plaintiff will state and allege that the parties are within the jurisdiction of this court, generally by the fact of their residence or possible minimum contacts. The allegations for cause of action should state the legally acceptable reason for filing the action, such as negligence.

Example 2.4 – Allegations:

Comes now the plaintiff and for his action against the defendant states and alleges:

1. That the plaintiff is a resident of Pulaski County, Arkansas.
2. That the defendant is a resident of Pulaski County, Arkansas.
3. That on September 12, 2006, the defendant did negligently and inattentively operate his motor vehicle at a high rate of speed while failing to keep a proper lookout and carrying on a cellular telephone conversation and did collide with the plaintiff's motor vehicle.

Prayers for Relief

The plaintiff will then enter a **prayer for relief** in the form of an **ad damnum clause**, specifying the monetary damages for reimbursement of the injuries to person and property or the specific equitable remedies, which will be discussed later.

Verifications and Acknowledgements

The complaint will be signed by the plaintiff under **oath**, with the penalty of **perjury** if the plaintiff has lied. An **acknowledgement** of a **notary public** will be necessary for the oath. To prevent clients who frequently lie from filing **frivolous litigation**, it is required in many jurisdictions for the filing attorney to confirm the cause of action and so state in a **verification** after the plaintiff's signature. This verification could be as simple as obtaining a police report of the automobile accident.

Service of Process

Personal Service

The defendant in the action must be given notice of the action filed against him or her. This is accomplished by **service of process**. The first, and most common, way of serving a defendant is by **personal service**. Personal service is conducted by a **process server**, usually a member of the local sheriff's department, by personally delivering a copy of the complaint, along with a **summons** or **writ** to appear, to the defendant. Personal service by this manner is considered **actual** service. Many states allow the process server to leave the summons and complaint with a person over a certain age at the last known address of the defendant, which is **constructive** personal service.

Substituted Service

Substituted service can be accomplished by delivery of the summons and complaint to the defendant's attorney, if known, or by certified mail, return receipt requested. Certified mail is usually used for personal service by long arm statutes on out-of-state defendants. Service by **publication**, or **warning order**, as it is sometimes called, can be made by publishing the notice in a newspaper of general circulation.

Service on Corporations

Service of process on a corporation, especially an out-of-state, known-as-foreign corporation, can be accomplished in several ways. Service can be made at three locations: (1) within the corporation's state of incorporation, (2) within its state of headquarters, or (3) within any state in which it is doing business and has minimum contacts. Generally, one can serve the Secretary of State in any one of these three locations as the **Agent for Service of Process** for a corporation.

Once the defendant has been served, the process server will execute a **return of service,** usually in the form of an **affidavit of service** filed with the court.

Defensive Pleadings

Initial Motions

Once served with notice of an action, the defendant has a specified time to respond to the complaint, usually 20 days. A defendant's pleading is considered an **entry of appearance** in the case.

Defendants can challenge the plaintiff's pleading as to its propriety by a **limited entry of appearance,** whereby the defendant makes a particular type of motion. A **motion to dismiss for failure to state a cause of action** or **demurrer** is a frequent motion seen at this point. Another one may be a **motion for a bill of particulars,** which is the defendant's request for more specific information about the cause of action, which will allow the defendant to more properly respond. A judge will **grant** or **deny** a motion.

Answer/Response

An entry of appearance by the defendant on the merits of the case is called an **answer** in a law action and a **response by a respondent** in an equity action. In the answer, the defendant can enter a **general denial,** denying all allegations of the plaintiff's complaint, or a **specific denial,** in which the defendant may admit the jurisdictional allegations and, in some cases, the event giving rise to the action, but specifically denies any fault or liability. It is imperative that a defendant answer a complaint; if he/she does not, a **default judgment** may be rendered against him or her.

Further within the answer may be **affirmative defenses,** which are legally accepted defenses that deny the plaintiff's right to bring a suit. The statute of limitations or **laches** would be two of many affirmative defenses, some of which will be discussed in the chapters covering substantive law.

Cross Claims and Counterclaims

The defendant also has the ability to **counterclaim** against the defendant. This is where the defendant has a cause of action against the plaintiff in relation to the event that gave rise to the original cause of action. In some states counterclaims are **compulsory,** even if the claim is not related to the plaintiff's cause of action.

Example 2.5:

The defendant may claim that the cause of an automobile accident was not his speeding, but instead the negligence of the plaintiff failing to yield at a stop sign.

The defendant may also file a **cross-claim** or a **cross-complaint**, in which he/she alleges that another party caused the injury for which the plaintiff seeks relief. Some states call this process **impleading a third-party defendant**. In both cases the plaintiff and the second defendant will be given additional time, usually 20 days, to respond. The plaintiff's response to a counterclaim is called a **reply**, whereas a third-party defendant's response is called an **answer**.

Amended Pleadings

During or after the process of pleadings, either party may find the need for filing **amended** or **supplemental pleadings** to change or add to prior pleadings. It would be wise to check your local court rules and procedures for determining if **leave of court**, or permission from the court (i.e., the judge), is necessary before filing.

Motions for Early Dismissal

At this point both the plaintiff and defendant have the opportunity to make **motion for judgment on the pleadings**. The **moving party** requests the judge to determine solely from the facts listed in the pleadings that one party is entitled, based on current law, to an early disposition of the case in his or her favor. This would be a **judgment on the merits** of the case and is quite rare.

A Summary Proceeding (2.3) – Pleadings

- Plaintiff/Petitioner Pleadings
  - Caption including identity of Court, parties, and case number
  - Allegations of jurisdiction and cause of action
  - Prayer for relief – Ad Damnum clause for monetary damages
  - Verification by attorney
- Defensive Pleadings
  - Limited entry of appearance to challenge Plaintiff/Petitioner pleadings
  - Answer by Defendant – Response by Petitioner
    - General or specific denial
    - Counterclaim against Plaintiff
    - Affirmative defenses of Defendant
    - Cross-claim/Cross-complaint to implead third-party defendant
  - Reply to counterclaim; Answer to cross-claim/cross-complaint

An Unusual Case

Occasionally there will be a party to a potential lawsuit who files an action and then effectively disappears. This is a **Motion for Interpleader** situation. One example of this would be an insurance company that is defending an insured for an automobile accident that has caused far more damages than the liability coverage on the insured's policy. As an example, assume that a person with $50,000 in liability coverage causes a highway pileup that results in 20 individuals sustaining property damage and personal injury in a total amount of $500,000. Who should get what amount? The individuals' damages are not equal, so an equal amount to each is not fair. The insurance company and the insured defendant, who is usually judgment proof, simply submit the case to the court and let the court sort it out. Both parties are no longer adversaries and have no stake in the outcome.

Discovery

The purpose of **discovery** in civil proceedings is to let each side discover what the other side has in terms of facts and evidence. Civil litigation is an attempt to resolve a dispute, not an attempt to ambush the other side with hidden evidence and witnesses. (Criminal discovery procedures exist for the defendant to determine what evidence the prosecution has, but generally the defense need not reveal its evidence.)

Oral Discovery

A frequently used type of discovery is the **deposition**, which is oral discovery. A party or a witness to a civil action, called the **deponent**, is **deposed**. The two attorneys reach an agreement to meet in an office with a court reporter and the deponent will verbally answer questions regarding his knowledge about the case. A deposition is testimony, is under oath, and is recorded and transcribed by the court reporter.

Written Discovery

Another frequently used discovery device is **interrogatories** or written questions **propounded** on a party to the case. Answers to interrogatories must be in writing.

Motions and Requests

Motions and **requests** are the next common type of discovery. A party may make a **Motion to Produce Documents** on the other party. Another is a **Request for Mental and Physical Exams**. There can also be **Requests for Admissions** by a party.

An Unusual Case

It may be necessary in some personal injury–automobile accident cases to request that a certain party admit that he or she was actually driving the car that caused the accident. Drivers who have suspended drivers' licenses or were driving while intoxicated have been known to claim that another individual was driving the car when the accident happened.

Pre-Trial Activities

As discovery processes come to an end, both attorneys and the judge will usually arrange for a pretrial conference. This meeting serves several purposes, as described in the following sections.

Settlements and Motions

The first purpose would be an attempt for both attorneys to reach a settlement. Some jurisdictions even refer to the meeting as a **settlement conference**. Approximately 95% of all civil lawsuits are settled. Another attempt to resolve a case immediately is through the filing of a **Motion for Summary Judgment**. The moving party feels that there are no issues of fact to be decided on by a trial and that, as a matter of law, the judge should rule in that party's favor. A judge may require the parties to submit **memoranda of law**, which includes precedent supporting the reasons why a motion should be **granted** or **denied.** Another possible early termination of the case could be a **Motion for Nonsuit** by the plaintiff. Here the plaintiff has decided that he or she should not proceed at this time, but wait for a later date. Usually a nonsuit granted to the plaintiff is **without prejudice**, which means the plaintiff may refile at a later date.

Two other pretrial motions can be seen at this conference. The first may be a **Motion for Recusal**. This is when a party asks the judge to step down due to bias. Note that the judge makes the actual decision whether or not he or she is biased. The second may be a **Motion in Limine**, which is a request that the court limit the introduction of evidence that may be improperly prejudicial to one side or that will be cumulative, such as several experts on one issue. In conjunction with the limiting of evidence is the concept of **stipulations**, in which both parties agree to the existence of certain facts in the case and that evidence will not be needed to prove those facts.

Subpoenas

Next would be the issuance of **subpoenas**, which are formal requests of the court for a witness to appear. Two types of **subpoenas** exist. The first is a **subpoena ad testificandum**, which is a request to appear and testify. The second, a **subpoena duces tecum**, is a request to appear and bring documents. With any subpoena it is wise to honor the request of the court and appear. If you fail to appear, you may be subject to a contempt citation. If for some reason you feel you should not have to appear as a witness in a case, you should have your attorney file a **Motion to Quash** the subpoena. A hearing will then be held to determine the granting or denial of such a motion.

The Court Calendar

Finally, the judge and both attorneys will have to schedule a date for the trial. The judge will list the agreed-on date or dates on the **court calendar** or **docket**.

A Summary Proceeding (2.4) – Discovery and Pretrial Conference

- Discovery Tools
  - Depositions – oral discovery
  - Interrogatories – written discovery
  - Motions to produce documents (Parties)
  - Requests for admissions and exams
- Pre-Trial Conference
  - Settlement discussions
  - Motions for Summary Judgment to terminate case
  - Motions in Limine to limit testimony
  - Stipulations as to agreed-on facts of case
- Motion for Nonsuit for plaintiff to refile at later date
- Motion for Recusal for judge to step down due to bias
- Issuance of Subpoenas for witnesses and documents
  - Subpoena ad testificandum
  - Subpoena duces tecum
    - Motion to quash
- Setting of trial date on court docket or court calendar

Conclusions of Law

The student should pay particular notice to not only the sheer amount of documents that can be filed in a case, but also the length of time that elapses during the pleading and discovery process. Service of process alone can take days. All answers or responses and replies can take weeks. Discovery can take months and years. The wait for the trial date can be several weeks or months or more. The process is intensive, time consuming, and expensive, and cases can be won or lost during this whole process. These are the reasons why Alternative Dispute Resolution is a rapidly growing field.

The Latin Language

Ad damnum – ad *dam*-num

Forum non conveniens – *four*-um non kun-*veen*-yuns

Motion in limine - in *lim*-uh-nee

Subpoena – Suh–pee-neh

Duces tecum – dooses *tee*-kum

Ad testificandum – ad tes-tuh-fuh-*con*-dum

Exercises – Chapter 2

True/False Correction Determine if the statement is true or false; if false, insert the correct term in the blank below the question for the term in bold to make the statement true.

_____ 1. A plaintiff's decision to withdraw a suit is a **recusal**.

____

_____ 2. A generic term for a party to a civil suit is an **interpleader**.

____

_____ 3. A **reply** is a defensive pleading to a counterclaim.

____

_____ 4. A **demurrer** is an entry of appearance on the merits.

____

_____ 5. A prayer for relief involving monetary damages is an **allegation**.

____

_____ 6. A case in controversy is **justiciable**.

____

_____ 7. A more detailed statement of a complaint is a **writ**.

____

_____ 8. Statutes of Limitation allow for the time in which an **equity action** is to be filed.

____

_____ 9. **Leave of court** is permission from the court.

____

_____ 10. An **answer** is the defensive pleading to a complaint.

____

_____ 11. An **allegation** is the document heading for a pleading.

____

_____ 12. The party who files a **petition** is the moving party.

____

Definitions Insert the correct legal term in the blank above the definition.

1. ____

   The initial pleading in an action at law

2. ____

   A statement that one swears to tell the truth

3. ____

   An attorney's fee calculated as a percentage of an award

4. ____

   Jurisdiction over a matter or a thing

5. ____

   The least amount of activity of a defendant to subject him or her to personal jurisdiction

6. ____

   The relocation of a trial to provide for fairness

7. ____

   A legal action by plaintiffs who have a similar cause of action

8. ____

   Proof that a process server has completed delivery of a summons to a defendant

9. ____

   The process to bring in a third-party defendant

10. ____

    A dismissal of a case without a decision on the merits allowing the plaintiff to refile

11. ____

    A formal request of a court to appear and testify

12. ____

    The process of disclosing facts to the adverse party in litigation

13. ____

    The request of a witness to be relieved from appearing to testify

14. ____

    A motion to exclude inflammatory evidence from being introduced at trial

15. ____

    A proceeding without another party

Matching/Word Association Match the term in the left column with the most appropriate term in the right column.

_____	1.	standing	A.	engagement letter
_____	2.	cause of action	B.	initial pleading in equity
_____	3.	conflict of interest	C.	jurisdiction over the matter
_____	4.	settlement in lieu of litigation	D.	laches
_____	5.	fee letter	E.	failure to answer or respond
_____	6.	ripeness	F.	prior representation of adversary
_____	7.	in rem	G.	attorney confirmation of cause of action
_____	8.	long arm statute	H.	prayer for relief
_____	9.	petition	I.	with prejudice
_____	10.	ad damnum clause	J.	entry of appearance
_____	11.	warning order	K.	aggrieved party
_____	12.	default judgment	L.	removal of judge
_____	13.	interrogatories	M.	writ
_____	14.	memoranda of law	N.	finality of harm
_____	15.	recusal	O.	statement in a complaint
_____	16.	judgment on the merits	P.	court calendar
_____	17.	ex parte	Q.	negotiated settlement prior to pleadings
_____	18.	verification	R.	action at law
_____	19.	summons	S.	oral testimony
_____	20.	allegations	T.	recognized reason to sue
_____	21.	answer	U.	without an adversary
_____	22.	deposition	V.	legal reasoning to support a motion
_____	23.	affirmative defense	W.	service by publication
_____	24.	docket	X.	propound questions
_____	25.	complaint	Y.	jurisdiction over a nonresident defendant

List/Fill in the Blank List the two adversaries in an equitable action:

1. ____________________

2. ____________________

List four types of attorneys' fees:

1. ____________________

2. ____________________

3. ____________________

4. ____________________

List two types of allegations in a complaint:

1. ____________________

2. ____________________

List five types of discovery tools:

1. ____________________

2. ____________________

3. ____________________

4. ____________________

5. ____________________

List two motions for dismissal prior to trial:

1. ____________________

2. ____________________

Chapter 3

Civil Litigation – Trial and Appeal

Opening Statements

Chapter 2 has led us to this point. Without a settlement or dismissal of the action, a trial is now necessary to resolve the dispute of two adversaries. Trials are nothing like the ones you see on television. They are basically a methodical presentation of facts and evidence to convince a judge or a **jury** that one party is entitled to relief. Some civil trials are **bifurcated**, or divided into two phases: the liability phase and the damages phase.

Trials

Not all trials are jury trials. Many are **bench trials**, in which the parties have waived their right to a jury trial or else an equitable issue is involved. In a bench trial the judge will be the **trier of fact**, or the person who decides the winner of the lawsuit. In a jury trial, the jury is the trier of fact. In both types of trials the judge is always the **trier of law**, or the person who makes rulings on points of law that arise during a trial. A jury in a civil case is referred to as a **petit jury**, as opposed to a **grand jury**, which is used only for certain criminal proceedings.

Jury Selection

Jury Pool

It is everyone's civic duty to serve on a jury as a **juror**. Consequently, if your name is on the property tax rolls, the registered voters' lists, or in the database of the local division of motor vehicles, you may receive a **summons for jury duty**. In the past people would go to great lengths to obtain an **excuse** from jury duty because they feel it will interfere with their already-busy lives. Rarely will judges grant excuses anymore except for those reasons stated in the state code or statutes. Failure to report for jury duty could lead to a **contempt citation** from the judge.

A common form of jury duty is now the **one day – one trial** situation. You will serve for three to six months and be on call for jury duty once a week. For instance, on Tuesday of every week the juror will call a recorded telephone line of the clerk or bailiff to determine whether they should show up on Wednesday for possible service on a jury. The trials are expected to be short, one full day at the most.

If called for jury duty, you will be one member of the **jury pool** from which a **jury panel** will be formed. Civil juries no longer require 12 members and no longer require a unanimous vote for a decision. Criminal trials still do, however.

Voir Dire

The process of weeding out the jury pool to the agreed-on jurors is called **jury selection** or **voir dire,** a French term meaning "to speak the truth." Voir dire utilizes a process of **jury challenges**, the purpose of which is to select jurors that are impartial or unbiased. Attorneys determine who they think is most appropriate to serve on a jury for a particular case by asking questions to a juror or group of jurors. Some of the usual questions are already presented in the form of a questionnaire sent with the jury summons.

If an attorney determines that the juror may be biased for whatever reason, a **challenge for cause** will be entered. There is no limit to the number of challenges for cause an attorney may make, but the judge will decide who is or is not excused due to cause. Each attorney will also have a limited number of **peremptory challenges**, which are challenges for no reason at all. The actual number of peremptory challenges may be set by statute or court rules, or at the pretrial conference. When the requisite number of jurors remain seated after voir dire, the jury is **impaneled or seated**.

A Summary Proceeding (3.1) – Jury Selection

Jury Pool determined by random selection of property owners, drivers, or registered voters within the jurisdiction

Summons for jury duty mailed out

Excuses for service on jury limited

Voir Dire process

- Challenges for cause (bias)
- Peremptory challenges

Jury impaneled (seated)

The Jury Trial

Once the requisite number of jurors have been selected, all parties and witnesses will be **sworn in** or take an oath in open court that they swear to tell the truth. Those who do not wish to swear an oath or swear an oath to God may be allowed to make an **affirmation**, to affirm that they will tell the truth. All witnesses will then leave the courtroom and be allowed back in only at the time they testify. Witnesses who are not present at this time, such as experts who come in for one appearance, will be sworn in immediately before their testimony.

The trial begins with the **opening statements.** The plaintiff's attorney will go first and tell the jury what he or she intends to prove in this case. The defendant's attorney may make his or her opening statement at this time or may reserve the right to "open" at a later time, when the defendant's case is presented. Length of time for these statements is usually decided on in the pretrial conference.

The Plaintiff's Case

The plaintiff then has the burden of presenting his or her **case in chief,** which must be a **prima facie case.** Prima facie means "on its face" and requires that the plaintiff's case be sufficient in facts and evidence to win if the defendant does not come forward with a case.

A party puts on a case by introducing evidence (to be discussed in Appendix 3A immediately after this chapter). Evidence is presented through **witnesses** who are **called** to the witness stand, or called to testify, by the plaintiff or defendant during their case. There are two basic types of witnesses: the **lay witness** and the **expert witness.** A lay witness can only testify as to first-hand knowledge, that is, that which they see or hear directly. An expert witness can testify as to opinions and conclusions about the facts presented.

The party calling the witness will conduct a **direct examination** of the witness asking the witness to offer **testimony** as to facts that will prove the party's case. After the direct examination, the opposing party's attorney will be allowed to **cross-examine** the witness. **Cross-examination** usually has the purpose of **impeaching the credibility** of the witness. The opposing party is trying to discount the value of the witness's testimony. **Leading questions**, which have the answer within the question, are frequently used on cross-examination. A witness on cross-examination is said to be **hostile.**

Example 3.1:

Witness W has just finished testifying on direct examination and provided evidence that the defendant was at fault in the automobile accident. Defendant's attorney would not ask how far away the witness was when they saw the accident, but rather, would phrase it this way: "Isn't is true that you were over 300 feet away from the accident when you saw it?"

Witnesses will also be used to introduce **exhibits** as evidence. Exhibits can be documents, diagrams, guns, photographs and just about any other type of physical evidence one can think of.

The Defendant's Case

The defendant must consider at this point a **Motion for Directed Verdict**, which asks the judge to instruct the jury that the plaintiff has failed to state a prima facie case and that the defendant must win. More often than not, the judge will deny this motion.

The defendant must now come forward with a case to dispute or deny the plaintiff's case or the defendant will lose. The defendant may have chosen, with permission of the court, to make his or her opening statement at this time rather than at the opening of the trial. The defendant will also go through the same procedure as the plaintiff in that witnesses will be called, direct and cross-examination will be conducted, and exhibits will be offered.

At the end of the defendant's case the plaintiff can make a Motion for Directed Verdict requesting that the court rule, as a matter of law, the facts and evidence are such that the jury must decide for the plaintiff. Again, more often than not, the judge will deny the motion and let the trier of fact determine who wins.

Rebuttal and Rejoinder

At this point the plaintiff may call new witnesses specifically for **rebuttal** of the testimony of the defendant's witnesses, and the defendant will then get a chance for **rejoinder** to respond to the rebuttal witnesses of the plaintiff. Testimony would now be complete.

Objections

At any time during the testimony of a witness, whether the plaintiff's or defendant's, the opposing attorney may raise an **objection** to the attempt to introduce certain evidence. The objecting attorney must offer a legal reason, such as hearsay, as to why the evidence should not be admitted. The judge will make a **ruling of law** as to the admissibility of the offered evidence and the attorney's objection. The judge will **sustain** the objection if he agrees that the evidence is improper and **overrule** the objection if he feels the testimony should come into evidence.

Closing Statements

At this time both the plaintiff and defendant, usually in that order, will summarize their case in a light most favorable to their client. This summary is called **closing arguments, closing statements,** or **summations.** This is where good speaking ability helps an attorney's presentation. Again there is the possibility of rebuttal and rejoinder statements.

Jury Instructions

It is now time for the judge to instruct or **charge** the jury as to the law that will be applied to the case at hand and used by the jury in reaching its decision. Most states have model guidelines for **jury instructions**. Each attorney will redraft the model instructions as they feel appropriate for their client and submit them to the judge. The judge, in a ruling of law, makes a determination of what the jury instructions will actually be. There is one clear jury instruction in all civil cases, and that is the instruction for the **burden of proof**. The burden of proof rests with the plaintiff. This means that the plaintiff must prove his or her case **by a preponderance of the evidence**. This standard has also been described as the "more probably than not" standard. Simply put, the plaintiff needs more evidence in favor of the case than the defendant has against the case.

Jury Deliberations

The jury will now **retire** for **deliberations**. Private rooms are usually adjoining the courtroom for the juries to use while discussing the case.

An Unusual Case

Occasionally a judge will feel that trial publicity is so great, especially in criminal trials, that jurors need to be **sequestered. Sequestration** involves isolating the jury from the public. Jurors may be placed in hotels and may not be allowed to watch television, make or receive phone calls, read a newspaper, or even talk with each other except when being shuttled to meals and back.

Juries should deliberate the evidence and not their own knowledge or biases. To do so would result in **jury nullification** and a **mistrial**. Juries may not be able to arrive at a decision, which results in a **hung jury** and a **mistrial** being declared by the judge. A mistrial means another trial – from the beginning.

Verdicts and Judgments

The jury **returns a verdict,** which is merely the jury's decision as to who wins. The jury should also include an **award** for the plaintiff if the jury's verdict is for the plaintiff. Awards will be discussed in detail a little later.

Obviously one party is going to disagree with the verdict. The losing party may first ask the judge to **poll** the jury to confirm the verdict. The losing party may also make a **Motion for Judgment Notwithstanding the Verdict (NOV)**. (The Latin phrase is **non obstante veredicto.**) This motion requests that the court overrule the jury and decide in favor of the moving party based on the fact that no reasonable jury should have returned that verdict.

The court will rarely grant this motion and accept the jury's verdict and enter a **judgment** that is final determination by the trial court. The winning party may make a **Motion for Additur**, or a request that the court add to the monetary award, while the losing party may make a **Motion for Remititur**, a request that the monetary award be lowered.

A Summary Proceeding (3.2) – The Trial

Jury is seated
Parties and witnesses are sworn in and witnesses are excluded from courtroom

Plaintiff puts on case in chief – prima facie case
    Direct examination of Plaintiff's witnesses
    Cross-examination of Plaintiff's witnesses by Defendant

Motion for Directed Verdict by Defendant
Defendant puts on case
    Direct examination of Defendant's witnesses
    Cross-examination of Defendant's witnesses by Plaintiff

Motion for Directed Verdict by Plaintiff

Rebuttal Witnesses for Plaintiff
Rejoinder Witnesses for Defendant

Closing statements
Jury instructions given by judge
Jury retires for deliberations
Jury returns a verdict and award
Polling of the jury

Motion for Judgment Notwithstanding Verdict by losing party
Motions for Additur or Remititur

Judgment entered

The Bench Trial

In the event that an action at law has a bench trial or there is no jury in an action in equity, there are distinctions in the process that should be noted. In the action at law, the judge will usually take a case **under advisement**, render his or her decision with **findings of fact** and

conclusions of law, and then enter a judgment with its corresponding award. In an equitable case, the judge would enter a **decree** with the appropriate equitable remedies.

Remedies

Remedies are part of the verdict that a jury returns in an action at law and the decree that a judge or chancellor issues in an equitable action. In actions at law the remedies are monetary damage **awards**, and in equitable actions the remedy is specifically designed for the case.

Monetary Damages

Monetary damages fall into specific categories as follows:

1. **Compensatory damages** – These are for out-of-pocket losses that the plaintiff has sustained. They may be such things as property damages, medical expenses, and lost wages and can be referred to as economic losses.

An Unusual Case

Plaintiffs may recover damages for pain and suffering. What if the plaintiff is unconscious or in a coma during part of his or her injury? Do those people feel pain and suffering? Many complaints will request damages for "conscious pain and suffering."

2. **Special or consequential damages** – These are reimbursement to the plaintiff for losses that are unique to the plaintiff and are also economic losses.

Example 3.2:

A college music student suffers throat burns when the plane she is riding in crashes and burns due to the negligence of the defendant. She will never be able to perform in a music career. These economic losses are recoverable.

3. **Punitive damages** – These are damages meant to punish a defendant for his or her intentional or grossly negligent acts.
4. **Nominal damages** – These are a very small amount of damages awarded for the principle of the matter. Nominal damages have historically been 6 cents on $1.

Equitable Remedies

Equitable remedies are tailored for the specific **irreparable harm** – harm for which monetary damages will not compensate – that the plaintiff has suffered. Three examples of equitable remedies are the following:

1. **Specific Performance** – This is a court order mandating the respondent to specifically perform some act. This remedy is usually seen when land or unique items are involved. The court may order the defendant to deliver to the petitioner a deed

to land for breach of contract to sell. Specific performance would not be used to order someone to perform a service, such as building a brick wall.

2. **Injunction** – This relief is when a court orders the respondent to cease conducting some activity that is irreparably harming the petitioner, such as ordering the respondent to stop playing loud music.
3. **Rescission** – This is when a court declares a contract to be **null and void** or, in other words, it no longer exists.

A SUMMARY PROCEEDING (3.3) – REMEDIES

Monetary Damages

Compensatory – for plaintiff's out-of-pocket losses

Special/Consequential – damages that are unique to the plaintiff

Punitive – damages that punish the defendant

Nominal – small amount of damages for the principle of the matter

Equitable Remedies

Specific performance – orders the respondent to act

Injunction – orders the respondent to cease an activity

Rescission – declares a contract null and void

The Appeals Process

The losing party may feel that the trial court made **errors of law** during the trial and that they should have won but for the errors of the court. This leads to the filing of an **appeal** with the appropriate court having **appellate jurisdiction**. (Most appeals are available to all parties who wish to appeal but that may not be so when attempting to appeal to the U.S. Supreme Court. The Supreme Court hears only a limited number of appeals per year and picks and chooses them carefully. If the Supreme Court decides to hear an appeal based on the appellant's **Petition for Writ of Certiorari**, it will grant the writ that orders the lower court to certify the record for appeal.)

Errors of law are rulings by the lower court judge that the appellant feels were wrong. Actions by the lower court such as overruling objections, denying motions, and reading improper jury instructions are frequently alleged errors of law. The appeals courts do not retry the case, nor do they normally review facts.

Filings

The first thing the **appellant**, the one who files the appeal, must do is give notice of appeal to the **appellee**, the winner at the trial court, and the courts, and pay the filing fees for the appeal. The appellant may have to post an **appeals bond** equal to at least the amount of the award of the lower court. These bonds have premiums that can be quite expensive. Finally, the appellant will have to obtain a copy of the **certified record** from the lower court. This will include all pleadings and documents from the trial and a transcript of trial proceedings from the court reporter.

In some cases the appellee will also be dissatisfied with the lower court decision and may file a **cross appeal**. Now, the appellee becomes the **cross appellant,** and the appellant becomes the **cross appellee**.

Briefs

The appellant will then file a written **brief** stating the errors of law committed by the lower court with supporting precedent. A paralegal may be responsible for researching quite a bit of the precedent for this brief. The appellee will then file a **response brief** defending the actions of the lower court. The appellee has also been referred to as the **defendant in error**. On major issues of law that are appealed to a Supreme Court level, the court may invite additional parties, usually experts as to the case, other than the litigants to submit briefs as "**friends of the court,**" or **amicus curiae** or **amici** if more than one "friend" submits a brief.

A Similar Case

When an appeals court receives a written brief on a case, they expect the brief to be exactly that: brief. Attorneys are not known for their brevity when writing and speaking. Therefore, most appeals courts limit the number of pages that can be contained in a brief and even go so far as to establish uniform margins and minimum-size type in the brief. Letter-sized paper (8.5 x 11 inches) as opposed to legal-size paper (8.5 x 14 inches) is almost universally required for all court documents.

Oral Arguments

Most appeals courts allow for **oral arguments,** or the opportunity for the attorneys to appear in front of the appeals judges and plead their case. The U.S. Supreme Court grants oral arguments very judiciously.

Holdings of the Appeals Court

Appeals courts reach decisions on a case called **holdings**. There are four basic holdings:

1. **Affirm** – This is where the appeals court agrees with the lower court's decisions and finds no **reversible errors** or **errors prejudicial** to the appellant. These are errors that affected the outcome of the case. Errors that are not prejudicial have been called **harmless errors** or errors which, if corrected, would not alter the outcome at the lower court.
2. **Modify** – The appeals court can modify the lower courts ruling especially as to the amount of the award and as to procedure the lower court should follow.
3. **Reverse** – The appeals court decides that the lower court did commit an error of law that was prejudicial to the appellant and dismisses the lower court decision, which now creates a finding in favor of the appellant.

4. **Remand** – More frequently than a reversal with dismissal is a reversal with a remand, which is an order to the trial court to retry the case de novo, which is now conducted according to the instructions of the appeals court.

Opinions of the Appeals Court

Written opinions of the appeals court, whether intermediate-level appeals courts or Supreme Courts, form the basis for our case law or precedent. Without this lawyers would be deprived of a major source of law. One of the more frustrating announcements of an appeals court is a one-word holding: Affirmed. With no attending opinion there is no true precedent.

The major opinions issued by appeals courts are as follows:

1. **Majority opinion** – Because most appeals courts have an odd number of judges, there is rarely a tie vote. The party that garners the most votes from the judges or justices wins. One of the voting members of the majority will be assigned to write the opinion.
2. **Dissenting opinion** – The party with fewer votes receives the dissent or dissenting opinion, which is written by one of the judges or justices who disagrees with the majority.
3. **Concurring opinions** – Both majority and dissenting opinions can have judges or justices who wish to agree with one side but wish to write their own analysis of how the law should have been applied.
4. **Per Curiam Orders** – These are anonymous opinions of the court as a whole rather than any one writing judge or justice.

An Unusual Case

An appeals court judge or justice is supposed to write an opinion regarding the issues that were presented in the case on appeal. Sometimes judges stray and opine as to what the law would be if another issue were presented or a particular fact was changed. This results in **obiter dictum** or **dicta.**

A Summary Proceeding (3.4) – Appeals Courts – Holdings and Opinions

Holdings

Affirm – upholds the lower court decision

Modify – alters the lower court awards

Reverse – changes the lower court's decision and dismisses the case

Remand – sends the case back to the lower court for a new trial

Opinions

Majority – written for the party successful on appeal

Dissent – written for the party unsuccessful on appeal

Concurring – a separate opinion agreeing with either the majority or the dissent

Per curiam order – anonymous opinion of the court as a whole

Enforcement of the Judgment

When a judgment becomes final and the matter is decided (i.e., **res judicata**), whether by appeal or lack thereof, the plaintiff is entitled to payment of monetary damages. Some defendants are unwilling to pay and assistance is needed from the court in enforcing the judgment.

The plaintiff can begin a proceeding to **levy execution** of the judgment or seek a **writ of execution.** The plaintiff can specify the writ to be a **writ of attachment** on personal property or a **writ of garnishment** on the wages of the defendant. In an attachment order the sheriff can take possession of the defendant's bank accounts or sell the defendant's personal property at auction. The plaintiff can also deliver the garnishment order to the defendant's employer, whereupon the employer must withhold a portion of the defendant's wages or salaries in favor of the plaintiff. Many states allow a judgment to be extended by the plaintiff for years at a time because some defendants have nothing to execute on and are **judgment proof.**

Conclusions of Law

Trials and appeals may be the ultimate in the practice of law, but they are simply a process within the process of law. Court rules and procedures dictate how a trial proceeds. Obviously, with the voluminous amount of documents from pleadings and discovery and the infinite number of things witnesses can say while testifying, the trial lawyer must be fully prepared for anything and everything. The paralegal will be part of the team that prepares the attorney for his or her job.

The Latin Language

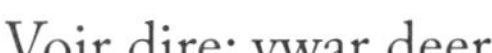

Voir dire: vwar deer

Prima facie: *pry*-muh *fay*-shuh

Non obstante veredicto: nawn ob–*stawn*-tay vera–*dik*-tow

Writ of Certiorari: rit of sir-shee-oh-*rare*-ree

Amicus Curiae: Ah-*mee*-kus *cure*-ee-I

Amici: Ah-*mee*-ky

Res judicata: race jew-duh-*cot*-uh

Appendix 3A

Evidence

Opening Statements

It is impossible to fully discuss trial practice and procedure without a discussion of some basic rules of evidence. Objections entered by an attorney during a trial have to do with the propriety of the evidence and how it is being introduced. Although paralegals will not be the party on the lookout for improper evidence while the trial is in session, nor, of course, will they be entering the objection, the paralegal may be called on to research evidentiary law for the attorney. As the paralegal becomes more experienced in civil litigation, they may be able to spot evidentiary issues in advance of the trial that could help the attorney tremendously in relation to the outcome of a case.

The Concept of Evidence

Evidence defined is anything that can prove or disprove the existence of a fact. For evidence to be entered at a trial it must be **admissible** as opposed to **inadmissible.**

Evidence generally must be the **best evidence**, namely, the actual piece of evidence that was involved in events creating the dispute and not a copy or prototype.

Example 3A.1:

Plaintiff is injured while using a product and claims the instructions on the bottle containing the product did not warn of possible harm. The actual bottle with instructions that the plaintiff used should be introduced into evidence because it is admissible, not a similar bottle from the local store, which would be inadmissible because it is not the best evidence. It is merely a copy.

Witnesses and Evidence

The way to introduce evidence is through a witness. All witnesses must be **competent** to testify. To be competent, a witness must understand the difference between the truth and a lie and recognize that an oath taken to tell the truth, when violated, could result in legal sanctions (i.e., perjury).

As stated previously, a lay witness can only testify as to first-hand knowledge; an expert witness can testify as to opinions and conclusions. In pretrial activities, experts will be presented to the court as such and the court will rule on their competency as an expert witness.

Witnesses are used to **lay the foundation** for the introduction of evidence. The police officer that found the gun at the scene of the crime should be the one who testifies to finding the gun. A party to a letter being introduced as evidence should be the one to introduce the letter as evidence.

Privileged Witnesses

Some individuals cannot be called as witnesses to testify in court. Communications that a party has with these individuals are said to be **privileged** or **confidential communications**. These categories are fairly well known and are listed here, but the student should note that there may be exceptions to the privileges.

1. **Husband/wife privilege** – Spouses cannot be compelled to testify against each other but can if the issue is a dispute between the husband and wife.
2. **Priest/penitent** – The sanctity of religious communication will not be violated.
3. **Doctor/patient relationship** – Communications with a medical doctor are kept confidential.
4. **Attorney/client** – Here the privilege extends not only to communications, but also to the attorney's **work product**. Work product generally revolves around the materials, investigations, and strategies that the attorney has prepared for the case.

Classifications and Types of Evidence

Direct vs. Circumstantial

Evidence can be **direct** or **circumstantial**. Direct evidence shows or tends to show the existence of a fact. Circumstantial evidence requires that one infer or deduce a fact from a collection of other facts.

Example 3A.2:

A promissory note signed by a defendant would be direct evidence of a loan. A person making payments to another on a periodic basis could be inferred as payments on a loan even though no promissory note exists.

Presumptions

Evidence may be shown by **rebuttable** or **conclusive presumptions**. A rebuttable presumption states that if Fact A exists, Fact B may or may not exist. A conclusive presumption states that if Fact A exists, Fact B must also exist.

Example 3A.3:

If it is raining, the pavement is wet. This is a conclusive presumption. If it is snowing, the pavement has snow accumulation on it. This is a rebuttable presumption, because one party may introduce evidence that the snow was dusty in nature and not sticking to the pavement.

Judicial Notice

Evidence may be admissible by the court taking **judicial notice** of a fact. This is a fact for which no evidence need be admitted to prove. Such things as the laws of physics are natural facts. The court could take judicial notice that the sun rises in the east.

Tangible vs. Demonstrative

Evidence may be **tangible,** that is, **real or physical,** as opposed to **demonstrative.** A bumper from a damaged car is tangible, real, and physical. A schematic drawing of the car showing the bumper is demonstrative.

Material and Relevant Evidence

Material evidence is evidence that pertains to the issue being litigated and will influence the trier of fact as to the existence or nonexistence of a fact. The fact that someone is tall has nothing to do with whether or not they pay their debts and is **immaterial. Relevant** evidence is that which probes the value of the evidence as opposed to prejudices the party against whom the evidence is admitted. Rape shield laws are excellent examples of the debate over the relevancy or of a rape victim's sexual history, some of which may be **irrelevant.**

The Hearsay Rule

If there is one singular rule of evidence that is bandied about, and usually erroneously, it is the hearsay rule. Generally the hearsay rule comes into play when a witness tries to testify as to what someone or something else, such as a document, says. The question is whether or not that other person's statement should be allowed as evidence, because it has truth of the matter inserted in the statement. Just because a witness starts off by saying, "She said," doesn't mean the statement is inadmissible hearsay. There are many, many exceptions to the hearsay rule. These rules revolve around other individual's verbal and written statements.

Exceptions to the Hearsay Rule

Verbal statements that are admitted into evidence for the truth of the matter asserted are usually made in situations in which the person would normally make a truthful statement. A group of these statements fall under the similar rules of **res gestae, excited utterances,** and **spontaneous declarations.** While, and immediately after, an event is occurring people make statements and do not have time to think up a lie. While someone is excited, they are not really thinking about what they are saying and usually speak the truth.

Another set of statements that are usually true or relate to the truth of the matter stated is the **admission** or **statement against interest.** Criminals bragging to their friends about "getting away with a crime" are frequently telling the truth. People don't normally admit to crimes. The other type of statement that is admitted to question another statement of a party is the **prior inconsistent statement.** If a defendant claims he was never in a certain city and then the police find out he was previously telling his friends about how scenic that city was, you have a prior inconsistent statement that can be entered to prove the truth about the defendant having the opportunity to have committed the crime, as well as being a liar or a person without credibility.

Written statements such as business, historical, educational, and public records and documents, or the lack thereof, may be introduced without the writer of the specific document or record being currently available. The actual clerk who prepared a marriage license would not have to testify as to its preparation. These documents are prepared so routinely that they are accepted as truthful. The lack of a business record for payment of an amount due could also be evidence that the payment was not made. Sometimes the lack of evidence is evidence.

A Summary Proceeding (3A.1) – Evidence

Admissible or inadmissible

Best evidence – the actual evidence involved in the dispute

Witnesses must lay a foundation for the introduction of the evidence

Competency of lay versus expert witnesses

Privileged witnesses: spouses, doctors, priests, and attorneys

Direct evidence versus circumstantial evidence needing inference

Conclusive and rebuttable presumptions that subsequent facts exist

Judicial notice – a fact accepted by the court without proof

Material evidence – that which influences the trier of fact as to the existence of a fact

Relevant evidence – that which is probative to a fact as opposed to prejudicial to a party

Real, tangible, or physical evidence vs. demonstrative evidence

Hearsay evidence – statements made and records prepared by others

- Exceptions: res gestae, excited utterances, and spontaneous declarations
  - Statements against interest and prior inconsistent statements
  - Routine records or the lack thereof

Conclusions of Law

As the evidence goes, so goes the trial. Evidence must be introduced in a specific, logical manner to be effective. Some of your evidence is admissible and some is not, but it is up to the attorney and the paralegal to research and know the ways evidence will and will not be admitted.

The Latin Language

Res gestae - rez *jes*-te

Exercises – Chapter 3 and Appendix 3A

True/False Correction Determine if the statement is true or false; if false, insert the correct term in the blank below the statement for the word in bold to make the statement true.

_____ 1. A **grand jury** sits for a civil trial.

____

_____ 2. Specific performance is a **monetary damage** remedy.

____

_____ 3. Appeals courts review **errors of law** made by the judge of the trial court.

____

_____ 4. Leading questions can be used on **direct** examination.

____

_____ 5. A **rebuttal** is when a plaintiff calls witness to counter a defendant's case.

____

_____ 6. When a judge agrees with an objection he/she **overrules** the objection.

____

_____ 7. A final decision on a case makes the case **res gestae**.

____

_____ 8. A jury challenge for no reason is a **peremptory** challenge.

____

_____ 9. A plaintiff's case in chief must be a **prima facie** case.

____

_____ 10. An **appellant** is sometimes called a defendant in error.

____

_____ 11. Damages unique to a plaintiff are called **nominal** damages.

____

_____ 12. Citizens receive a **writ** to appear for jury duty.

____

Definitions Insert the correct legal term in the blank above the definition.

1. ______________________________

   A confession heard by another that is admissible under a hearsay exception

2. ______________________________

   Evidence that requires one to draw an inference

3. ______________________________

   Judge's remarks in an opinion that do not relate to the issue of the case being reviewed

4. ______________________________

   A trial with the judge as the trier of fact

5. ______________________________

   Injuries that cannot be compensated for with monetary damages

6. ______________________________

   Examples of this term would be denial of motions and sustaining objections

7. ______________________________

   Damages that reimburse a plaintiff for out-of-pocket losses

8. ______________________________

   The term for a defendant that cannot pay the damages awarded a plaintiff

9. ______________________________

   The act of a jury refusing to consider evidence and deciding a case on other facts

10. ______________________________

    A statement made while emotional, which is admissible under a hearsay exception

11. ______________________________

    An original of a document admitted into evidence as opposed to a copy

12. ______________________________

    The legal concept of a judge assuming a fact to be true without evidence

13. ______________________________

    An appeals court holding that upholds the lower court's ruling

14. ______________________________

    The appeals court opinion that disagrees with the majority opinion

15. ______________________________

    A jury that is deadlocked and cannot reach a decision

Word Association Match the term in the left column with the most appropriate term in the right column.

_____	1.	remedies	A.	irreparable harm
_____	2.	judge	B.	summation
_____	3.	voir dire	C.	mistrial
_____	4.	punitive damages	D.	probative value of evidence
_____	5.	equitable action	E.	conclusions and opinions
_____	6.	garnishment	F.	hearsay exception
_____	7.	jury nullification	G.	impeach witness credibility
_____	8.	per curiam order	H.	seated jury
_____	9.	expert testimony	I.	alternative to oath
_____	10.	cross-examination	J.	punishment
_____	11.	brief	K.	wages
_____	12.	relevant	L.	equitable remedy
_____	13.	attachment	M.	bias of juror
_____	14.	impaneled	N.	damages and injunctions
_____	15.	confidential communication	O.	charges
_____	16.	affirmation	P.	first-hand knowledge testimony
_____	17.	closing statements	Q.	execution on personal property
_____	18.	rescission	R.	trier of fact
_____	19.	sustained	S.	"he said"
_____	20.	lay witness	T.	jury selection process
_____	21.	remand	U.	written argument on appeal
_____	22.	burden of proof	V.	tangible
_____	23.	challenge for cause	W.	anonymous opinion of the whole court
_____	24.	friends of the court	X.	preponderance of the evidence
_____	25.	jury instructions	Y.	amici
_____	26.	jury	Z.	liability and damages phases
_____	27.	excited utterance	AA.	attorney's work product
_____	28.	physical evidence	BB.	trial de novo
_____	29.	hearsay	CC.	trier of law
_____	30.	bifurcated trial	DD.	ruling on an objection

List/Fill in the Blank List four types of monetary damages:

1. ______________________________

2. ______________________________

3. ______________________________

4. ______________________________

List four holdings an appeals court can issue:

1. ______________________________

2. ______________________________

3. ______________________________

4. ______________________________

List four privileged witnesses:

1. ______________________________

2. ______________________________

3. ______________________________

4. ______________________________

List two challenges to a juror:

1. ______________________________

2. ______________________________

List two types of presumptions:

1. ______________________________

2. ______________________________

Section II

Criminal Law

Chapter 4

Criminal Procedure

Opening Statements

Criminal law is not like it is on television, where the emphasis is on criminal investigation (although a few aspects of investigation involving search warrants will be discussed in Appendix 4A). Television has heightened the knowledge people have of criminal law, however.

Crimes are wrongs against society for which the government **prosecutes** to maintain order in society. The **prosecutor,** known frequently as the **District Attorney** or **Prosecuting Attorney** in most local jurisdictions, or **U.S. Attorney** in the federal system of justice, represents the "state" and not the victim, although many states have introduced victims' assistance programs to aid those who have been injured by a criminal act.

Criminal laws are enforced by the police, or law enforcement agents, such as officers, sheriffs, marshals and federal agents. All of these individuals possess "**color of authority**" to act on behalf of a government, the results of which may restrict your freedoms and liberties; therefore, the U.S. Constitution will play a major role in criminal law and criminal procedure. Criminal law has its basis in **common law**, but many states have modified common law to account for social change and the neverending ways in which people find to injure others. A portion of the states have adopted uniform laws such as the **Model Penal Code**, which helps create consistency across the nation for precedent. Otherwise, criminal law and criminal procedure tend to be very state specific.

Arrests

When an individual is placed under **arrest,** or is detained in custody, the process of applying criminal law begins. There are two basic ways arrests come about: First is the **arrest warrant**, and second is the **indictment**.

Arrest Warrants

When the police are comfortable that they have identified a criminal, they will seek a warrant based on **probable cause** from a **neutral magistrate**. Probable cause is generally defined as a reasonable belief, based on the knowledge of the officer, which may include reliable information the officer has received, that a person has committed a crime. The neutral magistrate is usually a judge.

A Different Case

A police officer does not need a warrant to make an arrest for a crime, felony or misdemeanor, if the officer witnesses the crime. The warrant can be prepared while the officer is processing the criminal through the "booking" process.

Indictments

An indictment is a decision by a **grand jury** that probable cause exists. The federal system of justice, especially, and some state systems will allow the prosecutor to **convene** a grand jury, which consists of 12 or more jurors, to hear the evidence and make the decision. This adds a level of independent or neutral review of the facts before one is arrested. Note, however, that a grand jury is exclusively the prosecutor's domain. The jury only hears the evidence against the suspect and not any defense evidence. Evidence is usually presented by the **information** or **affidavit** of the prosecutor.

An Unusual Case

A grand jury proceeding is so exclusively a proceeding of the prosecutor that a running joke in criminal law is that a grand jury can indict a ham sandwich.

A grand jury is a closed proceeding; it is not open to the public. Although a record is kept, the proceeding is not public; violating the secrecy of a grand jury can result in a contempt citation and possibly a criminal charge. It also should be noted that a grand jury has investigative powers and can issue subpoenas for any person, including the defendant, to appear and testify. Although a defendant cannot be represented by counsel in a grand jury, the defendant can elect to refuse to testify against him or herself. A grand jury returns a "**true bill**" if there is probable cause to indict and a "**no bill**" if there is not.

The Arraignment

Once a person has been arrested they must be **arraigned** within a short period of time. An **arraignment** is a short procedural hearing in front of a judge in which the defendant is formally advised of the **charges**, or **accusations**, which may be **separate counts** or one charge for each separate offense. Counts of crimes may include **lesser included offenses.** In other words, if you are charged with murder, battery is automatically included. You cannot murder someone without battering them. The defendant is also advised of his or her constitutional rights, allowed to request a **public defender** if the defendant is **indigent** or unable to afford an attorney, allowed to enter a **plea**, and allowed to request **bail**.

Pleas

The four basic pleas in a criminal case are as follows:

1. guilty
2. not guilty
3. not guilty by reason of insanity
4. nolo contendere

Guilty and not guilty are self-explanatory, but it should be noted that *not guilty* is not the same as *innocent*. Not guilty by reason of insanity brings into play the issue of intent and will be discussed later. Nolo contendere is the unusual plea. **Nolo contendere** means "I do not contend," and is sometimes called pleading **no contest**. It is not an admission of guilt, but the punishment you receive will be the same as if you were found guilty. What this plea does is that it shields the defendant from automatic liability in a civil action for his or her crime, which may also be a tort. This is because the burden of proof is higher in a criminal action than in a civil action and if you meet a higher burden of proof, then you have automatically met the lower burden of proof.

Bail

Bail is a constitutional issue to be discussed in Appendix 4A, as well as a practical issue for the defendant. Obtaining bail usually means paying a bail bondsman a fee to **post bail** for you. In some instances no bail is granted, especially when the crime is serious, such as murder. In other situations no bail is required due to the integrity of the defendant, and the defendant is released on his **own recognizance** (O.R.). The purpose of bail is to ensure the appearance of the defendant at trial.

The Preliminary Hearing

For those individuals arrested via warrant, and not an indictment, the next step is a **preliminary hearing**, sometimes called a **probable cause hearing**. This proceeding is public and the prosecutor must display a sufficient amount of evidence to confirm probable cause to **bind the defendant over** for trial. The defendant should be represented by counsel at this stage. Some defendants prefer to go **pro se,** or represent themselves, which attorneys consider a bad idea. In this case, the presiding judge will make the determination if a pro se request is to be granted and may appoint an attorney to advise the defendant.

Plea Bargaining

Before, and even during a trial, the prosecutor and the defendant, through their attorneys, may reach an agreement whereby the defendant pleads guilty, usually to a lesser charge, in return for a lighter sentence. Many cases are **plea bargained** or **pled out** by the defendant, which relieves the clogged criminal court system. Most plea bargaining is as a result of the defendant's right to discover the evidence against him or her in the possession of the prosecutor. This includes any evidence that might be **exculpatory** or evidence that tends to prove the innocence of the defendant. It is at this point that many defendants will make a **Motion to Suppress** to keep evidence out of a trial under constitutional principles, which also will be discussed in Appendix 4A.

In some, but not many cases, the prosecutor may feel that the case is just not winnable and will enter a **nolle prosequi**, Latin for "I will prosecute no further." The prosecutor may enter this as to one count or all counts against the defendant.

A Summary Proceeding (4.1) – Criminal Prosecutions – Pre-trial

- Arrest – Custodial detention
  - Grand Jury indictment – closed proceeding of prosecutor
    - True Bill of indictment
    - No Bill of indictment
  - Arrest Warrant – based on probable cause, signed by neutral magistrate

- Arraignment
  - Notice of charges and counts
  - Appointment of Counsel for indigents
  - Pleas – guilty, not guilty, nolo contendere, not guilty by reason of insanity
  - Bail – bondsmen
    - Released on own recognizance

- Preliminary Hearing
  - Determination of probable cause under arrest warrant
  - Public proceeding – defense present

(Continued)

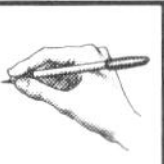

A Summary Proceeding (4.1) – (Continued)
Plea bargaining Discovery of exculpatory evidence Motion to Suppress Nolle Prosequi

Criminal Trials

There are a few differences between criminal trials and civil trials that require mention. The first and most important is the burden of proof concept. In a criminal trial the prosecutor must prove his or her case by the standard of **beyond a reasonable doubt,** which is a higher standard than by a preponderance of the evidence. Much argument exists as to a definition of reasonable doubt, because two people may differ dramatically as to what "reasonable" means. A judge will have instructions for the jury as to what constitutes reasonable doubt in that jurisdiction.

The second difference involves a discussion of the **bifurcated trial**. In a criminal case, the two phases of the trial are the **guilt phase** and the **punishment phase**. **Capital cases**, or cases in which the defendant may receive the **death penalty**, known as **capital punishment,** use the bifurcated trial to comply with U.S. Supreme Court decisions on the death penalty. In the punishment phase, the prosecution will offer evidence of **aggravating circumstances**, such at kidnapping and rape before murdering a victim, while the defendant will offer **mitigating circumstances**, such as childhood abuse. The jury must select the option of putting a defendant to death.

Next, rarely are there motions for early disposition of the case by a judge. Motions for judgments on the pleadings, summary judgment, or directed verdict are not present, but in some jurisdictions it is possible for the judge to overrule a jury verdict with a motion similar to a Motion for Judgment NOV in a civil case.

Another interesting aspect of criminal trials involves the testimony of witnesses. In some cases, another party to the crime may be given **immunity** from prosecution in return for testimony against a defendant. Immunity may prohibit the prosecutor from any use of the testimony to prosecute the witness or any information the witness provides as to a certain criminal transaction.

Criminal Defenses

Criminal defendants have a very limited number of defenses. Generally, these defenses are **alibi, justification, insanity, incompetency to stand trial,** and **diminished capacity**.

Alibi

An **alibi** is simply proof that the defendant was somewhere else at the time of the crime.

Justification

A **justification** is a legal excuse for committing a crime. The most common is **self-defense,** which means you are allowed to use force, including deadly force, when you are in fear of your life. In some cases, **defense of third parties** who also may be in fear of their lives allows the use of force or deadly force. Generally, **defense of property** does not allow for the use of deadly force, only reasonable force, in most states. Most states do recognize the **castle doctrine**, which states that one is not required to flee from their home (i.e., their "castle") during the commission of a crime and may use deadly force inside their home. Other states may qualify this doctrine and say that you still must be in fear of your life inside your house to use deadly force.

Insanity

Insanity is an issue that will be addressed more fully at a later point; however, a change in many states' laws requires a discussion of an additional verdict other than **not guilty by reason of insanity** that can be rendered by a criminal jury when insanity is offered as a defense. That verdict is **guilty but insane.** The defendant will be incarcerated either in a mental institution or a prison for the term of sentence imposed, even if the insanity is alleviated by medical science.

Incompetent to Stand Trial

Another twist on the insanity issue is the defendant who is **incompetent to stand trial.** If a defendant is unable to assist in his or her defense or unable to understand the concept of criminal proceedings, he or she cannot be placed on trial for a crime.

Diminished Capacity

Finally, there is the **diminished capacity** defense, which some used to call the *temporary insanity* defense or the *irresistible impulse* defense. Here the defendant raises a lack of mental capacity to due drug or alcohol intoxication, emotional trauma, or mental disease or defect that precluded the defendant from conforming his or her conduct to the requirements of the law.

Punishment and Sentencing

A jury can find a defendant not guilty, which is an **acquittal,** or the jury can find the defendant guilty. Once a guilty verdict has been returned by the jury and the judge accepts the verdict, the next step is sentencing the defendant to some sort of punishment. There can be **monetary fines** (which are self-explanatory), non-incarceration sentences, and **incarceration.**

A Different Case

A finding of not guilty is not a finding of innocent. "Not guilty" means the prosecutor failed to prove his or her case beyond a reasonable doubt. It is still quite possible that the defendant actually committed the crime.

Non-Incarceration Punishments

Non-incarceration punishments can include **probation,** which is a stated period of time during which the defendant may not commit another offense or the probation will be **revoked** and incarceration may occur. With a **suspended sentence,** the defendant receives a sentence for imprisonment but the judge revokes the implementation of the sentence. In other words, you are sentenced to jail or prison, but do not actually have to go. Some states have a procedure called **suspended imposition of sentence** or **deferred sentencing**, in which the judge will wait for a period of time before actually determining the punishment. If during that time the defendant does not commit another offense, or makes **restitution** for certain acts, the judge will reduce or eliminate the sentence.

Incarceration

Incarceration is confinement to jail or prisons. Jails are generally found in cities and counties and house **misdemeanants**. Prisons are state institutions that generally house **felons.** Sentences can be **indeterminate**, such as a sentence of no less than one year nor more than five years, or **mandatory**, such as a ten-year or a life sentence. Sentences can be reduced by a decision of the judge for **time served**, which is the time the defendant spent in jail while awaiting trial. When multiple offenses have occurred, the judge may order the sentences for each crime to run **concurrently**, or at the same time, or **consecutively,** which is one right after another. **Habitual criminal** statutes may provide for extended incarceration for **recidivists**, or repeat offenders. Of course, the ultimate sentence is the **death sentence,** which is referred to as **capital punishment**.

An Unusual Case

Habitual criminal statutes have also been called the "three strikes, you're out" rule. On the third criminal conviction, whether the convictions are felonies or misdemeanors, the criminal can be imprisoned for life without parole.

Post-Trial Activities

Appeals

Many defendants believe that an appeal as to an error of law made by the judge in a lower court will lead to their freedom. Unfortunately very few criminal cases are reversed on appeal; more often than not, a remand of the case occurs with a new trial or the lower court decision is affirmed.

Just as in civil appeals, the defendant gives notice of the appeal, pays filing fees, and files a brief alleging errors at law. In some cases the defendant is allowed to remain **free on bond** pending the appeal. The prosecutor, frequently through the state Attorney General's office, will file response briefs. Otherwise, the criminal appeals process is quite similar to the civil appeals process.

The basis for overturning a criminal case will be the finding of a **prejudicial, harmful,** or **reversible** error warranting the reversal of the trial court decision. **Harmless errors,** those that would not have changed the outcome of the trial, will not result in a reversal or reversal with remand. Note that a new trial for a criminal defendant is not a violation of the concept of **double jeopardy** under the U.S. Constitution.

Two very common reasons for criminal appeals are **ineffective assistance of counsel** and the **newly discovered evidence** rule. Ineffective assistance of counsel arises when the criminal defense attorney fails to perform his or her duties in a reasonable fashion. **Capital cases** generally see this claim because defendants in capital cases tend to be represented by **public defenders,** who tend to be young and have little experience in such cases. Newly discovered evidence has become quite popular as a grounds for appeal with the process of **DNA testing,** a procedure that was not available to defendants just a very few years ago.

Releases from Incarceration

Most prison sentences allow for the possibility of **parole,** which ends the incarceration but not the sentence. **Parolees** will remain on **probation** for the remainder of their sentence. Violating any condition of parole will lead to a **revocation** of the parole and reincarceration.

Other releases can come from **executive clemency,** a decision of the governor of the state that eliminates or reduces the sentence and sometimes the conviction. **Commutation,** which means substitution, can change a sentence to **time served** or can reduce a death sentence to life in prison. A **pardon** is a complete forgiveness of the act. **Expungement,** or a complete erasing of the criminal proceeding, usually occurs in juvenile cases when the juvenile reaches a specified age, most frequently 18 or 21.

A Summary Proceeding (4.2) – Criminal Prosecutions – Trial and Post-Trial Activities

Burden of Proof – beyond a reasonable doubt

Bifurcated Trial – capital cases – guilt and punishment phases

- Aggravating and mitigating circumstances

Defenses – justifications, insanity, alibi, diminished capacity, incompetency to stand trial

Verdicts – guilty, not guilty/acquittal, not guilty by reason of insanity, guilty but insane

Sentencing – fines, incarceration, non-incarceration penalties

Appeals

- Errors of Law – prejudicial/reversible, harmless

(Continued)

A SUMMARY PROCEEDING (4.2) – (CONTINUED)

Post-Prison Releases

Parole – revocation

Executive clemency – pardon or commutation

Expungement

Conclusions of Law

Criminal law, like civil law, is a process. The major difference is that criminal law is public law involving the government as a representative of society. It has been said that the United States has the worst system of criminal justice in the world … until you compare it to all of the other systems of criminal justice in the world. Many of the aspects of criminal law in the United States have become major constitutional issues, and those will be discussed in the Appendix to this chapter.

THE LATIN LANGUAGE

Nolo contendere – *noh*-loh kuhn-*ten*-duh-ree

Nolle prosequi – *nol*-ee *pros*-i-kway

Pro se – pro say

Appendix 4A

Criminal Procedure and Constitutional Law

Opening Statements

Beginning in the 1960s, the U.S. Supreme Court began applying portions of the Articles and the first ten Amendments to the U.S. Constitution, commonly referred to as the **Bill of Rights**, to the states through a process called **selective incorporation** under the **Due Process clause** of the **Fourteenth Amendment**. This meant that state and local governments would be subject to scrutiny for their actions with regard to the enforcement of criminal laws and the treatment of criminal defendants as they passed through the system. These cases led to many claims that criminals were "getting off on technicalities." A review of these principles of constitutional law is absolutely necessary for the legal professional working in a firm that practices criminal defense law.

Articles

Two provisions of Article 1, Section 9 of the U.S. Constitution have been applied to state criminal laws and procedure. The first is the **ex post facto** provision. This provision prohibits the application of retroactive laws or laws that were passed after an act occurred and made the act illegal.

Example 4A.1:

Assume you park your car at a curb without any "no parking" signs present. While you are away, the city places a "no parking" sign next to your car. You return to find a parking ticket on your car.

The second provision is the **habeas corpus** provision. This provision is used by imprisoned criminals to claim that they are being illegally confined as a result of the criminal process. The criminal petitions the court for a **Writ of Habeas Corpus** in the hopes that a federal court will hear the case and grant a release. Rarely are they successful, however. Grounds for the requested release are usually based on alleged violations of the Amendments to the U.S. Constitution.

Amendments

Fourth Amendment

The Fourth Amendment deals with searches and seizures of property and persons. It protects against **unreasonable searches and seizures** and requires **warrants** to be based on **probable cause.** Unreasonable searches and seizures are usually claimed to have occurred when a warrant is not present. The first question to answer is whether or not a warrant is required.

The general rule is that warrants are required for a search, and a warrantless search must fall within a recognized exception to the warrant requirement to be reasonable. All searches with or without a warrant must be based on probable cause. **Probable cause** has been defined as a reasonable belief, based on knowledge of the officer or reliable information the officer has obtained, that a crime is being or has been committed by a certain person, which belief is supported by an **affidavit**.

Some of the more common exceptions to the requirement of a warrant are the following:

1. **Plain view exception** – This is where the evidence of criminal activity is within plain view of the officer. Plain view generally means in open sight for all of the public to see.
2. **Exigent circumstances exception** – In the case of an emergency where there is imminent danger to a person or the public, an officer can search immediately.
3. **Automobile exception** – Because automobiles are mobile and evidence can disappear quickly in an automobile, no warrant may be required in this situation.
4. **Terry Stop exception** – Here the officer may conduct a "pat down" or "stop and frisk" if he or she has reasonable suspicion that a person is armed.
5. **Border search** – Law enforcement can search anyone crossing a border into or out of the country.
6. **Consent search** – Police can obtain a person's consent to search even without telling the person they have the right to refuse the search.
7. **Search incident to arrest** – If the officer has executed a valid arrest, then the officer may search the area immediately adjacent to the suspect for evidence of a crime.

If a search and seizure has been suspected as unreasonable, the defendant may make a **Motion to Suppress** and the illegally obtained evidence may not be admissible in a trial under the **Exclusionary Rule.** An extension of the Exclusionary Rule is the **Fruits of the Poisonous Tree Doctrine**, which basically says that evidence obtained as a result of evidence obtained in an unreasonable search is also excluded.

Example 4A.2:

If the search of a car is determined as unreasonable and a slip of paper showing the location of stolen goods is found in the car, then the stolen goods are excluded as well as the slip of paper.

Fifth Amendment

The Fifth Amendment protects against **double jeopardy** and **self-incrimination**. *Double jeopardy* is being tried twice for the same crime, or better stated, two crimes that have the same elements. It should be noted that a defendant can be tried twice for the same crime in two different jurisdictions, such as Federal District Court and State Court.

Self-incrimination is the popular term for being compelled to be a witness against one's self. No criminal defendant is required to take the witness stand in his or her trial nor can they be coerced to confess, but they can voluntarily confess. An exception to the self-incrimination rule is that the Fifth Amendment applies only to testimony, not physical evidence such as fingerprints, hair, blood, etc.

Sixth Amendment

The Sixth Amendment guarantees a **speedy jury trial** for all criminal defendants. States have enacted various provisions determining the time in which the trial must begin depending on the arrest date, the arraignment date, or the preliminary hearing date.

The right to the **assistance of counsel** is also guaranteed under the Sixth Amendment. This has led to the creation of **Public Defender** offices, which provide attorneys for **indigents,** or those who cannot afford an attorney.

The Miranda Warnings

The United States Supreme Court in the landmark decision of Miranda v. Arizona determined that the Fifth and Sixth Amendment when taken together were so important in establishing the rights of an accused that the accused must be advised of his or her rights, generally known as the **Miranda Rights.** This advice must be given to the accused no later than a **critical stage** of the process. Critical stage has at least occurred when the suspect is placed under arrest.

Eighth Amendment

Issues of **bail** and **cruel and unusual punishment** are addressed by the Eighth Amendment. The prohibition of **excessive bail** is what the amendment addresses, not the right to bail. Bail need not be set in all crimes, but if it is set, it cannot be excessive. The death penalty has asserted as failing the prohibition of cruel and unusual punishment. Most cruel about the death penalty was its application not the actual penalty of death **per se.**

The Fourteenth Amendment

The Fourteenth Amendment guarantees that no person shall be deprived of life, liberty, and property without due process of law. As to what constitutes due process, there has been a separation of concepts producing procedural due process and substantive due process. **Procedural due process** covers the process of criminal prosecutions such as arrests, searches, and trials. **Substantive due process** looks to the actual law itself and what acts constitute crimes.

Activities such as **vagrancy** have been declared criminal activity at one time or another. The U.S. Supreme Court has disagreed that such activity should be criminal under the **void for vagueness** doctrine. If a law cannot be defined so that a reasonable person can determine if his or her acts constitute a crime, then the law must fail for lack of due process under the doctrine of fundamental fairness.

Conclusions of Law

Without the U.S. Constitution and its Amendments, our criminal justice system would be drastically different. The extension of rights as against state and local governments not only changed the way attorneys talked, but also the way they practiced. Extensive legal research in federal law is now required to practice criminal law, which previously limited its research to state law.

A Summary Proceeding (4A-1) – Criminal Prosecutions and the U.S. Constitution

Articles of the Constitution

- Ex Post Facto – no retroactive application of the law
- Habeas Corpus – no illegal confinement of the person

Amendments to the Constitution

- Fourth Amendment – unreasonable search and seizure
  - Exceptions – Plain view, exigent circumstances, incident to arrest, Terry stop, automobile, border search, consent search
  - Exclusionary Rule/fruits of the poisonous tree doctrine
- Fifth Amendment – double jeopardy and self-incrimination
- Sixth Amendment – speedy trial and right to counsel
  - Miranda rights – read to suspect at critical stage
- Eighth Amendment – prohibition of excessive bail and cruel and unusual punishment
- Fourteenth Amendment – Procedural and substantive due process
  - Void for vagueness doctrine

The Latin Language

Habeas corpus – *Hay*-be-us *core*-pus

Exercises – Chapter 4 and Appendix 4A

True/False Correction Determine if the statement is true or false; if false, insert the correct word in the blank below the question for the term in bold to make the statement true.

_____ 1. A criminal trial with a guilt phase and a punishment phase is a **bifurcated trial.**

____

_____ 2. Evidence showing the innocence of a defendant is considered **incompetent**.

____

_____ 3. To compensate a crime victim for their losses is said to make **bail.**

____

_____ 4. The stage of the criminal process where the defendant pleads is the **indictment**.

____

_____ 5. Defendants who cannot afford an attorney are said to be **indigent**.

____

_____ 6. To testify without fear of prosecution is said to testify with **information**.

____

_____ 7. To assemble a grand jury is said to **seat** a grand jury.

____

_____ 8. To be placed in prison or jail is said to be **under color of authority**.

____

_____ 9. A suspect who is somewhere else at the time of the crime has **a justification**.

____

_____ 10. Having a sentence reduced to time served is called a **pardon**.

____

_____ 11. Allowing a law enforcement official to search your suitcase is a **border search**.

____

_____ 12. Separate charges for multiple crimes are called **counts**.

____

Definitions Insert the correct legal term in the blank above the definition.

1. ______________________________

The representative of any government that brings and tries criminal actions

2. ______________________________

A custodial detention

3. ______________________________

A reasonable belief, along with reliable information, that a crime has been committed

4. ______________________________

The inability to conform your conduct to the law due to severe emotional trauma

5. ______________________________

The document under oath or affirmation supporting a request for a warrant

6. ______________________________

Evidence offered by a defendant in a capital case to avoid the death penalty

7. ______________________________

A sentence of no less than one year nor more than three years

8. ______________________________

Two sentences both of which run at the same time

9. ______________________________

An entry with the court of the decision by a prosecutor not to proceed further

10. ______________________________

An agreement by a defendant to plead guilty in return for a lighter punishment

11. ______________________________

The attorney appointed to represent a defendant without monetary means

12. ______________________________

A place of extended incarceration of felons

13. ______________________________

A law that is applied retroactively

14. ______________________________

The term for representing oneself in a trial

15. ______________________________

The process of completely erasing a criminal proceeding of a juvenile

Word Association/Matching Match the term in the left column with the best corresponding term in the right column.

_____	1.	capital punishment	A.	illegal confinement
_____	2.	U. S. Attorney	B.	custodial detention
_____	3.	nolo contendere	C.	imminent danger to public
_____	4.	acquittal	D.	county jail
_____	5.	prejudicial error	E.	6th Amendment
_____	6.	habeas corpus	F.	federal prosecutor
_____	7.	exclusionary rule	G.	jury verdict
_____	8.	exigent circumstances	H.	parole violation
_____	9.	revocation	I.	home
_____	10.	excessive bail	J.	grand jury decision
_____	11.	justification	K.	life in prison
_____	12.	misdemeanants	L.	death penalty
_____	13.	true bill	M.	DNA evidence
_____	14.	motion to suppress	N.	stop and frisk
_____	15.	guilty but insane	O.	beyond a reasonable doubt
_____	16.	castle doctrine	P.	reversible error
_____	17.	Terry stop	Q.	bind over for trial
_____	18.	critical stage	R.	unreasonable search
_____	19.	mandatory	S.	defense of third person
_____	20.	ineffective counsel	T.	capital murder trial
_____	21.	plain view	U.	no contest plea
_____	22.	district attorney	V.	Bill of Rights
_____	23.	bifurcated trial	W.	deferred
_____	24.	speedy trial	X.	fruits of the poisonous tree
_____	25.	public defender	Y.	open sight
_____	26.	burden of proof	Z.	grounds for appeal
_____	27.	suspended imposition of sentence	AA.	not guilty verdict
_____	28.	newly discovered evidence	BB.	attorney for indigent
_____	29.	selective incorporation	CC.	local prosecutor
_____	30.	preliminary hearing	DD.	Eighth Amendment

List/Fill in the Blank List four types of pleas a criminal defendant may enter:

1. ______________________________

2. ______________________________

3. ______________________________

4. ______________________________

List five defenses a criminal defendant may use:

1. ______________________________

2. ______________________________

3. ______________________________

4. ______________________________

5. ______________________________

List seven types of warrantless searches that may occur:

1. ______________________________

2. ______________________________

3. ______________________________

4. ______________________________

5. ______________________________

6. ______________________________

7. ______________________________

Chapter 5

Criminal Law

Opening Statements

This chapter will concentrate on what constitutes a crime or the substantive law of crimes, as opposed to the procedural law found in Chapter 4 and Chapter 4A. It will not be limited to a discussion of criminal acts, but will also consider the elements of a crime, the classifications and degrees of crimes, as well as the parties involved in a crime. Much of the discussion will center on common law principles, with acknowledgement that common law no longer controls the concept of criminal law – statutory law does. The total number of crimes that now exist has expanded dramatically since most states began enacting statutes. Again, a warning must be issued: Criminal law is very much a local or state matter, and your state and local criminal codes must be referenced in any and all research related to criminal law. Computer-related crimes, or cybercrime, as some are now calling it, is still so much in its infancy that only a cursory discussion is presented.

Elements of a Crime

The two most common elements of almost all crimes are **mens rea**, the intent to commit a crime, and **actus reus,** the act of committing the crime. Both should be present unless the crime is a **strict liability** crime, in which the mere act may be considered the crime.

A Different Case

Mens rea is a Latin word used in the plural, while *actus reus* is used in the singular. While it may – or may not – take more than one thought for the commission of a crime, it usually takes only one act.

Mens rea

To expand on the definition of mens rea would first be to describe it as evil or criminal intent or a guilty mind. The Model Penal Code has classified four mental states of **culpability** to describe criminal responsibility: purposely, knowingly, recklessly, and negligently. **Purposely** is conscious engagement in an act with the objective of causing a result. **Knowingly** is awareness that an act will cause a result. Knowledge that an act is illegal or will cause a particular result is also known as **scienter. Recklessly** means to disregard the risk that an act will cause a result, and **negligently** is the awareness that a risk exists that will cause a result.

Example 5.1:

Pointing a loaded gun at a person and pulling the trigger would be purposeful intent. Shooting a gun into a crowd could be knowing intent. Shooting a gun into the air would be a reckless action, and cleaning a loaded gun inside your house with children present may be a negligent act. The differences between each level of intent, especially knowingly and recklessly, become very fine and are subject to debate. Inferences, or deductions, must be drawn from the circumstances to help define the guilty state of mind.

Insanity

No discussion of intent can be complete without a discussion of the inability to form intent, or the concept of **insanity**. From the common law **M'Naughten Rule** to the Model Penal Code, the definition of insanity remains fairly constant. Basically, the rule is defined as follows: When, as a result of a **mental disease or defect**, a person cannot appreciate the nature and consequences of his or her act, they are considered insane and cannot form the requisite intent to be guilty of a crime. More popular is the question of whether the defendant knows the difference between right and wrong. The first requirement of an insanity plea is that a mental disease or defect must exist. Here, a medical expert will testify as to its existence. Then it must be shown that the person did not believe the act to be criminal in nature, and furthermore, did believe that there would be no penalties for his or her actions. Most individuals lose their possible insanity plea by covering up after the crime, which shows that the person knew there would be consequences and tried to hide his or her act.

Insanity is generally considered an **affirmative defense**, which means the defendant must prove insanity. This is the rare exception to the requirement that the prosecution must prove all elements of a crime beyond a reasonable doubt. A few jurisdictions require the prosecution to prove sanity once the defendant has raised the defense of insanity.

An Unusual Case

It should be noted that there is no such medical term as insanity. Insanity is a legal term.

Actus reus

Because one of the most basic premises of law is that law governs conduct, not thought, there must be an act, **actus reus**, or acts, **actus rea**, for a crime to occur. The law cannot prosecute anyone for their evil thoughts, no matter how evil the thoughts are.

An issue with an act is the voluntary aspect of the act, as in whether the person acted by their own volition or free will. Defenses such as **duress** are sometimes entered to preclude a prosecution or a guilty verdict. Examples of duress include someone forcing or coercing you to act, or possibly an act committed while sleepwalking, where you are completely unaware of your actions.

An Unusual Case

Is it a crime to be a drug addict? The answer is no. There is no act present for a crime to be committed. A person's **status** generally does not make one a criminal.

A Different Case

Is it a crime to be a sexual predator? The answer is again no, because there is no current act present, even after release from prison, to constitute a crime. Only the status is present. State laws giving notice of the presence of sexual predators do not make the predator a criminal.

Classification of Crimes

The most general classifications of crimes come from the common law concepts of **mala in se** and **mala prohibita**. *Mala in se* refers to crimes that are evil in nature and generally require knowledge and intent to act wrongly. *Mala prohibita* refers to crimes that are failures to follow rules such as regulations or ordinances, and the acts are sometimes referred to as **violations** or **infractions**. These acts are frequently **strict liability** crimes and do not require intent or knowledge to be proven as an element.

Example 5.2:

If you are pulled over for speeding, it does no good to tell the officer that you did not realize you were speeding or that you did not intend to speed. You were speeding. That's all that counts.

A Different Case

In some states speeding is a strict or absolute offense. In other words, the only defense you have is that you weren't speeding. In other states, a speeding ticket is only a prima facie case of speeding. If you can offer a justification for speeding – that is, a legal excuse for speeding – then you could be absolved.

Capital Crimes

The highest classification of crimes is the **capital crime**. This is an act, usually murder, for which, if convicted, you will be subjected to **capital punishment** or the **death penalty**. Only a select number of murders will fall into this category. Murders of children and public officials, as well as more than one murder in a single event, or murders while in the commission of a specific felony (e.g., robbery), will receive the death penalty. Other murders, in which **premeditation** and **malice aforethought** are involved, may also receive the death penalty. **Heinous** or particularly vicious murders may also be classified as capital crimes.

Felonies and Misdemeanors

Felonies are the more serious crimes, those that result in serious injury and substantial property damage or monetary losses. They are usually caused by violence creating substantial danger to an individual or society. Felonies frequently involve the use of weapons and potentially deadly force. Felonies have been equated to the term **high crimes**, as found in the U.S. Constitution. Felonies result in prison sentences for long periods of time, sometimes up to life. Monetary fines can be substantial.

Misdemeanors are the lesser crimes. The term *misdemeanor* literally means "bad behavior." Misdemeanors usually result in jail time in a local or county jail and involve smaller monetary fines. It should be noted that many states include traffic (i.e., moving and parking) violations in state codes under **Rules of the Road** statutes. Your speeding or parking ticket may be a misdemeanor, and not just a municipal **violation** or **infraction**. This allows for uniform ticketing and enforcement by all county, city, and state law enforcement officials. Rules of the Road do not normally preclude a city or county from enacting additional ordinances that would classify as violations or infractions.

Constitutional Crimes

There is only one **enumerated**, or listed, crime in the U.S. Constitution, and that is **treason.** *Treason* is defined as levying war against the United States or giving (or attempting to give) aid and comfort to the enemy. Treason must be proved by either a confession in open court by the defendant or on the testimony of two witnesses to the act of treason. Punishment for treason can be the death penalty.

Attempt and Conspiracy

Attempt can be easily defined as a crime that failed. If a person takes a **substantial step** toward the completion of a crime and, but for an intervening cause, the crime would have been completed, the person is guilty of attempt.

Example 5.3:

If a person walks into a store with a mask on and a gun in his pocket and meets up with a police officer who is paying for his coffee at the cash register who subdues the criminal, there can be a charge for attempted robbery.

Conspiracy is an agreement between or among two or more parties to commit a crime with an overt act taken toward the completion of the crime.

Example 5.4:

If two people discuss and agree to rob a bank, no crime has been committed. But if those same two go to the effort of obtaining the floor plans for the bank, an overt act may have been committed and conspiracy charges may be brought.

In a conspiracy situation it is possible that one of the individuals may **renunciate** or refuse to participate in the crime. In this situation, the individual should contact law enforcement before the crime actually occurs to be absolved of guilt. Another unusual aspect to conspiracy is that a defendant can be charged with conspiracy for the planning of a crime and then be charged separately with the actual commission of the crime.

Finally, it is possible in some jurisdictions to be charged with conspiracy without taking an overt act toward the completion of the murder. Some states have made conspiracy to commit murder a crime per se. Any discussions toward a murder-for-hire agreement are conspiracy. Actually delivering advance payment for the murder would be a sufficient act to complete the conspiracy, even though no act toward the actual murder ever occurred. Some jurisdictions make the act of questioning another for assistance in committing murder the crime of **criminal solicitation**.

Degrees of Crimes

Not only can you say that all crimes are not alike, but also that all crimes within a specified type of crime are not alike. **Degrees** of crimes have been established to differentiate a crime within a crime. Degrees are based on several different factors, such as the extent of intent, the severity of the crime, the severity of the injury, the amount of property damage, and the victim of the crime as to age and gender. Degrees have helped meet the adage that the punishment should fit the crime.

Parties to a Crime

The person or persons who commit a crime are considered to be **principals**. In the past, the term **accomplice** has been used to differentiate principals such as lookouts or getaway drivers. These parties may not have actually been the party who committed the robbery, for instance, but were present at the scene when the crime occurred. Many states classify accomplices as principals, while others classify accomplices as **accessories.**

Those who help a criminal commit a crime but are not present at the criminal act have also been called accessories. An **accessory before the fact** assists before the criminal event, and an **accessory after the fact** assists the criminal after the event with knowledge that the crime has occurred. Assistance occurs if the accessory hides the criminal or aids the criminal in fleeing law enforcement.

A more generic type of law for those who participate or help in the criminal event without being present is the **aiding and abetting** statute. This statute could cover any and all accomplices and accessories involved with a crime.

A Summary Proceeding (5.1) – Elements, Classifications, and Parties to a Crime

Elements of a Crime

mens rea – intent

- insanity – affirmative defense to intent and crime

actus Reus – voluntary act

Classifications of Crimes

- mala in se vs. mala prohibita
- capital crime – capital punishment – named victims or premeditation/malice aforethought
- felony – serious or high crimes with imprisonment
- misdemeanor – lesser crime with fines and jail terms
- violations and infractions – municipal ordinances and regulations
- constitutional crime – treason

Attempt – crime that failed

- substantial step toward completion

(Continued)

A Summary Proceeding (5.1) – (Continued)

Conspiracy – criminal agreement
- overt act
- renunciation
- murder – strict liability or criminal solicitation

Degrees of Crimes – based on injuries, damages, and intent

Parties to a Crime
- principal – commits the crime
- accomplice – present at crime
- accessory – before the fact vs. after the fact
  - aiding and abettiing

Crimes Against Property

Arson

Arson is the deliberate, willful, or malicious burning of a building or structure. The burning of the structure can be directly caused by starting a fire, or indirectly by an explosion, which results in destruction of the structure or building. Arson should not be confused with **insurance fraud**, which is a separate crime (but may be the reason why arson is committed). Although the two crimes frequently occur together, they would be separate counts or charges within a prosecution.

Bribery

Bribery is the offering of something of value to a public official for the purpose of influencing the official. Some regulatory agencies, especially those connected with finance or banking, also have criminal regulations involving bribery. These regulations are strict liability in nature. If you accept value in excess of a specified amount, you have accepted a bribe.

Burglary

At common law, **burglary** was defined as the breaking and entering of a dwelling at night with the intent to commit a felony therein. Statutory law has expanded the definition of burglary dramatically. No longer must the structure be a dwelling, and the crime need not take place at night. Any structure within an enclosed area surrounding the dwelling, known as **curtilage**, may be burglarized. Businesses may be burglarized as well. Other states have created **breaking and entering** or **unlawful entry** statutes for situations in which no felonies or misdemeanors are conducted inside a structure. **Criminal trespass** statutes may also punish entry onto the land of another without an entry into a structure, as well as the remaining on another's land after being instructed to leave.

Forgery and counterfeiting

The creation or alteration of printed matter with the intent to defraud is considered **forgery**. Printed matter can be another's signature, as well as the document itself. Copying or imitating a document of value is **counterfeiting**. Transferring or negotiating the falsified document for value would be classified as **uttering**.

Example 5.5:

Printing a copy of a bank's cashiers' check on your computer is counterfeiting. Signing someone else's name to their blank check, which has somehow come into your possession, is forgery. Cashing a forged check is uttering.

Larceny

Larceny, also known as **theft**, is the unlawful taking of personal property, without the consent of the owner, for the purpose of converting the property to the use and possession of a nonowner. Larceny is usually divided into **grand** or **felony larceny** and **petit** (petty) or **misdemeanor larceny**, based on a defined statutory amount. Larceny does not involve any threats, force, or violence. Larceny statutes have been expanded to cover **theft by deceit** or **false pretenses** to prosecute "con artists," as well **as theft by receiving**, formerly known as **possession of stolen property**.

Embezzlement

Embezzlement occurs when a person, such as an employee or trustee, entrusted with custody or possession of money or property, converts that money or property to theirs. It is a specific form of larceny. Embezzlement is most frequently seen with bank tellers and company bookkeepers. Other terms to describe embezzlement are **misappropriation** and **pilferage**.

Robbery

Simply stated, **robbery** is theft by force or fear of force. It is not only a crime against property, but becomes a crime against a person when force or violence is used against the person. The student should compare robbery and **extortion**. Extortion is the obtaining of something of value by force or fear of force. Extortion is not theft.

A Summary Proceeding (5.2) – Crimes Against Property

Arson – deliberate burning of a structure by fire or explosion

Bribery – the offering of something of value to a public official to influence the official

Burglary – the unlawful entry into a structure of another

Forgery – the unauthorized printing or creation of a document with intent to defraud

Uttering – the negotiation or transfer of a forged document

(Continued)

A SUMMARY PROCEEDING (5.2) – (CONTINUED)

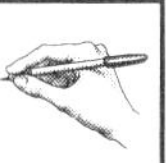

Counterfeiting – the copying or imitating of something of value

Larceny – theft of personal property

  Grand Larceny – larceny with a value over a statutory amount

  Petit Larceny – larceny with a value under a statutory amount

Embezzlement – theft of money entrusted to another

Robbery – theft by force or fear of force

Extortion – the obtaining of something of value by force or fear of force

Crimes Against Persons

Assault

Assault is any act of force that gives rise to a reasonable fear of imminent danger or harm. The act must be by someone who has the capability of carrying out the act. Assault can also be described as an attempted battery. There need not be any physical contact, or **battery**, for assault to occur.

Assault can be divided into degrees. The most popular division is **aggravated assault** and **simple assault**. Some jurisdictions classify assault as felony and misdemeanor assault. *Aggravated assault* usually involves weapons with a threat to use the weapon to commit another crime such as battery or murder. *Simple assault* usually involves words with threatening conduct that bodily harm will occur. Mere words do not constitute assault, however.

Terroristic Threats

Terroristic threatening statutes have evolved in situations in which no conduct or act is involved, but merely threats to cause bodily harm are made. If the threat is to cause death or **maiming**, then **felony terroristic threatening** exists. Otherwise, the threat is usually considered **misdemeanor terroristic threatening**.

Battery

Battery laws still follow the basic common law definition, which is the unconsented to striking or touching of another which is harmful or offensive. Battery also includes the use of objects, as well as objects put in motion by the actor. Battery laws are also divided into degrees. Many states use first-, second-, and third-degree battery laws defined by the amount of injury inflicted.

Example 5.6:

If someone slaps you, that could be third-degree battery. If they hit you with their fist and break your nose, that could be second-degree battery. If they beat you badly and break your nose, knock out teeth, blacken your eyes, and render you unconscious, requiring hospitalization, that could be first-degree battery.

Kidnapping

Kidnapping is the taking or carrying away of a person against their will by force or threat. Kidnapping can occur with the slightest act on the part of the criminal. If a robber orders a store clerk to move to a bathroom so he/she can be locked in, a kidnapping has occurred. Some kidnappings involve a **ransom** or a monetary demand in return for the release of the kidnapped victim.

Homicide

Homicide is defined as the killing of a human being. The categories of homicide are numerous:

1. **Justifiable homicide** – When a crime is justifiable, there is a legal excuse for the crime. Self-defense could make a homicide justifiable.
2. **Capital murder** – This is the killing of a named individual with special or aggravated circumstances. The punishment is the death penalty.
3. **First-degree murder** – This is a murder with specific intent. It is the intentional and premeditated killing of a human being.
4. **Second-degree murder** – This is a murder with general intent. It is an intentional killing with malice aforethought.
5. **Voluntary manslaughter** – This is an intentional killing due to passion or provocation. It is also called the "heat of passion" crime.
6. **Involuntary manslaughter** – This is an unintentional killing while committing an act with reckless indifference to human life.
7. **Negligent homicide** – This is an unintentional killing while committing a negligent act. Many states include deaths due to driving under the influence of alcohol or drugs in this category.
8. **Felony murder** – When a criminal, in the commission of a named felony, causes the death of another, the criminal may be charged with first-degree, or possibly, capital murder. Named felonies are such things as rape, kidnapping, robbery, and burglary.

Example 5.7:

If a police officer fires a weapon at a robber brandishing a weapon, misses the robber, and kills an innocent bystander, the robber will be charged with capital or first-degree murder.

A Summary Proceeding (5.3) – Crimes Against Persons

Assault – acts that give rise to reasonable fear of imminent danger
- aggravated assault – use of weapon
- simple assault – lack of aggravation

Battery – unconsented to striking or touching that is harmful or offensive
- degrees of battery based on extent of injury

Terroristic Threatening
- use of word to threaten bodily harm
- felony and misdemeanor

Kidnapping – taking or carrying away of another against their will
- ransom – monetary gain for release of kidnapped victim

Homicide – the killing of a human being
- justifiable – self defense
- capital murder – killing of named individual or special circumstances
- first-degree murder – killing with premeditation
- second-degree murder – killing with malice aforethought
- voluntary manslaughter – intentional killing in heat of passion or provocation
- involuntary manslaughter – unintentional killing during reckless act
- negligent homicide – unintentional killing during negligent act; DUI/DWI
- felony murder – causing a death in commission of named felony

Family and Sex-Related Crimes

Rape

Rape, as defined by common law, was the forced or unconsented to sexual intercourse with a woman or sexual intercourse with a girl under the age of 11 years. Today's rape statutes expand the definition dramatically.

Rape can be committed by both men and women. Rape victims can be both men and women. Rape can be committed with the use of an object and has been called "object rape." At common law a wife could not be raped, but that is no longer so. Some states have reclassified rape according to degrees and others classify rape as **sexual battery**.

Statutory Rape

Statutory rape crimes are mostly designed to protect minors or those under the age of consent, generally considered to be 18 years. The laws are gender neutral, namely, women can commit statutory rape as well as men. Many states use an age differential factor to determine statutory rape. For example, if one party is over the age of 21 and the other party is under the age of 18, then a statutory rape has occurred.

Historically, statutory rape was a **strict liability crime** in that there need be no intent; if sexual intercourse occurred, then there was statutory rape. Many states now allow the defendant to offer evidence of mistaken belief as to age as a defense to statutory rape.

Prostitution

The general definition of **prostitution** is having sexual relations in return for compensation. Prostitution is considered to be a **victimless crime** in that no one is injured by the act. The student must remember, however, that crimes are wrongs against society.

Incest

Having sexual relations with family members is **incest**. Some states have renamed incest to **sexual abuse**.

Bigamy/Polygamy

Having two spouses is considered **bigamy**. Having more than two spouses is **polygamy.** Religious reasons for multiple spouses are not justifications for bigamy or polygamy.

Sodomy

Acts of oral and anal sex between two people have historically been considered a crime. Recent U.S. Supreme Court decisions have decriminalized **sodomy** between consenting adults, including those adults of the same sex. Coerced sodomy is still a crime.

Fornication/Assignation

Having sexual relations with a person who is not your spouse is still considered illegal in many states. Most states do not prosecute such crimes.

A Summary Proceeding (5.4) – Family- and Sex-Related Crimes

Rape – unconsented to or forced sexual relations
Statutory rape – sexual relations with a person under the age of consent
Prostitution – sexual services in return for compensation
Incest – sexual relations with a family member
Bigamy – having two spouses
Polygamy – having more than two spouses
Sodomy – oral or anal sexual relations
Fornication – sexual relations with one who is not your spouse

Computer-Related Crimes

Identity Theft

Identity theft is the acquisition of personal identification information, such as social security numbers, credit card numbers, and checking account information of others for the purpose of obtaining financial gain through the fraudulent use of such information. Much identity theft occurs as a result of **hacking** or **cracking**.

Pornography

Pornography is **obscene** material that is not protected free speech under the U.S. Constitution. Pornography is not a new issue to crime, but the Internet has expanded its presence. Child pornography is especially prevalent on the Internet.

For pornography to be considered obscene the material as a whole must meet three basic tests:

1. The material, according to community standards, must appeal to **prurient interests**,
2. The material must depict sexual activity as **patently offensive**, and
3. The material must lack any **serious literary, political**, or **scientific value**.

A Summary Proceeding (5.5) – Computer-Related Crimes

Identity theft – acquiring another's personal information for fraudulent gain
Pornography – obscene material that is unprotected free speech

Conclusions of Law

Crimes and their definitions vary tremendously by state. New crimes are being created every day. Sometimes it seems as if the criminals are always ahead of the legislators in devising ways to commit crimes against property. Things that used to be crimes are no longer crimes, such as sodomy between consenting adults. Some crimes are rarely enforced, such as fornication laws, yet they remain in the criminal code. Criminal law is a very serious area of law, however, for the violation of criminal laws can result in not only a loss of freedom, but a loss of life.

The Latin Language

Mens rea – menz *ray*-uh

Actus reus – *ak*-tus *ray*-us

Mala in se – *maw*-la in say

Mala prohibita – *maw*-la pro-*hi*-buh-tuh

Scienter – see-*en*-ter

Exercises – Chapter 5

True/False Correction Determine if the statement is true or false; if false, insert the correct word in the blank below the question for the term in bold to make the statement true.

_____ 1. A **conspiracy** is a crime that failed.

____

_____ 2. The offering of money to a public official to influence the official is **extortion**.

____

_____ 3. An intentional killing caused by provocation is **involuntary** manslaughter.

____

_____ 4. Having more than two spouses is considered **bigamy.**

____

_____ 5. A defense to the element of criminal intent is **insanity**.

____

_____ 6. Copying or imitating a document for fraudulent purposes is **forgery**.

____

_____ 7. Transferring a forged document for financial gain is **pilferage**.

____

_____ 8. An accessory after the fact could be charged with **aiding and abetting**.

____

_____ 9. Insanity is generally an **affirmative defense**.

____

_____ 10. Sexual intercourse with a person under the age of consent is **rape**.

____

Definitions Insert the correct legal term in the blank above the definition.

1. ______________________________

The theft of property above a statutory amount

2. ______________________________

Breaking and entering a dwelling at night to commit a felony therein

3. ______________________________

The enclosed grounds and structures around a dwelling

4. ______________________________

The theft of property by one in possession or custody of the property

5. ______________________________

The monetary demand in order to release an individual taken against their will

6. ______________________________

The killing of a named individual or the killing with aggravated circumstance

7. ______________________________

The unconsented to striking or touching of another which is harmful or offensive

8. ______________________________

The Latin term for a type of crime that violates a regulation

9. ______________________________

The type of act that must be present as an element to prove conspiracy

10. ______________________________

The sale of sexual services

11. ______________________________

Theft by force or threat of force

12. ______________________________

Conduct that gives rise to imminent fear of bodily harm

Word Association/Matching Match the term in the left column with the best corresponding term in the right column.

_____ 1.	mens rea	A.	breaking and entering
_____ 2.	renunciation	B.	theft by force
_____ 3.	justifiable homicide	C.	inherently evil
_____ 4.	arson	D.	disregarding risk
_____ 5.	premeditation	E.	bad behavior
_____ 6.	unlawful entry	F.	self defense
_____ 7.	capital punishment	G.	misappropriation
_____ 8.	mala in se	H.	high crime
_____ 9.	felony	I.	obscenity
_____ 10.	treason	J.	substantial step
_____ 11.	misdemeanor	K.	knowledge
_____ 12.	attempt	L.	criminal intent
_____ 13.	criminal solicitation	M.	driving while intoxicated
_____ 14.	pilferage	N.	murder for hire
_____ 15.	prostitution	O.	words of intent to harm
_____ 16.	pornography	P.	specific intent
_____ 17.	incest	Q.	coerced sexual intercourse
_____ 18.	robbery	R.	constitutional crime
_____ 19.	negligent homicide	S.	theft
_____ 20.	scienter	T.	abandonment of conspiracy
_____ 21.	reckless	U.	affirmative defense
_____ 22.	insanity	V.	victimless crime
_____ 23.	terroristic threatening	W.	death penalty
_____ 24.	rape	X.	sexual abuse
_____ 25.	larceny	Y.	intentional burning

List/Fill in the Blank List the four mental states of culpability under the Model Penal Code:

1. ____________________
2. ____________________
3. ____________________
4. ____________________

List six types of sexual crimes:

1. ____________________
2. ____________________
3. ____________________
4. ____________________
5. ____________________
6. ____________________

List six types of homicide:

1. ____________________
2. ____________________
3. ____________________
4. ____________________
5. ____________________
6. ____________________

List the two primary elements of a crime:

1. ____________________
2. ____________________

Section III

Traditional Civil Law

Chapter 6

Contract Law

Opening Statements

The law of contracts as derived from common law may seem mundane to attorneys that specialize in complex business transactions, but it plays a major role in the day-to-day activities of the average individual. People negotiate, buy and sell, and transact in an infinite number of ways that bring the law of contracts into play. There are myths that exist about contracts. One of the most common myths is that all contracts have to be in writing – that is not true. Many who sign a contract do so without reading it, which can be a dangerous thing to do. Many claim that contracts are not easily understandable, which can be true. Hopefully, this chapter will enlighten the reader as to the ways with which contracts can be managed. The contracts discussed in this chapter are not necessarily business contracts, that is, contracts that involve a merchant and the sale of goods. Those contracts are covered by the **Uniform Commercial Code** (UCC), and will be discussed in more detail in a later chapter. This chapter's contracts are those that exist between two individuals. The contractual relationship between two parties is called **privity of contract**.

Definition of a Contract

As with any common law concept, it is best to start with a definition. A **contract** is a set of promises between or among two or more people, the breach of which the law provides a remedy or the performance of which the law recognizes as a duty. **Breach** is another legal term that will be discussed in greater detail at a later point, but for the moment, it will suffice to say that a breach is a failure to keep a promise.

Types of Contracts

Formal and Informal Contracts

A **formal contract** is one that must contain specific language to be enforceable. One common formal contract is a **negotiable instrument**, such as a check. The formalities of writing a check will be discussed later in the chapter on the UCC. Most contracts are **informal** in nature. Two people can agree on practically any provisions or type of language in a contract.

Bilateral and Unilateral Contracts

In a **bilateral** contract, two people make a promise to perform some activity. In a **unilateral** contract, one party promises to perform and the other party must perform some act for the contract to be enforceable.

Example 6.1:

A contractor gives you a bid to build a brick wall. You accept his bid and agree to pay him $1,500 for the wall. Each party has made a promise and a bilateral contract exists.

Example 6.2:

An insurance company agrees to provide you with car insurance. You must pay the premiums for the insurance company to cover you for liability in an accident. The insurance company has made a promise and you must perform. This is a unilateral contract.

Executed and Executory Contracts

An **executed** contract isn't one that has been signed; it is a contract that has been performed by both parties. An **executory** contract is one that is yet to be performed.

Example 6.3:

Farmer A signs a contract to sell and deliver his crop to the local crop buyer. Farmer A dies before the crop is harvested. The contract is executory in nature. The **executor** of Farmer A's estate can execute the contract and deliver the crop after his death.

Express and Implied Contracts

An **express** contract is one that has been stated orally or in writing. An **implied contract** is one that is inferred from the conduct of the parties or the circumstances. An implied contract can be **implied in fact**, from the conduct of the parties, or **implied in law** to prevent **unjust enrichment**. Implied in law contracts are also called **quasi contracts** and can be enforced under a concept called **quantum meruit**, or "for what it is worth."

Example 6.4:

Mr. A looks out his window and sees a bricklayer building a brick wall in front of his house. Mr. A didn't order a brick wall, but lets the bricklayer finish and then refuses to pay. Mr. A has been unjustly enriched by his knowledge of the bricklayer making a mistake. The court will imply a contract and require Mr. A to pay the bricklayer the value of the brick wall.

Adhesion and Unconscionable Contracts

An **adhesion** contract is basically a "take it or leave it" contract. If you sign the contract, you are "stuck" with whatever provisions exist within the contract. Lease agreements and insurance policies are examples of this type of contract. Courts usually scrutinize these contracts and interpret the contract "as against the drafter" or the party who wrote the contract, and will not bargain. An **unconscionable** contract is one a court may not tolerate. In this situation, one party has superior bargaining power and the other party has no alternatives.

Example 6.5:

A family has lost their home to a hurricane. The closest motels are charging higher-than-normal rates and requiring longer-than-normal stays to obtain a room. The court may void this contract at the request of the renter when the renter tries to move out early.

Option Contracts

An **option contract** gives one party the right, but not the duty, to perform within a specified period of time. During that time, the party who has granted the option, usually as a result of a payment of some type, cannot revoke the option, but must let the contract **lapse**, or in other words let the agreed-on period of time expire.

Output and Requirement Contracts

In an **output contract**, one party agrees to sell or buy the entire output produced by one party, whereas in a **requirement contract** one party is required to sell all products requested by the other party. The problem with these contracts is the unspecified amounts of products involved with the contract.

Example 6.6:

Farmer A signs a contract with Local Buyer to sell all of his chickens to Local Buyer. Local Buyer agrees to buy all of the chickens. This is an output contract.

Example 6.7:

A gasoline station agrees to sell to Company A all the gasoline Company A needs each month to run its delivery trucks. This is a requirement contract.

Problems with these contracts occur when Farmer A raises twice as many chickens as Local Buyer can reasonably afford, or the price of gasoline increases dramatically in less than a month and Company A substantially increases its purchases of gasoline.

A Summary Proceeding (6.1) – Types of Contracts

Formal contract – must contain specific language; a negotiable instrument
Informal contract – no specific language required

Bilateral contract – a contract with two promises
Unilateral contract – a contract with one promise and one performance

Executed contract – a contract that has been performed
Executory contract – a contract that is yet to be performed

Express contract – a contract stated orally or in writing
Implied contract
- Implied in fact – contract inferred by the conduct of the parties
- Implied in law – quasi-contract to prevent unjust enrichment

Adhesion contract – a take-it-or-leave-it contract
Unconscionable contract – one party with superior bargaining power; the other party has no alternatives

(Continued)

A Summary Proceeding (6.1) – (Continued)

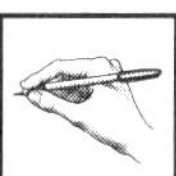

Option contract – where one party has the right to perform by a specified date

Output contract – one party must buy or sell its entire production
Requirement contract – one party must provide all products requested by other party

The Statute of Frauds – Written Contracts

Only certain contracts must be in writing. Therefore, all other contracts could be oral, and therefore valid, enforceable contracts. Certain contracts are so susceptible to fraud that the law eventually determined they should be in writing to determine the rights and duties of the parties to the contract. The following is a list of the eight types of contracts that should be in writing, the first six of which are pursuant to the **Statute of Frauds**:

1. Contracts for the transfer of ownership interests in land. A sale of land would fall in this category. Some states require that any transfer of *any* interest in land, such as a **lease**, must be in writing.
2. Contracts, the performance of which will exceed one year. States that don't require all leases to be in writing would require a lease of greater than one year to be in writing.
3. Contracts in consideration of marriage must be in writing. These are **antenuptial** or **prenuptial** agreements. **Postnuptial** agreements such as **property settlements** on divorce should be in writing as well.
4. Contracts greater than a statutory amount should also be in writing. An example would be contracts for the **sale of goods** over $500 must be in writing under the UCC. Contracts for services rendered depend on each state code to determine the threshold amount.
5. Contracts to pay the debts of others.
6. Contracts of a **personal representative**, such as an executor, to personally pay the debts of a **decedent**.
7. Formal contracts such as **negotiable instruments**, which include **checks** and **promissory notes**, are required to be in writing pursuant to the UCC (to be discussed in Chapter 11).
8. Agreements to provide for another in a **will** should be in writing according to the case law of many states.

Another issue that needs to be discussed is the sufficiency of the writing to satisfy the Statute of Frauds. There are two basic requirements for the writing to be sufficient. First, the writing must state the **material and essential terms** of the contract. Second, the writing must be **signed by the party to be charged** or the party against whom enforcement is sought.

Example 6.8:

Car Seller sends a signed letter to Car Buyer stating that he agrees to sell his 1968 red and white Corvette convertible for $12,000. Car Seller can be required to sell the Corvette because he has signed the writing, but Car Buyer cannot be liable for not buying the car because he has not signed the writing.

A Similar Case

The student should note that this is the second time the term "the Statute of ..." has been used. In Chapter 2, the Statute of Limitations was used to define the time period during which a legal action, civil or criminal, must be brought. Here, the Statute of Frauds defines those contracts that should be in writing and the sufficiency of the writing. What is so special about these legal concepts as to require the special designation of "the Statute of ..."? These concepts were so widely recognized through common law cases that they were some of the first to be converted to statutory law in England.

A particular rule of evidence comes into play with written contracts. It is the **parol evidence rule** that prohibits the use of oral statements, made with the execution of a written contract, which vary, alter, or contradict the written terms. The written document controls for contract interpretation.

A Different Case

Do not confuse *parole*, which is an early release of a felon from prison, and *parol* in the parol evidence rule. Here, the word "parol" means oral or verbal.

A Summary Proceeding (6.2) – The Statute of Frauds

Contracts which must be in writing

- Transfer of ownership interest in land
- Contracts with performance greater than one year
- Contracts in consideration of marriage
- Contracts to pay the debts of another
- Contracts over a statutory amount
- Contract of a personal representative to personally pay debts of decedent
- Formal contracts such as negotiable instruments
- Contract to provide for another in a will

(Continued)

A Summary Proceeding (6.2) – (Continued)

Writings to satisfy the Statute of Frauds

Material and essential terms

Signed by the party to be charged

Parol evidence – oral statements cannot vary the terms of a written contract

Contract Formation

At common law there were fairly strict requirements for establishing a contract. There are four basic concepts of contract law that must be met for a contract to exist. Because many states still follow common law as reported in case law, these requirements still exist today.

Competent Parties

Two or more **competent parties** must exist to form a valid, enforceable contract. Competency has also been called the **capacity to contract**. Two types of individuals may not have the capacity to contract. They are minors and individuals with diminished capacity.

Minors

Minors are those who have not reached the age of **majority**. The general age of majority in most states is 18 years, but exceptions exist, such as the age of majority to buy alcohol. If a minor enters into a contract, it may or may not be enforceable or, in other words, it is **voidable**. Various scenarios must be discussed to determine if the contract with the minor is enforceable.

The minor may choose to **disaffirm** the contract or have it declared void. If the subject matter of the contract was **necessaries**, such as food, clothing, and shelter, the contract is generally enforceable against the minor. If the contract is not for necessaries, the minor must make **restitution** of the goods (i.e., give the goods back). If the minor has damaged the goods he or she may be liable for the damage. The minor may choose to **ratify** the contract after reaching the age of majority. **Ratification** is retroactive to the original date of the contract in this situation.

Diminished capacity

Those who have been adjudged legally **incompetent**, such as a **ward** under **guardianship**, are presumed by the law to be incompetent and the contract is **void**. Others who suffer from diminished capacity without a judgment of **incompetency**, also known as **impaired parties**, may or may not be held to terms of a contract. Their contracts are **voidable** depending on the circumstances of each case. The question to answer is whether or not the incompetent could understand the nature of the contract as to duties and liabilities under the agreement.

Lawful Purpose

The purpose of the contract must be lawful or have a legal objective. Illegal contracts and contracts which are **contrary to public policy** need discussion.

Any contract purpose that violates state or federal laws is an **illegal contract**. Illegal contracts are considered **unenforceable**. Examples of illegal contracts include gambling contracts and **usurious** contracts. **Usury** is the charging of an interest rate on a loan in excess of the amount allowed by state law and has been called *loan sharking*.

Contracts contrary to public policy include unconscionable contracts, **exculpatory** contracts, and **contracts in restraint of trade**. In an exculpatory contract, one party inserts language that they will not be responsible for any damages in relation to the contract.

Example 6.9:

A parking valet provides a receipt that states that the valet service is not responsible for damage to your car. The valet drives your car negligently and damages it. The exculpatory language does not relieve the valet from liability for damages.

An example of a contract in restraint of trade is a contract with a **covenant not to compete clause**. To be enforceable the covenant must be reasonable as to time, extent of prohibition, and geographic area.

Example 6.10:

A weather forecaster signs a contract not to appear on the air for any other local television station for two years if he resigns before the end of his two-year contract. He can resign and work at another station; he just can't appear on the air. This would not be contrary to public policy.

Mutual Assent

Mutual assent has also been called an **agreement**, a **meeting of the minds**, and a **striking of a bargain**. Mutual assent is evidence of **intent to contract**. The process of establishing intent is the process of **offer** and **acceptance**.

Offers

An **offeror** extends an offer to an **offeree**. The offer is a promise to do something or refrain from doing something. The offer must be serious, or not made in jest, definite or reasonably certain, and communicated to the offeree before **performance** or **acceptance** by the offeree.

Example 6.11:

If a person rescues a dog from traffic and returns the dog to the owner listed on the dog tags and then returns home to see an ad in the paper listing a reward for the dog, the finder cannot now claim the reward. The offer was not communicated before the performance of returning the dog.

Offers can be terminated by **revocation** (i.e., taking back the offer), or **rejection** of the offer by the offeree. A **counteroffer** by the offeree carries with it an implied rejection. Offers also terminate by lapse of time as in an option contract. Offers may also terminate automatically by **operation of law**. Death or disability of a party, destruction of the subject matter of the offer, and **intervening illegality** terminate offers.

Example 6.12:

(1) If a person makes an offer to buy a bar and grill and the bar and grill burns down, the offer terminates by operation of law.

(2) If the county in which the bar and grill is located votes to go "dry" or prohibit the sale of alcohol after the offer is made, the offer to buy is terminated.

(3) If the offeror to buy the bar dies or is adjudged incompetent, the offer is terminated.

Acceptance

Acceptance by the offeree would create a contract, as acceptance is an agreement to the terms of the offer. An acceptance must be **unconditional**, which has been called the **mirror image rule** in common law. The offeree must accept exactly what is offered. If the offeree changes the terms of the offer it is considered a **counteroffer,** which is also a **rejection** of the offer. The acceptance must be in a reasonable fashion and communicated to the offeror. In some cases, performance is considered acceptance.

An Unusual Case

Assume an offer has been made by mail. The offeree places the acceptance in the mail at the same time the offeror places a revocation of the offer in the mail. Is the offer accepted or revoked? The **mailbox rule** states that the acceptance is valid when placed in the mail and the revocation is effective only when received by the offeree. There is a contract.

Consideration

Consideration is defined as something of value. The offeror/promisor must receive some benefit from the promise of the offeree, and the offeree must suffer some detriment from his or her promise.

Example 6.13:

Father promises to pay Daughter $10,000 if she agrees not to get married until she has obtained a Bachelors' degree. Daughter accepts his offer and promises not to get married. Daughter stays single for four years of college until she earns her diploma. Valid consideration exists. Daughter has suffered a detriment by giving up her right to get married, and Father has received the benefit that which he requested. Father has suffered the detriment of paying $10,000 and Daughter has received the benefit of receiving $10,000.

Adequacy of consideration is an issue courts prefer not to address. Courts are not here to protect individuals from making bad deals unless the consideration given is grossly disproportionate to the consideration received.

An Unusual Case

It is possible for no consideration to exist and a contract to be found. If a promise is made that would reasonably expect **detrimental reliance** on the part of the promisee, then the promisor may be liable under the concept of **promissory estoppel.**

Example 6.14:

Mr. A wishes to have an ABC Company franchise. ABC Company tells Mr. A that if Mr. A leases a certain-size store and buys a set amount of equipment (shelving, tables, chairs, and cash registers), that he would qualify to receive a franchise. Mr. A leases a store and purchases all of the equipment, but ABC does not grant the franchise. A contract exists under which damages may be recovered by Mr. A.

Mistakes and Lack of Intent

During negotiations to reach a contract, parties may be mistaken as to material information about the deal. These mistaken beliefs go to the heart of mutual assent or the intent to contract. Had the mistake not been present, the deal would not have been done.

Unilateral mistakes

A **unilateral mistake** occurs when one party is mistaken as to a significant or material fact involving the contract. If the mistake is obvious to the other party, then the contract is not enforceable.

Mutual mistakes

Mutual mistakes are where both parties are mistaken as to the bargain itself.

Example 6.15:

Farmer A wishes to sell a sterile cow at a very low price to Farmer B, who wishes to buy a sterile cow at a very low price. The cow turns out to be pregnant. Neither party bargained for the sale of a pregnant cow, and the contract is void.

Fraud

Fraud may be the most difficult of all causes of actions to prove. There are seven elements necessary to be proven to establish fraud, and they will be discussed in the chapter on torts. Fraud clearly **vitiates** or eliminates the intent to contract of the defrauded party.

A Summary Proceeding (6.3) – Contract Formation

- Two competent parties
  - Minors – contracts are voidable
    - Contracts for necessaries are enforceable
    - Disaffirmed contracts – minor must make restitution
    - Minor may ratify contract after reaching age of majority
  - Wards – Contracts are void
  - Impaired parties – contracts voidable depending on circumstances

- Lawful purpose
  - Illegal contracts not enforceable
  - Contracts contrary to public policy
    - Exculpatory contracts – cannot avoid liability by language of contract
    - Contract in restraint of trade: covenant not to compete – voidable contract

- Mutual assent
  - Offer must be reasonable, certain, not made in jest, and communicated to offeree
  - Offers can be terminated by revocation or operation of law
  - Offers can be rejected by counteroffer
  - Acceptance must be unconditional – mirror image rule
  - Acceptance posted in mail creates contract – mailbox rule

- Consideration – something of value
  - Benefit to offeror
  - Detriment to offeree
  - Adequacy of consideration not a justiciable issue
  - Promissory estoppel – no consideration necessary

(Continued)

A SUMMARY PROCEEDING (6.3) – (CONTINUED)

Mistakes

Unilateral mistake – if obvious then contract not enforceable

Bilateral mistake – mistake as to the bargain – contract void

Fraud – vitiates intent

Performance, Discharge, and Breach

If all parties to a contract perform as required under the terms of the contract, each party is discharged. When a party doesn't perform, there may or may not be **discharge** depending on many circumstances. There may, in fact, be a **breach of contract**, which is more formally defined as the wrongful, or unexcused, nonperformance of a contract.

Third-Party Performance

Parties may be able to have a third party perform under a contract. With an **assignment**, a party can **transfer rights** under a contract. Under the concept of **delegation**, a party can **transfer duties** to perform under a contract. A party to a **personal service contract**, such a famous painter engaged to paint a portrait, usually cannot delegate duties.

Example 6.16:

A landlord who has a right to receive monthly rent may assign that rent as collateral for a loan. It also may be possible for the tenant to delegate the duty to pay rent through a sublease.

A Different Case

Although the words *assignment* and *assignation* may appear similar in nature, they should never be confused. Assignation is another term for fornication or illegal sexual intercourse between unmarried individuals.

Third-Party Enforcement

It is possible for a party who is not a party to a contract to seek enforcement of the contract. This third party may be an **intended beneficiary** of the contract. This concept is seen most frequently with life insurance contracts. The insured and the insurer are the parties to the insurance contract. The beneficiary to the policy may seek enforcement of the policy to collect death proceeds.

Some states also recognize a **third-party creditor beneficiary** situation. In this situation, Lender loans Borrower $100. Borrower makes a promise to Lender that he will pay

Creditor the $100 because Lender owes Creditor $100. Creditor may be able to collect from Borrower if Lender doesn't pay.

Discharge by Novation

One party to a contract may agree to let the other party out of a contract by substituting a new, or third, party. The new party will sign a contract with the remaining party and a **novation** has occurred. The original party is discharged.

Discharge by Agreement

Two parties to a contract may agree to terminate the contract. This acts as a discharge for both parties and is considered a **mutual rescission**.

Discharge by Substantial Performance

If one party substantially performs under a contract, the other party cannot withhold total payment. The party who completes **substantial performance** is entitled to be paid for the value of his or her work and is discharged as to that amount. As to what constitutes substantial performance is a question of fact. If substantial performance is not found to exist, then the nonperforming party is in **material breach** of the contract. The nonbreaching party has now been discharged.

Discharge by Accord and Satisfaction

Two parties who are in dispute as to the terms of the contract may resolve their dispute by agreeing to new terms which is an **accord**. If each party now performs under the new terms, then there is a **satisfaction**. Both parties are discharged as to the original contract and the revised contract.

Discharge by Anticipatory Breach

One party to a contract may try to **repudiate** the contract and commit **anticipatory breach**.

Example 6.17:

On April 1, Supplier indicates to Manufacturer that he will not be able to deliver the supplies Manufacturer ordered for May 1. Supplier has committed an anticipatory breach. Manufacturer is discharged from the contract and may order the supplies from another Supplier without fear of liability. The repudiating supplier may be liable for damages.

Discharge by Occurrence of Conditions Precedent, Concurrent and Subsequent

Contracts may not become operational until the occurrence of some event before the expected performance. This event is a **condition precedent**. If the event does not occur, then performance is not required and discharge occurs.

Example 6.18:

Rock Band agrees to perform an outdoor concert on May 1 if 5,000 advance tickets are sold by April 1. 4,000 tickets are sold as of April 1. The parties are discharged from performance.

Parties may also be discharged for the failure of a **condition concurrent**, or an event that must take place at the same time as performance of the contract.

Example 6.19:

Rock Band agrees to play outdoors only if it is not raining. It begins to rain 5 minutes before Rock Band is scheduled to appear on stage. The parties are discharged from the contract.

Finally, parties may be discharged on the occurrence of a **condition subsequent** to the contract. In this situation, an event occurs that terminates the contract and discharges both parties.

Example 6.20:

Rock Band agrees to perform encores as long as the crowd continues to cheer and applaud. The crowd leaves after the first encore. All parties are discharged.

Discharge by Legal Excuse

Discharge may occur if certain legal excuses exist. These legal excuses will relieve the breaching party from liability on failure to perform.

Legal impossibility of performance may be **objective** or **subjective**. **Objective impossibility** would occur with death or disability under a personal service contract and with destruction of subject matter under other contracts. **Subjective impossibility** has been interpreted as the **Act of God** or **force majeure** rule. Although natural disasters may increase the expense or difficulty of performing, they do not necessarily discharge a party.

Some jurisdictions have adopted the **impracticality** rule, as opposed to the subjective impossibility rule, from the Restatement of Contracts 2nd, where extreme difficulty, injury, or loss will discharge a party. Very few jurisdictions have adopted the **frustration of purpose** doctrine.

Example 6.21:

ABC Company rents a floor of hotel rooms from which they will watch a parade. A snowfall cancels the parade. Although the purpose of renting the rooms is frustrated, the loss suffered by paying for the rooms is not extreme.

Discharge by Operation of Law

Finally, a party to a contract may be **discharged by operation of law**. This usually happens when one party to a contract files bankruptcy. The other party may contract with another ongoing business and will not incur any liability.

A SUMMARY PROCEEDING (6.4) – PERFORMANCE, DISCHARGE, AND BREACH

Third-party performance
- Assignment of rights
- Delegation of duties – not allowed in personal service contracts
- Novation – new contract with substituted third party

Third-party enforcement
- Intended Beneficiary
- Creditor Beneficiary

Mutual Recission – both parties agree to discharge

Substantial performance – no material breach – party discharged as to performance

Accord and Satisfaction – performance of renegotiated terms

Anticipatory Breach – repudiation discharges other party

Conditions
- Failure of conditions precedent and concurrent discharges parties
- Occurrence of condition subsequent terminates contract

Legal Excuses
- Discharge occurs with objective impossibility
- No discharge with subjective impossibility or frustration of purpose
- Possible discharge with impracticability

Discharge by operation of law – bankruptcy of party

Remedies

A nonbreaching party, which can now be defined as a discharged party, is entitled to remedies from the breaching party who has not been discharged. Remedies are similar to tort remedies with a few differences. Remedies may be damages or equitable remedies.

Monetary Damages

Compensatory damages are for out-of-pocket losses sustained by the nonbreaching party. **Special and consequential damages** are for losses unique to the contract or the nonbreaching party and are granted if the breaching party has notice of the unique situations.

Example 6.22:

Supplier fails to deliver $1,000 of materials on the specified date. Manufacturer must buy the materials for $1,500. Because of the delay, Manufacturer cannot deliver his finished product on time and suffers a penalty under his contract with Retailer. The $500 additional cost will be compensatory damages and the amount of the penalty Manufacturer suffers under his contract with Retailer is consequential damages. Note that Supplier is not normally responsible for consequential damages unless Supplier was aware of Manufacturer's contract penalty with Retailer. Manufacturer could have inserted a **time is of the essence** clause in the contract with Supplier to alert Supplier to possible losses based on time.

Some contract damages are considered to be **liquidated**, or determined in advance. These are frequently seen in construction contracts in which the builder is penalized a certain amount per day if a building is not complete by the contract date.

Mitigation of damages is required of the nonbreaching party. Mitigation is a lessening of damages.

Example 6.23:

If a tenant to a 1-year, $500-per-month lease contract vacates early, the landlord must attempt to re-let the apartment. The landlord cannot just sit back and expect a breaching party to pay. If the landlord re-lets the apartment at less than $500 per month, the breaching tenant is responsible for the difference. However, if the landlord re-lets the apartment for $600 per month, the breaching tenant cannot profit from a breach.

Equitable Remedies

Remedies for irreparable harm are unique to the breach of contract action. Equitable remedies are applied when monetary damages will not compensate for the injury.

Specific performance is where the court orders a breaching party to perform. This usually occurs when land and unique items are involved. The court can order the breaching seller of land to deliver a deed to the petitioner.

An **injunction** is a remedy ordering a breaching party to do or refrain from doing an act. A court could order an employee who has breached his covenant not to compete to close his business.

Restitution is the remedy that makes a nonbreaching party whole again. In the case of a minor who disaffirms a contract, the minor must return the goods undamaged or pay for the damaged goods.

Reformation is rare. Only occasionally will a court actually reform a contract by rewriting the provisions. Courts will, however, **sever** clauses that are in dispute if the clauses would be unenforceable anyway. Some contracts will provide the authority for a court to sever an unworkable condition or clause.

A Summary Proceeding (6.5) – Remedies for Breach of Contract

- Monetary damages
  - Compensatory – out-of-pocket damages
  - Special/Consequential – unique to the plaintiff
    - Notice of special damages – time is of the essence clause
  - Liquidated – determined in advance
  - Mitigation – nonbreaching party must lessen damages
- Equitable remedies
  - Specific Performance – court orders breaching party to perform
  - Injunction – court order to act or refrain from acting
  - Restitution – making nonbreaching party whole
  - Reformation – court rewrites contract or severs provisions

Conclusions of Law

This chapter clearly shows that the law of contracts can be complex and tedious. That is simply because the number of contracts as well as the number of clauses within contracts can be not only complex and tedious, but also infinite. It almost goes without saying that the number of cases resolving contract disputes will probably be never-ending.

The Latin Language

Quantum meruit – kwan-tum meh-rue-it

Majuere – mah-*jher*

Exercises – Chapter 6

True-False correction Determine if the statement is true or false; if false, insert the correct term in the blank below the question for the word in bold to make the statement true.

_____ 1. A minor may **revoke** a contract.

____

_____ 2. A contract based on promises of both parties to a contract is called **unilateral**.

____

_____ 3. A party to a contract who lacks capacity to contract due to age is a **minor.**

____

_____ 4. Performance of a contract by both parties results in **breach**.

____

_____ 5. The person who receives an offer is the **offeror.**

____

_____ 6. Food, clothing, and shelter are generally considered **necessaries** for a minor.

____

_____ 7. Contract damages determined in advance are called **consequential** damages.

____

_____ 8. Taking back an offer is called **rejection**.

____

_____ 9. Reducing the damages due to a breach is called **reformation.**

____

_____ 10. **Mutual assent** is based on the concept of intent to contract.

____

Definitions Insert the correct legal term in the blank above the definition.

1. ______________________________

The relationship between two parties to a contract

2. ______________________________

A contract that is yet to be performed

3. ______________________________

The common law requirement that an acceptance be unconditional

4. ______________________________

The wrongful failure to perform under a contract

5. ______________________________

A contract requiring a party to buy or sell all goods produced

6. ______________________________

A contract with language that relieves a party from their wrongful actions

7. ______________________________

The type of beneficiary generally found in an insurance contract

8. ______________________________

A court order mandating that a party act or refrain from acting

9. ______________________________

A contract inferred to exist from the conduct of the parties

10. ______________________________

Consideration derived from a waiver of a right

11. ______________________________

A clause that may allow for consequential damages due to untimely performance

12. ______________________________

A type of contract in which delegation of duties is generally not allowed

Matching/Word Association Match the term in the left column with the best corresponding term in the right column.

_____	1. formal contract	A. antenuptial agreement
_____	2. executory contract	B. detrimental reliance
_____	3. implied in law	C. severable clauses
_____	4. prenuptial agreement	D. destruction of subject matter
_____	5. parol evidence	E. property settlement on divorce
_____	6. ratification	F. quasi-contract
_____	7. reformation	G. repudiation
_____	8. meeting of the minds	H. restraint of trade
_____	9. consideration	I. void contract
_____	10. contrary to public policy	J. after the fact agreement
_____	11. counteroffer	K. impracticability
_____	12. objective impossibility	L. lapse
_____	13. anticipatory breach	M. negotiable instrument
_____	14. offeror	N. make whole
_____	15. ward under guardianship	O. predetermined damages
_____	16. competency	P. benefit and detriment
_____	17. option contract	Q. agreement in writing
_____	18. restitution	R. land and unique items
_____	19. accord	S. yet to be performed
_____	20. promissory estoppel	T. capacity to contract
_____	21. liquidated	U. implied rejection
_____	22. subjective impossibility	V. offer and acceptance
_____	23. Statute of Frauds	W. satisfaction
_____	24. postnuptial agreements	X. promisor
_____	25. specific performance	Y. oral statements

List/Fill in the Blank List the four elements necessary to form a common law contract:

1. ____
2. ____
3. ____
4. ____

List four equitable remedies for a breach of contract:

1. ____
2. ____
3. ____
4. ____

List two types of mistakes in the formation of a contract:

1. ____
2. ____

List two types of implied contracts:

1. ____
2. ____

List three possible conditions to contract performance:

1. ____
2. ____
3. ____

Chapter 7

Property Law

Opening Statements

Property law may be the most misunderstood law of all. In the first place, people do not really "own" property. They may have rights to use, possess, and control property, they may have title to property, and they may possess estates and interests in property, but ownership is a very broad term not easily applicable to property. There are really only two types of property: real property and personal property, but personal property can become part of real property and real property can be converted to personal property. Real property is generally a matter of local or state law and is extensively regulated. Personal property is also a matter of local law but can be extensively regulated by federal law as well.

Definitions of Property

Real property is defined as land and anything permanently or solidly attached to it. Air, water, minerals, and trees are things that are permanently or solidly attached to land. Structures such houses and buildings are considered real property by most, but are actually known as **fixtures.** Fixtures come from personal property such as lumber and concrete. Fixtures are better defined as any item of personal property that when so attached or removed from land materially affects the value of the land. Things that are attached to land such as minerals and trees can also be removed from land and become personal property.

Personal property is everything that is not considered real property. Personal property is divided into two categories: **tangible** and **intangible. Tangible** personal property is moveable and touchable. **Intangible** personal property comes from thought and ideas and is known as **intellectual property.** Intangible property can also be property represented by documents such as stocks and bonds. You cannot touch an ownership interest in or a debt of a corporation, but you do possess a **chose in action,** or the right to take legal action to defend an interest that accrues from possession.

Parties to a transfer of real property are generally referred to as the **grantor** or the transferor and the **grantee** or transferee. The transfer of land is called a **grant** and the transfer can be by **deed** or **will.**

Estates in Real Property

The estates most commonly considered ownership estates are **freehold estates.** There are two basic types of freehold estates: **fee simple estates** and **life estates.**

Fee simple estates

A **fee simple absolute** is the highest form of ownership under the law. The owner has the broadest rights to use or dispose of the property as he or she sees fit. Without language to the contrary in the **deed** received, all property granted is presumed to be a fee simple absolute.

A **fee simple defeasible** limits the owner's right to use the property and may limit the duration of the owner's interest. If the owner conducts activities not in accordance with the deed granting the interest, the interest may be lost and **revert** back to the grantor or the grantor's heirs or a third party.

Life Estates

A grantor can transfer his or her interest in land for a length of time equal to the life of an individual. The transferee is called a **life tenant** and possesses a present interest. At the end of the life estate (i.e. the death of the life tenant), the interest, known as a **remainder** or **future interest,** passes to a **remainderman.** It is especially important to note that a life tenant does not hold **title** to the property for purposes of **conveyance** or sale, but can sell the rights to their life estate.

An Unusual Case

Mrs. S transfers (**devises**) a life estate in her apartment building to her Daughter in her will. The remainderman is Grandson. Daughter can sell her future rights to rent from the apartments to Buyer. Buyer now has an **estate pur autre vie,** or a life estate for the life of another. Buyer will "own" the apartment building only so long as Daughter is alive. At Daughter's death, the apartment building will go to Grandson.

Leasehold Estates

Anyone who has ever rented an apartment or a house has possessed a **leasehold estate.** It is a nonownership estate, as no title passes to a **lessee** from a **lessor.** Leasehold estates are now considered either part of contract law or a separate set of laws known as Landlord-Tenant laws and will be discussed in greater detail later in the chapter.

Concurrent Estates

Two or more people can own an estate in the same piece of land. These are commonly referred to as *joint interests* but that terminology is not precise. More precise terminology includes the following:

1. **Tenancy in common** – In this estate two or more people own an undivided interest in the whole as to a piece of real property. At the death of one **tenant in common,** that tenant's pro-rata interest goes to his or her heirs.
2. **Joint tenancy with right of survivorship** – In this estate two or more people own an undivided interest in the whole, but at the death of one **joint tenant** the surviving joint tenant or tenants acquire the pro rata interest of the deceased tenant.
3. **Tenancy by the entirety** – This tenancy is simply a joint tenancy with right of survivorship between husband and wife.
4. **Community property** – This tenancy applies to property acquired by a husband and wife, other than property acquired by gift or will, which is called **separate property,** during a marriage. There is no right of survivorship as to this **marital** or **community property** so there is a similarity to tenancies in common. Several states now adopt community property rules for marital property as opposed to concurrent estate rules.

Common Ownership

New forms of ownership that were not contemplated under common law principles have developed over time. Statutory forms of ownership such as **condominiums, cooperatives,** and **timeshares** have become common forms of "ownership" of real estate.

Condominiums generally operate under the concept of **fee ownership** whether or not the fee is actually attached to the land. It is better described as a fee interest in an apartment. Cooperatives operate more like a corporation, with each apartment owner purchasing an **equity interest** in the cooperative equal to the value of the apartment. In either case, all owners also own a pro-rata interest in the common grounds such as the lawns, sidewalks, and swimming pools. Timeshares are a form of **multiple ownership** of a fee interest but exist for a limited amount of time, which is usually a designated number of weeks during any year.

A SUMMARY PROCEEDING (7.1) – ESTATES IN REAL PROPERTY

Freehold Estates

- Fee simple absolute – highest form of ownership of real property
- Fed simple defeasible – limits use and duration of estate – may revert to grantor, grantor's heirs, or third party

Life Estates

- Life tenant – first beneficial interest in property
- Remainder – future interest resulting after death of life tenant
- Estate pur autre vie – life estate for the life of another

Leasehold Estates – landlord-tenant law

Concurrent Estates

- Tenancy in common – succession to heirs of tenant in common at death
- Joint tenancy with right of survivorship – succession to surviving joint tenants
- Tenancy by the entirety – joint tenancy with right of survivorship between husband and wife
- Community property – tenancy in common as to marital property

Common ownership

- Condominiums – fee interest in apartment
- Cooperatives – equity interest equal to value of apartment
- Timeshares – multiple fee interests at designated time

Conveyance of Real Property

A **deed** is a document that transfers or **conveys** title to real property. Deeds are generally classified as **warranty** deeds or **quitclaim** deeds.

A **general warranty deed** contains **covenants,** or warranty clauses, whereby the grantor of the real estate guarantees the title as against anyone or any action of the past that would create a claim on the property or a defect in the title. A **special warranty deed** guarantees against only the grantor's actions or events while the grantor was **seised** or in possession of title. Personal representatives of estates and sheriffs at foreclosure sales usually execute special warranty deeds.

A general warranty deed can be created solely by the granting clause without the deed actually stating it to be a general warranty deed. Certain words such as **"grant,"** **"bargain,"** or **"sell"** or the phrase **"with warranty covenants"** create the warranties. Without these special words or phrases, the deed will be assumed to be a special warranty deed.

A **quitclaim** deed does exactly what is says it will do: The grantor will quit any claim he or she may have in a parcel of land. The grantor of a quitclaim deed is releasing any interest he or she may have in the property. A quitclaim deed will usually deny the existence of any warranty. Quitclaim deeds are frequently used in divorces and to clear any defect in the title to the land.

A Different Case

A **deed of trust** conveys **legal title** to land to a third party while the grantor, who is the buyer of the property, keeps **beneficial title** and lives on the property. A deed of trust is actually more of a security device for the lender. The trustee owns legal title to the property and can sell the property on default in payment by the purchaser without foreclosure.

A Different Case

In our mobile society, it is not practical to look to a grantor or seller of property to actually come back and defend the title to property sold. **Title insurance** has replaced the concept of a seller actually defending title.

A Summary Proceeding (7.2) – Deeds

Warranty deeds

- General warranty – warrants title as to all previous owners
- Limited warranty – warrants title as to duration of possession by grantor

Quitclaim deeds – no warranties; quits all claims to property

Deed of trust – security device for lender – legal title with trustee; beneficial title with grantor of deed of trust

Title to Real Property

The first step in determining who has title to property is to conduct a **title search.** Documents reflecting previous transactions as to the owners or the tract of land are on file at the county courthouse. The most popular index for record searches is the **grantor-grantee index.** The grantor index lists all parties who sold or conveyed the property, whereas the grantee index lists all parties who have bought or received an interest in the property. A few states still use the **tract index,** which lists all transactions that relate to a designated tract or **parcel** of land. All court records, lien records, and tax records must also be researched.

An **abstract** is then assembled. An abstract is merely a compilation of references to documents that affect the land. Attorneys will rely on an abstract to provide an opinion as to title; insurance companies also use the abstract to issue title insurance policies.

If a document in the **chain of title** reveals a **defect** or a **cloud** on the title, curative action must be taken. This may be something as simple as seeking a quitclaim deed from a prior owner or heir of the prior owner, or as drastic as filing an **Action to Quiet Title.** This action gives all parties who may have a claim as to the property involved an opportunity to appear and assert their claim. The court will rule as to who does or does not have a valid claim. States may have a specific statute of limitations as to claims against title. Title to property can be traced back to the original **land grant** of property from the United States.

An Unusual Case

Many jurisdictions offer utility services, especially water and sewer, directly through a city or county, as opposed to a private utility company, and may consider your utility bill, or a portion of it, a tax. Failure to pay this utility bill may create a cloud on a title.

A Summary Proceeding (7.3) – Title to Real Property

Title search
- Grantor-Grantee index – search by previous owners
- Tract index – search by parcel of land
- Search of court records, lien records and tax filings

Abstract – compilations of references to documents connected to parcel establishing chain of title back to land grant

Cure of defects and clouds
- Quitclaim deeds
- Action to quiet title

Attorney opinion and title insurance issued based on abstract

Legal Descriptions

Legal descriptions can be complex and vexing but they must be precise. There are three basic ways to describe property.

Metes and Bounds

A **metes and bounds description** is a statement of the boundary lines to a parcel of property based on the length of the line **(metes)** and the direction of the line **(bounds).** A fixed starting point such as a surveyor's mark or monument or a natural element such as a creek, tree, or rock is absolutely necessary. Then, you simply follow the directions as to how far to measure in each direction and where to turn, and you should end up back at the starting point which encloses the property.

Rectangular Survey

The most complex legal descriptions come from the **rectangular survey.** The earth is defined by lines of latitude and longitude. Each square of land within these lines is 24 miles square. This block of land is then broken into 16 squares called **townships,** which are 6 miles square. Each township is then broken into 36 squares, each 1 mile square. These 1-square-mile areas are called **sections** and comprise 640 acres. Each section is then divided into quarter sections of 160 acres each. These quarter sections can be broken down into even smaller areas of differing size. This way of describing land came up with the phrase "the north forty." (This is actually an abbreviated description of rectangular surveys and does not reference the designation of all lines within each division.)

Plat Descriptions

Plat descriptions are by far the easiest to understand and describe in a document of transfer. Any parcel, or division of land, can be defined by its boundary lines. Then the parcel is broken into smaller parcels known as **lots** and **blocks.** A common plat description could be Lot 4 of Block 6 of the Hillcrest Addition to the City of Little Rock, County of Pulaski, State of Arkansas. The Hillcrest Addition would have the plat description defining its boundary lines. This concept, along with the rectangular description, came to be known as **subdividing land** and **subdivisions.**

An Unusual Case

Although land can be sold in various-sized parcels, a common small parcel of land that many end up owning perpetually is a **plot**... for your grave.

A Summary Proceeding (7.4) – Legal Descriptions

Metes and Bounds – length and directions of boundary to property starting and beginning at surveyor's mark or natural element

Rectangular – division and subdivision of earth into squares based on latitude and longitude

Plat description – subdivision of land into lots and blocks

Recording Statutes

Parties to certain transactions involving real estate should record the documents of the transaction to put the world on notice as to their interest. Such documents are usually filed with a county official such as the **county clerk, recorder of deeds,** or **registrar of deeds.** Deeds, mortgages, liens, judgments, and easements are normally recorded. Recording statutes allow for a determination of who has priority in a claim to real estate when two competing interests appear. Recorded documents should be **acknowledged** by a notary public, and fees and **transfer taxes,** sometimes called **revenue stamps,** are sometimes collected by the recording office. The grantee is the party with the duty to record. Three general types of recording statutes are **race statutes, notice statutes,** and **race-notice statutes.**

Race Statutes

Race statutes are very simple. The recorder of the document must "race" to the courthouse to be the first to record to acquire priority.

Notice Statutes

Notice statutes establish priority of the recorder based on whether the subsequent taker of an interest in real estate knew or should have known of a prior taker of interest in the parcel of land.

Example 7.1:

If there are two successive buyers to the land and Buyer #2 becomes Recorder #1, Buyer #2 does not have priority if he knew or should have known about Buyer #1. Buyer #2 only has priority if he has no notice and paid value for the land. There is no weight given to who records first.

Race-Notice Statutes

In race-notice statutes weight can be given to who records first and to who did or did not have notice of a prior transaction.

Example 7.2:

If Buyer #2 has no notice of Buyer #1 and records first, he has priority. If Buyer # 1 records first, he has priority even if Buyer #2 paid value for the property and Buyer #1 did not and received the property as a gift.

A Summary Proceeding (7.5) – Recording Statutes

Race statutes – race to the courthouse; first to record has priority

Notice statutes – recorder without notice of prior transaction has priority

Race-notice statutesfirst to record without notice has priority

Real Property Servitudes

Private ownership of real property is not always completely private. A piece of property may serve the interests of parties other than the owner. These interests of others are usually limited as to time and use.

Easements

An **easement**, also known as a **right of way**, is the right of a nonowner to use a piece of property for a specific reason. A common easement is the right of a nonowner to pass over the land of another to reach the nonowner's property. The nonowner's property receiving the benefit of the easement is the **dominant tenement**. The property over which the nonowner passes is the **servient tenement**.

Easements can be created in a variety of ways, and there are various types of easements. One of the most common easements is that which a utility company has to run electrical, phone, and natural gas lines over property. Another common easement is the **easement of access**, which allows an individual to reach their property from a public way. A more unusual type of easement is a **prescriptive easement**, which is also known as **adverse possession**. This is where someone uses your land and ends up owning it. Adverse possession is also known by more colorful terms such as "homesteading" and "squatters' rights." The elements necessary for adverse possession to exist are (1) **actual** use of the property by the claimant, (2) the use by the claimant must be **adverse** or **hostile** to the owner, (3) the use must be **open and notorious**, and (4) the use must be **continuous** for a period of time established by state law.

Example 7.3:

Property A and Property B are **contiguous** or **abut** each other. The owner of Property A builds a new driveway 1 foot over the property line into Property B. This condition continues for several years. The owner of Property A now owns the 1-foot strip of land on which the driveway was built.

License

A **license** is similar to an easement but is more temporary in nature and can be revoked by the owner of the property. Allowing the neighborhood children to take a shortcut across your backyard when coming home from school would be an example of a license. To revoke the license, the owner could merely put up a sign stating "keep out."

Profit

A **profit** or **profit a pendre,** also known as **royalties,** is the right of another to enter land and remove or extract timber, crops, minerals, or just dirt. A profit is actually similar to an easement with the right to remove part of the land of the servient tenement.

Restrictions on Use of Real Property

The most common restriction on use of land is **zoning. Land use or land use planning** applies not only to the activities that are conducted on the land, but also the structures that may be built on the land. Cities will have agencies called a "zoning board" or "land use planning commission" that regulate the use of land pursuant to a **master plan**. Exceptions to zoning regulations can occur, especially with land that was in use before the zoning plan being adopted. This is the concept of **grandfathering** a **nonconforming use**. Zoning boards can also change the category of use of and allowable structure on any parcel though **exceptions** and **variances.**

A Summary Proceeding (7.6) – Servitudes and Restrictions on Real Property

Easements – Right of way – right enter another's property for limited purpose

- Dominant tenement – served by another's property
- Servient tenement – serves another's property

Adverse possession – prescriptive easement

- Must be actual entry
- Must be hostile and adverse to owner
- Must be open and notorious
- Must be continuous for period under state law

License – temporary right to use another's property for limited purpose – may be revoked

Profit – right to enter another's property and remove land, minerals, timber, or crops

Zoning – restrictions on the use of property

- Grandfathering of prior nonconforming uses
- Exceptions and variances granted by zoning board

Landlord-Tenant Law (Leasehold Estates)

At common law, leases or rentals of property were considered a **leasehold estate** or a **tenancy** under property law. Today, however, leases are considered contract law or, in some states, are governed by specific landlord-tenant statutes. In common law, the landlord was the **lessor** and the tenant was the **lessee**. Many legal concepts of common law are still embodied in the state codes. Leasehold estates are nonownership estates in that the lease does not transfer any title, but only an interest to possess and use the property. Although not required by all states, leases should be in writing with clauses that specifically govern the use of the land and the rights and responsibilities of each party.

Tenancies

Tenancies are generally determined by the length of the lease. The four main tenancies that still exist are the following:

1. **Tenancy for years** – The length of this lease is more than 1 year and may be up to 100 years in some jurisdictions. The Statute of Frauds requires this lease to be in writing.
2. **Periodic Tenancy** – The length of this lease is 1 year or less. A year-to-year lease or a month-to-month lease would be the normal terminology to define the length.
3. **Tenancy at will** – This lease arrangement is for an indefinite duration and would end on the occurrence of a particular event, usually the giving of **notice to quit and vacate** by either the lessor or the lessee.
4. **Tenancy at sufferance** – This tenancy has nothing to do with the length of the lease. It exists to describe a tenant who has failed to quit and vacate a property at the end of a lease. The tenant is described as a **holdover tenant**.

Covenants of a Lease

Although leases should be in writing and should specifically address the rights and duties of the landlord and the tenant, many leases do not conform to these standards. Many **covenants**, or promises of the parties, exist as implied, as opposed to express covenants.

The landlord provides a **covenant** or **warranty of habitability**. This means that the landlord must provide premises that are habitable or premises that possess livable conditions. Another implied covenant is the **covenant of quiet enjoyment**. This protects the tenant from being divested of his or her right to occupy and use the property by a third party or the lessor.

Example 7.4:

An example of something that does not constitute a breach of the landlord's implied warranty of habitability would be the air conditioning going out on a long, hot Fourth of July weekend when it can be repaired in a few days.

The tenant has duties as well. Other than paying rent, the tenant shall not engage in **waste**, defined as destruction of the premises. Waste can occur by **commission**, in which the tenant affirmatively damages the property. An example of waste by commission would be punching holes in the wall. There can also be **waste by omission**, in which the tenant fails to notify the landlord of a condition that is damaging the premises, such as dripping drainpipes under a sink.

Eviction

Eviction is the reclaiming of property by a landlord. On a breach of the provisions of a lease, especially the nonpayment of rent, a landlord can institute a legal action known as **unlawful detainer** or **ejectment** to remove the tenant. This process is civil litigation and can take weeks, if not months, to remove a tenant. Some jurisdictions have created new forms of legal action to speed up the process of either rent collection or eviction. One of those is known as the **Municipal Court Procedure** or the **Misdemeanor Procedure**. Here, the landlord gives the tenant a 10-day notice to pay rent or vacate if the tenant has defaulted on the rent. If the tenant fails to pay or vacate the premises within the 10-day period, the landlord can file a complaint with the local prosecuting attorney and a summons to appear in municipal or district criminal court will be served on the tenant. The tenant may be found guilty of a misdemeanor and fined, but not jailed.

When the landlord takes steps to remove a tenant it is considered **actual eviction**. If the landlord allows conditions to exist that prevent the tenant from using the premises as intended there may be **constructive eviction**, and the tenant can take action to terminate the lease.

Example 7.5:

A neighboring tenant continues to play loud music at all hours of the day and night. The landlord refuses to take action to stop the nuisance created. The tenant may file a legal action against the landlord for constructive eviction.

Finally, a landlord cannot take action to evict a tenant who reported the landlord to authorities for violations of law. This would be **retaliatory eviction**.

A Summary Proceeding (7.7) – Leasehold Estates/Landlord-Tenant Law

Tenancies

- Tenancy for years – term of lease greater than 1 year
- Periodic tenancy – year-to-year or month-to-month lease
- Tenancy at will – indefinite duration of lease term
- Tenancy at sufferance – holdover tenant

(Continued)

A SUMMARY PROCEEDING (7.7) – (CONTINUED)

Lease Covenants
- Landlord
  - Warranty of habitability – livable conditions of premises
  - Covenant of quiet enjoyment – no interference with tenant possession
- Tenant – Waste
  - Waste by commission
  - Waste by omission

Eviction – also known as ejectment or unlawful detainer
- Actual eviction – court process
- Constructive eviction – conditions preventing tenant from expected use
- Retaliatory eviction – eviction after tenant reports landlord to authorities

Mortgages

A **mortgage** is a document that pledges real estate as collateral for a loan. The person who grants the mortgage is the **mortgagor** and is usually the buyer of property who borrows money to purchase the land. The **mortgagee** is the lender of the money who will have the mortgagor sign a promissory note, called a **mortgage note,** for repayment of the loan as well as the mortgage document itself.

If a mortgagor **defaults,** that is, fails to pay the mortgage note payments, the mortgagee may begin **foreclosure** proceedings. Foreclosure proceedings usually result in a public sale of the property. The proceeds of the sale will be used to pay the balance due on the mortgage note. If the proceeds of the sale are insufficient to pay the balance of the note, the mortgagor is responsible for the **deficiency**.

Prior to the foreclosure sale a mortgagor has the right to **equity of redemption,** which means that the mortgagor can cure the default by paying the outstanding amounts on the mortgage note and redeem his or her property. After the foreclosure sale the mortgagor still has a period of time, usually between 6 months and 2 years, to redeem the property under a **right of redemption**.

A SUMMARY PROCEEDING (7.8) – MORTGAGES

Mortgage – document to pledge real estate as collateral for a home loan

Parties to a mortgage
- Mortgagor – grants the mortgage/mortgagee – receives the mortgage

Foreclosure – on default of mortgagor payment
- Public sale – deficiency judgment possible
- Right of redemption period

Personal Property

Personal property issues revolving around tangible personal property include **bailments** and **lost, stolen,** and **abandoned** property. Intangible personal property includes issues of intellectual property such as patents, trademarks, trade secrets, and copyrights.

Bailments

When possession of personal property is transferred without intent to pass title, a **bailment** occurs. The person transferring the property is the **bailor** and the person receiving the property is the **bailee.** The actions of the bailee while in possession of the property may create many legal issues.

Example 7.6:

When a car is given to valet to be parked, a bailment has occurred. The car owner is the bailor; the valet is the bailee.

Lost, Stolen, and Abandoned Property

The basic rules of who owns lost, stolen, or abandoned property are fairly clear. The finder of **lost property** owns the property except as against the true owner. He who possesses **stolen property** has no ownership rights. As to **abandoned property**, the finder possesses ownership rights. States can vary as to these basic rules.

Intellectual Property

Intellectual property is intangible personal property that comes from thought. Intellectual property can be protected by common law concepts, such as priority in use, or by **registration**, usually with the U.S. Government. The major legal issue with intellectual property is the unauthorized use known as **infringement**. The following four primary types of intellectual property need to be discussed:

1. **Patents** – Patents are granted to protect the exclusive right to use, manufacture, or sell a device or process. They last for 20 years.
2. **Trademarks** – Trademarks are a commercial mark, design, logo, or motto used to sell or advertise a product. The symbol ® is used to identify a registered trademark.
3. **Copyrights** – Copyrights are granted to authors for original literary, artistic, or intellectual works. The symbol © designates a registered copyright. A copyright for an individual lasts for the life of the author plus 70 years.
4. **Trade Secrets** – Trade secrets are confidential information as to a commercial or industrial process. Trade secrets are not registered and can be protected by the civil cause of action of **misappropriation**.

A Summary Proceeding (7.9) – Personal Property
Bailments – transfer of personal property without intent to pass title
Lost property – finder owns except as against true owner
Stolen property – possessor has no ownership rights
Abandoned property – possessor has ownership rights
Intellectual Property – intangible property from thought
Patent – exclusive right to manufacture, sell, and use
Copyright – granted to author of original works
Trademark – commercial symbol
Trade secret – confidential information of a business process

Conclusions of Law

Obviously property law is as complex as any other field of law. Litigation involving property disputes are numerous because individuals are basically territorial. Disputes involving landlords and tenants were so numerous that many states began developing their own statutory law to resolve the issues. Even the concept of ownership is never complete ownership as property, real or personal, is subject to extensive regulation.

Exercises – Chapter 7

True-False Correction Determine if the statement is true or false; if false, insert the correct term in the blank below the question for the word in bold to make the statement true.

_____ 1. A remainder is a **present** interest in real estate.

____

_____ 2. Confidential business information as to a manufacturing process is a **trademark**.

____

_____ 3. The transfer of personal property with no intent to pass title is a **conveyance**.

____

_____ 4. Default of payment on a mortgage note may result in **foreclosure**.

____

_____ 5. The property that benefits from an easement is the **servient** tenement.

____

_____ 6. A compilation of documents to reflect chain of title is a **land grant**.

____

_____ 7. A legal description of land by lots and blocks is a **plat description**.

____

_____ 8. An estate that can be divested by a future event is a fee simple **absolute**.

____

_____ 9. Intangible personal property from thought is **intellectual** property.

____

_____ 10. A transfer of an interest in land is a **conveyance**.

____

Definitions Insert the correct legal term in the blank above the definition.

1. ______________________________

An item of personal property attached to land that materially affects the value of land

2. ______________________________

The common law estate of landlord and tenant

3. ______________________________

An amount on a mortgage note not covered by a foreclosure sale

4. ______________________________

A lease term stated as month-to-month

5. ______________________________

The concept of multi-ownership of real estate

6. ______________________________

The party who grants a security interest in real estate as collateral for a real estate loan

7. ______________________________

The notice to terminate a tenancy-at-will

8. ______________________________

The right of a landowner to redeem property after a foreclosure sale

9. ______________________________

A covenant of a lessor that addresses a third party interfering with a tenant's possession

10. ______________________________

A legal term for two pieces of real property that touch each other

11. ______________________________

An index of real estate transactions that list transactions by parcel of land

12. ______________________________

The process of recording the rights to intellectual property

Matching/Word Association Match the term in the right column with the best corresponding term in the left column.

_____	1.	community property	A.	unauthorized use
_____	2.	intangible personal property	B.	non-payment of rent
_____	3.	holdover tenant	C.	chose in action
_____	4.	profit a pendre	D.	sections and townships
_____	5.	tract	E.	conveyance at death
_____	6.	eviction	F.	cloud
_____	7.	covenants	G.	movable and touchable
_____	8.	tangible	H.	husband and wife
_____	9.	infringement	I.	release of real estate interest
_____	10.	defect in title	J.	Registrar of deeds
_____	11.	quitclaim	K.	revenue stamps
_____	12.	remainder	L.	first to record
_____	13.	transfer tax	M.	marital property
_____	14.	will	N.	notorious
_____	15.	rectangular description	O.	prior nonconforming use
_____	16.	adverse possession	P.	parcel
_____	17.	county clerk	Q.	license
_____	18.	open	R.	royalties
_____	19.	life estate	S.	prescriptive easement
_____	20.	race statute	T.	tenancy at sufferance
_____	21.	default	U.	unlawful detainer
_____	22.	tenancy by the entirety	V.	estate pur autre vie
_____	23.	grandfather	W.	warranties of lessor
_____	24.	servitude	X.	equity interest in land
_____	25.	cooperative	Y.	future interest

List/Fill in the Blank List the two tenements to an easement:

1. ______________________________

2. ______________________________

List three types of recording statutes:

1. ______________________________

2. ______________________________

3. ______________________________

List three types of evictions:

1. ______________________________

2. ______________________________

3. ______________________________

List two parties to a mortgage:

1. ______________________________

2. ______________________________

List two types of warranty deeds:

1. ______________________________

2. ______________________________

Chapter 8

Tort Law

Opening Statements

Tort law may be better known as "personal injury law"; however, that definition is woefully inadequate to define and discuss torts. A legal dictionary can tell you that the word "tort" comes from a Latin word meaning "to twist," but that doesn't help much either. Other definitions say that a tort is a breach of duty to society, but that comes close to the definition of a crime (which some torts are). A step-by-step look at the definition of a tort, the parties to a tort, the categories of torts, and the elements of a given tort is the best way to learn the language of torts.

Definition and Parties

A **tort** is most easily defined as a civil wrong, other than a breach of contract, which causes injury to another person or his or her property. The person who commits a tort is called a **tortfeasor** and engages in **tortious** conduct.

Categories of Torts

There are three basic categories of torts:

- *Intentional torts* – Actions or conduct that is designed and meant to produce the specific result of injury is an **intentional tort.** Intent is inferred from the circumstances. Intentional torts can be committed against persons and property.
- *Negligence* – The failure to use the standard of care a reasonable or prudent person would use in the same or similar circumstances is **negligence**.
- *Strict and Absolute Liability* – When a tortfeasor is liable regardless of intent, negligence, or fault, a **strict or absolute liability tort** has occurred. The most well-known strict liability tort is product liability.

Intentional Torts – Injury to Persons

Assault

Assault is conduct that gives rise to a reasonable fear or apprehension that an injury is imminent. Assault has also been called *attempted battery*. Basically, this is the same common law definition of the crime of assault. Here marks the major difference in a tort and a crime. A person can be convicted of the crime of assault, but that is not a judicial decision that awards the injured party damages. The civil action of assault is to recover damages. Occasionally a criminal court will order a defendant to make restitution for damages for not only assault, but also battery.

Battery

The unconsented to striking or touching of another that is harmful or offensive constitutes **battery**. The contact with another may only be an offensive touching as well as a physical striking.

An Unusual Case

Battery laws, both civil and criminal, eliminated the need to fight duels. When two "gentlemen" would engage in a verbal dispute that resulted in a slap or punch in the face, honor was restored by a duel. Battery actions have less dramatic results than duels.

False Imprisonment

False imprisonment is the intentional confinement of a person without that person's consent. It consists of acts that restrain liberty or freedom to leave. This cause of action is most frequently filed against shopkeepers who suspect shoplifting or police officers who unlawfully detain suspects by arrest or otherwise.

Invasion of Privacy

Basically, **invasion of privacy** is interfering with a person's right to be left alone. It can occur from publication of private information about the person as well as unauthorized or unreasonable use of one's likeness.

Example 8.1:

Opening a bar and grill, calling it "Slick Willy's," and placing the facial likeness of a local citizen named William who was just acquitted of a controversial crime of fraud on the front doors to the establishment could result in an invasion of privacy lawsuit.

Defamation

An act that is false and intentionally injures the reputation of another is **defamation**. The act may be an oral statement, which is **slander**, or printed material, which is **libel**. In either event, the statement or material must be communicated to a third party, which is the element of **publication**.

At common law certain defamatory acts were considered to be **per se**, or automatic defamation. If the defamation occurred, there was liability for damages. Such things as injury to business reputation, impugning the chastity of a woman, or accusing someone of being a felon or having a dread disease constituted **defamation per se**.

A Different Case

Libel is written defamation. *Liable* is to be responsible for damages in a civil action.

Malicious Prosecution and Abuse of Process

The filing of a groundless criminal complaint against another that results in an acquittal is **malicious prosecution**. The parallel cause of action for the filing of a groundless civil action against someone is called **abuse of process**. Again, the defendant must win the civil trial to have this cause of action.

Fraud and Misrepresentation

One of the most difficult torts to prove is **fraud**. In its simplest terms, fraud is the use of false statements to gain something of value. Several other elements of fraud include the fact that the statement must be material and known to be false by the maker, that the statements were made to induce someone to act and the reliance on the statements were reasonable, and that the false statements caused the injury. In business fraud actions there must also be a professional relationship between the parties. Fraud can also occur through knowing **concealment** of a material fact.

Example 8.2:

When selling a house, the seller openly states that a new roof was installed just last year when, in reality, the roof is 10 years old and starting to leak. That would be fraud. If the seller just says nothing to a buyer about an old, leaking roof, there could be fraud by concealment.

Intentional misrepresentation occurs when one acts intentionally to deceive another without the purpose of financial gain. **Negligent misrepresentation** occurs when one unknowingly makes a false statement that creates harm for the one who relied on the statement.

Intentional Infliction of Emotional Distress

Intentional infliction of emotional distress, also known as the tort of **outrage**, is conduct that is so outrageous that a victim would suffer **mental anguish**. Mental anguish is psychological harm. Examples of such harm would be shock, grief, fear, and even embarrassment. Generally the conduct is such that a person of ordinary sensibilities would be severely traumatized by the actions of the tortfeasor. In some jurisdictions, one act is not enough to constitute the tort; a series of acts or continuous acts is necessary to prove the tort.

Some jurisdictions have created categories of this tort to address the intent issue. Proving that the tortfeasor intended the results of emotional harm from his or her acts is difficult. Proving that the tortfeasor intended to commit the acts alone without specific intent to create the trauma has resulted in **reckless infliction of emotional distress**. Other jurisdictions have extended this tort to **negligent infliction of emotional distress**. Here it must be shown that the tortfeasor breached a duty of care, which resulted in distress to the victim. Practical jokes form the basis for some of these actions.

SUMMARY PROCEEDING (8.1) – INTENTIONAL TORTS – INJURY TO PERSONS

Intent – inferred from the circumstances – acts meant to cause a specific result

Intentional Torts – injury to persons

- Assault – conduct giving rise to reasonable fear of imminent danger
- Battery – unconsented to striking or touching of another that is harmful or offensive
- False Imprisonment – unconsented to confinement of a person
- Invasion of privacy – interfering with a person's right to be left alone
- Defamation – false statement or material injuring one's reputation
  - Slander – oral defamation

(Continued)

Summary Proceeding (8.1) – (Continued)

Libel – written defamation

Defamation per se – automatic defamation without showing of damages

Malicious prosecution – filing of groundless criminal action

Abuse of process – filing of groundless civil action

Fraud – the use of false statements to gain something of value

Concealment – the hiding of facts to gain something of value

Intentional misrepresentation – acts to deceive another

Negligent misrepresentation – unknowingly making false statements that injure

Intentional infliction of emotional distress – the tort of outrage causing emotional harm

Intentional Torts – Injury to Property

Trespass

Trespass to land is the entry onto another person's real property without consent of the owner. There need not be any knowledge that the land is private property, and there need not be any harm to the land. Trespass is usually considered a strict liability tort. Trespass can occur without a person entering the land. Throwing trash onto another's land is trespass. It is the interference with the exclusive use and possession of property that is in issue.

Trespass to chattel or personal property can occur when one interferes with the exclusive use and possession of another's personal property without consent.

Example 8.3:

Sitting on the hood of another person's car without permission could be trespass to chattel and could also create liability for damages caused to the finish of the car.

Conversion

When a theft occurs, someone is exercising dominion and control over your personal property – or, in other words, they have stolen your property and may have damaged it in the process. The action to recover damages for this theft is **conversion.** The injured party may even have to file an action to have the property returned known as **replevin** if the party retaining the personal property is a law enforcement or judicial official.

Nuisance

Nuisance is the interference with someone's enjoyment of land. There can be a **private nuisance**, which interferes with one individual's land, or a **public nuisance**, which interferes with the public's enjoyment of common rights such as the environment. The nuisance could be **mixed** and affect both an individual and the public. There can also be a **nuisance per se** as a result of a violation of the law.

A Summary Proceeding (8.2) – Intentional Torts – Injury to Property

Trespass to Land – entry onto another's land without consent

Trespass to Chattel – interference with exclusive use of another's personal property

Conversion – the exercise of dominion and control over another's property

Nuisance

- Private nuisance – interference with the land of another
- Public nuisance – interference with the rights of the public
- Mixed nuisance – a private and a public nuisance from one act
- Nuisance perse – an automatic nuisance from a violation of law

Defenses to Intentional Torts

Consent

Consent means that a victim of an intentional tort agrees to the intentional tortfeasor's actions. This consent must be **voluntary** and **informed.** *Informed* means that the victim was aware of the consequences of the actions and not just the actions themselves.

Consent can be **express consent** or **implied consent.** Express consent is consent that is stated orally or in writing, whereas implied consent is inferred from the circumstances.

Example 8.4:

Signing a contract to box in a professional fight would be express consent to be battered. Merely stepping into a boxing ring and lacing on the gloves could be implied consent to be battered.

An Unusual Case

Surgeons will inform patients of the risks of any type of surgery and obtain informed, express consent before the operation. If the surgeon operates on the wrong limb or organ he or she may be liable for battery as well as medical malpractice, as the patient did not give consent to be touched in a harmful way with the wrong surgery.

Self-Defense, Defense of Third Parties, and Defense of Property

Self-defense is probably the most well known defense to the intentional torts of assault, battery, and false imprisonment. Only **reasonable** or **necessary force** can be used, and **escape** must be considered to avoid the attack unless the attack is in the home and under the **castle doctrine. Defense of third parties** basically follows the same rules, except the victim is another person. **Defense of property** is reasonable force to protect property from damage or wrongful taking of the property. Reasonable force to protect property may be less force than to protect self or third parties.

Privilege

Privilege is defined a legal justification for acting to accomplish a greater good or a compelling social goal. Privilege can be a defense for torts against persons and torts against property. One may have a privilege to trespass to save a child in danger. One may also have a privilege to reasonably discipline a child without battery occurring. These are generally considered **conditional privileges** and are determined by the circumstances.

Certain individuals may have an **absolute privilege**. Judicial officers, law enforcement officials, and administrative officials may not be held liable for their otherwise tortious acts while in the performance of their duties.

Example 8.5:

Judges cannot be held liable for defamation for finding a criminal defendant guilty even though the defendant might have been innocent. Police officers do not commit battery when they physically take a defendant into custody.

Necessity and Mistake

Such things as trespass and battery may be necessary to avert a greater harm. These acts of **necessity** usually occur in **emergency** situations.

Example 8.6:

Jumping a fence and trespassing on another's land may be necessary if you are avoiding a charging dog. Pushing an individual out of the way of an out-of-control vehicle would not make you liable for battery.

In the defense of third-party situation, a **mistake** can be made. A mistake is an unintentional act usually based on incorrect assumptions. The following example shows how easy it might be to make a mistake in this era of child disappearances.

Example 8.7:

Passerby is driving home for lunch when he sees a poorly dressed man carrying a screaming/kicking child to a car waiting at the curb. Passerby jumps from his car, tackles the man and holds him down on the ground until the police arrive. The child runs back inside the house and locks the door. The police determine that the poorly dressed man was the child's father. The father had been doing yard work in some old clothes and had parked the car on the street to move yard equipment up and down the driveway when he remembered that he needed to take the child to the doctor. The child hated going to the doctor and threw a fit when the father reminded her of the appointment, necessitating that the father carry the daughter to the car.

Defenses to Defamation

Two general defenses are available to those sued for defamation. The first is **truth as a defense.** If what you say about someone is true, then unless the statement is made with **malice** liability does not exist. The **public figure** defense is also available for defamation cases. Public figures should expect statements, some of which may be false or misleading, to be made about them. Unless the statement is made with **malice**, no defamation has occurred.

Defense to Nuisance

Jurisdictions are split on the defense of "**coming to the nuisance.**" This defense is basically the creator of the nuisance saying, "I was here first and you knew that these conditions existed." Other jurisdictions follow the rule that a nuisance is a nuisance and therefore should be eliminated.

A Summary Proceeding (8.3) – Defenses to Intentional Torts

- Consent – voluntary and informed agreement with tortfeasor's actions
  - Express consent – stated orally or in writing
  - Implied consent – inferred from the circumstances
- Self-Defense – use of reasonable force to protect self
  - Castle doctrine – no need to attempt escape in home
- Defense of third party – use of reasonable force to protect third party
- Defense of property – use of reasonable "lesser" force to protect property
- Privilege – legal justification to accomplish a greater good
  - Conditional privilege – based on the circumstances
  - Absolute privilege – afforded to judicial, law enforcement, and administrative officers
- Necessity – emergency situations to avert a greater harm
- Mistake – unintentional acts based on incorrect assumptions
- Defamation defenses
  - Truth as a defense unless malice present
  - Public figures should expect some false statements without malice
- Nuisance defense – coming to the nuisance

Negligence

Negligence may be the most litigated tort of all. Defining negligence as the failure to use the standard of care that a reasonable or prudent person would use in the same or similar circumstances leaves much room for dispute. Negligence is proved through the four elements of the tort.

Duty

Duty is a legal obligation imposed by law to act or not act. Determining when one has a duty is the main issue. The **forseeability** rule is generally applied. If it is reasonably foreseeable that your actions or inactions may result in harm, then a duty of ordinary care is imposed. The standard of care for some individuals, such as experts, may be higher than ordinary care. In this situation, the duty of care is the standard of care other experts would use in the same or similar circumstances.

Example 8.8:

Gift Shop has been located at the base of a mountain for over 50 years. In that time, no rocks have ever fallen from the mountain through the roof of the store. One day a rock does fall through the roof and seriously injures Customer. Customer sues, but must prove that Gift Shop reasonably foresaw such an event and had a duty to warn Customer or take other reasonable actions to prevent the injury.

Breach of Duty

Breach is the wrongful, or unexcused, failure to perform a duty.

Causation

The breach of duty must be the act that causes the plaintiff's injury. **Causation** is a complex subject and has been discussed in several ways:

1. **Direct causation** or **causation in fact** – This is known as the "**but for**" or **sine qua non** theory of causation. Without the first event, the injury would have never occurred. In other words, Event A causes Event B, which causes Event C, which injures the plaintiff. Courts do not use this form of causation in negligence actions.
2. **Proximate causation** – This is the forseeability rule applied to causation. Was the act reasonably connected to the injury and was it reasonably foreseeable that the breach would cause the injury? Every lawyer knows the famous *Palsgraf* case (see Example 8.9), which goes into the depth of the proximate cause issue. What do you think should be the outcome of the case?

Example 8.9:

Mrs. Palsgraf is waiting to catch a train and is sitting quietly on the railway platform next to a set of scales used to weigh cargo. As a train pulls out of the station, a late-arriving passenger with a package under his arm runs to catch the train. The conductor on board the train reaches to help the passenger board, while a conductor on the platform pushes the passenger up the train steps. The platform conductor pushes the package out from under the arm of the passenger. The package contains fireworks, which explode as they hit the train rails and wheels. The fireworks shoot across the platform, hit the scales, and topple the scales onto Mrs. Palsgraf. Mrs. Palsgraf sues the railroad company for negligence.

A rule frequently used with the proximate causation rule is the **intervening cause rule.** This is where one person is negligent, but that negligence only creates an injury due to the negligence of another who intervenes into the situation and, in fact, **supersedes** the negligence of the first negligent party.

Example 8.10:

Car A is sitting at a stoplight. Car B stops just a few inches away from the rear of Car A, which may be negligence because it is reasonably foreseeable that Car A may have a stick shift, which causes Car A to roll backward on an incline. Car C hits the rear of Car B, which causes Car B to damage Car A. Had Car A rolled back into Car B, the driver of Car B would have been liable for negligence. However, because Car C intervened and caused the events of damage, the driver of Car C has superseded the negligence of Car B and is therefore liable.

3. Substantial factor rule – The **substantial factor** rule has also been called the **legal cause** rule. A simple question must be answered: Was the breach of duty a substantial factor in causing the injury?

Damages

Monetary damages are sought for injuries sustained to person and property in a tort action. The student should closely review the damages discussed in **Chapter 3** as a refresher. Equitable remedies should be reviewed as well.

A SUMMARY PROCEEDING (8.4) – NEGLIGENCE

Definition – the failure to use the standard of care a prudent person would use in similar events

Elements of negligence

- Duty – a legal obligation based on forseeability of harm
- Breach – the failure to exercise a legal obligation
- Causation
  - Direct causation – the "but for" or sine qua non rule
  - Proximate causation – based on the forseeability rule
  - Intervening causation – separate event superceding original negligence
  - Substantial factor – legal cause rule
- Damages – compensatory, special or consequential, punitive, and nominal

Defenses to Negligence

Assumption of Risk

When a plaintiff acts in spite of a known and obvious danger, the defendant can assert **assumption of risk** as a defense.

Example 8.11:

An ice storm has covered Grocery Store's parking lot and entryways. The store puts up signs and tape alerting Shopper to use another entryway, which has been cleared of ice. Shopper crosses the warning tape and begins to "skate" across a sheet of ice. The shopper falls, breaks his hip, and sues Grocery Store for negligence. Grocery Store asserts assumption of risk as a defense.

Contributory Negligence

At common law, if the plaintiff contributed any negligence to the event causing the injury, the plaintiff was completely barred from recovery under the **contributory negligence** doctrine. However, if the plaintiff could prove the defendant had **the last clear chance** to avoid the event and injury, the plaintiff could proceed.

Comparative Negligence

Almost all jurisdictions have replaced the contributory negligence defense with the **comparative negligence** defense. Here, the jury decides what percentage of fault lies with each party. Only if the plaintiff were more than 50% at fault would he or she be barred from recovery. The problem with comparative negligence as to liability is that it not only gets easily confused with damages, but it also allows the jury to arbitrarily assign percentages of fault.

Example 8.12:

Parker parks his car on the wrong side of the street with the front of the car facing the flow of traffic. This is a violation of law in many jurisdictions, and therefore, **negligence per se.** Drunk Driver hits the front of Parker's car, totaling the car with a loss of $20,000. Had the car been parked correctly, the damages would have been only $8,000. Who is more at fault with their actions, and whose actions caused more of the damages?

Sovereign Immunity

The concept of **sovereign immunity** means that you cannot sue the government; they are immune from liability. There are exceptions to this rule that have effectively eliminated the concept. First, the **Federal Tort Claims Act** specifies that certain tort actions can be filed against the U.S. Government. Second, many states have set up **Claims Commissions** within the legislative function to address individual claims. Finally, some jurisdictions allow for **direct actions**, whereby the party injured by the government can file litigation against an insurance company issuing a liability policy covering the state.

Charitable Immunity

A longstanding concept of common law was that charities, those who conduct benevolent activities, should not be liable through litigation (i.e., **charitable immunity**). Many states now allow charities to be sued, but limit the liability to the amount of charitable assets and shield individual members of the charity from litigation.

Statute of Limitations

Although a Statute of Limitations will bar almost all legal actions, except prosecution for murder, there are two unique applications of the Statute of Limitations in regard to negligence. These are the "**knew or should have known**" rule and the **fraudulent concealment** situation. Both allow for a **tolling** of the period of limitation. For a Statute of Limitation to **toll** means that it does not run.

Example 8.13:

The Statute of Limitations for medical negligence is 1 year. Surgeon leaves an instrument inside of Patient. Patient doesn't discover the instrument for 13 months, when symptoms begin to appear. Only when the symptoms appeared did Patient know or should have known of the negligence. Patient has one year from the date he or she knew of the negligence to sue.

Example 8.14:

The Statute of Limitations for ordinary negligence is 3 years. Contractor installs the wrong type of insulation underneath a house in a shoddy fashion and installs only half of the insulation, stopping about halfway back. The insulation begins to rot, smell, collapse, and fall 5 years after the installation. Homeowner discovers the problem when a pest control inspector makes a special inspection 5 years after the installation to find the source of the smell. Because Contractor fraudulently concealed his failure to finish, used improper insulation and installation techniques, and only an expert could detect the impropriety, Homeowner has three years from the date of discovery to file a lawsuit.

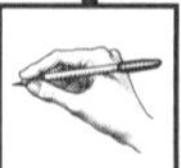

A Summary Proceeding (8.5) – Defenses to Negligence

- Assumption of risk – plaintiff is aware of a known and obvious risk
- Contributory negligence – any negligence contributed by plaintiff bars lawsuit
  - Last clear chance doctrine – if defendant had last chance to avoid injury, plaintiff can sue
- Comparative negligence – jury compares the negligence of both parties for liability
- Sovereign immunity – governments cannot be sued
  - Federal Tort Claims Act used to sue U.S. Government

(Continued)

A SUMMARY PROCEEDING (8.5) – (CONTINUED)

State Claims Commissions to resolve disputes with citizens
Direct action lawsuits against state insurance carriers allowed
Statute of Limitations
Tolling for knew or should have known rule and fraudulent concealment rule

Additional Negligence Concepts

Gross Negligence

Gross negligence has been described as excessive negligence or actions that shock the conscience of the jury. It is the first step toward assuring the award of **punitive damages** to punish the defendant.

Willful and Wanton Conduct

Willful and wanton conduct consists of negligent actions you intend to commit not for the purpose of injuring anyone, but that do injure someone in the process. Punitive damages are clearly sought in these actions as well as in intentional tort cases.

Example 8.15:

Driving 35 MPH in a 25 MPH zone would be negligence. Driving 35 MPH in a 25 MPH school zone at 3:00 p.m. while it is raining would be gross negligence. Drag racing would be willful and wanton conduct.

Attractive Nuisance

Certain conditions are so enticing to children (and sometimes adults), that their very nature incurs liability if someone is injured even though the victim is a trespasser or is negligent. Swimming pools, ladders leaning against a tree, and trampolines are three very common **attractive nuisances**.

Res Ispa Loquitur

Translated, **res ipsa loquitur** means "the thing speaks for itself." The injury could not have occurred without negligence being present and a presumption of negligence exists.

Example 8.16:

A tourist is walking through an industrial district at the turn of the twentieth century. A barrel falls on his head. The barrel rolled out of an open loft door above the sidewalk. It is obvious that someone left a loft door open with rolling objects close to the doors. This is obviously negligence on someone's part.

Premises Liability

Premises liability has been nicknamed the "slip and fall" cases. Someone is injured as a result of a dangerous condition on property. Two competing theories of law are used to decide these cases. The first is the "**status of the plaintiff**" theory and the second is simple negligence.

The status of the plaintiff can be a **trespasser**, a **licensee**, or an **invitee**. An owner of property owes no duty to a trespasser and therefore cannot be liable. The owner owes a duty of ordinary care to a licensee, such as those who are allowed to cross his or her property, and may be liable for negligence. The owner owes a high duty of care to invitees, such as business customers, and could be easily liable for slight negligence.

Problems evolve when a business customer walks into an area restricted to employees. Is the customer now a trespasser? Other problems evolve when a licensee, such as a friend who stops by to go to lunch with the business owner, decides to purchase a product from the business. Is the friend now an invitee or a licensee? Some jurisdictions have resolved this problem by applying standard rules of negligence to all premises liability cases, but other problems have evolved from the application of simple negligence theories to premises liability cases. What is your opinion of the following Unusual Case?

An Unusual Case

Storeowner's shop is located in a high-crime section of town. Storeowner places bars over the front windows and doors for safety and security. No bars are placed over a rear door to the shop, which opens to an old, rotten staircase leading down to a storage room in the basement of the shop. Burglar breaks in the back door, falls down the stairs, and breaks his leg. Burglar sues Storeowner for negligence under the theory of premises liability. The jury must answer the following question: was it reasonably foreseeable that a burglar would break in to a store through an unprotected back door in a high-crime area? If the answer is yes, then Storeowner owed a duty to Burglar to repair the stairs and may be liable for Burglar's injuries.

Other Tort Concepts

Survival and Wrongful Death Actions

Certain torts that cause death, such as battery, survive the death of the victim. The heirs of the victim can sue in place of the deceased. The torts that give rise to **survival actions** are usually established by state statute.

A similar type of action is a **wrongful death action**, in which the heirs of the deceased can bring a suit based on the tortious conduct of the person responsible. This suit is for the damages to the heirs of losing a loved one.

Example 8.17:

A man with two children by his ex-wife kills his ex-wife and a friend of hers by slashing each person's throat, which is battery. The heirs of the friend of the ex-wife can file a wrongful death action based on battery for the pain and suffering due to the loss of a loved one. The estate of the deceased mother could file a battery action against the ex-husband. In the battery action, the children do not have to testify against their father as to their pain and suffering. Merely proving the battery results in liability against the defendant ex-husband.

Vicarious Liability

Vicarious liability is a situation in which one person is responsible for another person's tortious conduct. At common law, the doctrine of **Respondeat Superior** meant the superior must respond and was well known as the **Master-Servant rule**. Most vicarious liability actions involve suing a business/employer instead of the agent/employee because the business has the "deep pocket" to pay a large award.

Another concept to establish vicarious liability is the doctrine of **negligent entrustment.**

Example 8.18:

Car Owner loans his car to Bad Driver, knowing that Bad Driver speeds and causes wrecks. If Bad Driver causes injury by negligent driving, Car Owner could be liable.

A Summary Proceeding (8.6) – Other Negligence and Tort Concepts

Gross negligence – excessive negligence

Willful and wanton conduct – intent to act negligently, but not to injure

Attractive nuisance – dangerous conditions that are enticing, especially to children

Res ipsa loquitur – the thing speaks for itself – a presumption of negligence

Premises liability – status

- Trespasser – no duty owed and no liability
- Licensee – duty of ordinary care – possible liability
- Invitee – high duty of care – probable liability

Premises liability – simple negligence applied

Survival actions – heirs may sue in place of deceased tort victim

Wrongful death actions – heirs may sue tortfeasor for pain and suffering of loss of loved one

(Continued)

A Summary Proceeding (8.6) – (Continued)

Vicarious liability – responsibility for the tortious actions of another

Respondeat superior – Master/servant

Negligent entrustment

Strict and Absolute Liability Torts

Strict and **absolute liability** torts have one common principle in that the tortfeasor is liable without a showing of fault. If a certain condition exists or event occurs, then liability exists. This is not to say there are not defenses to strict or absolute liability torts. There are very limited defenses, but there are very few strict liability torts.

Product Liability

Any seller of a product that is **defective, unreasonably dangerous**, and causes injury to person or property is liable for the injuries under the concept of **product liability**. This liability exists even though the injured party does not prove negligence of or privity of contract with the business.

Example 8.19:

Car Company sells a T-top car that was not designed with roll bars to support the passenger compartment. Teen Driver drives the car at an excessive speed after drinking alcohol, wrecks the car, and ends up a paraplegic. The car is unreasonably dangerous and defective and Car Company is liable. Car Company cannot defend with comparative negligence on the part of Teen Driver because Teen Driver does not have to prove negligence.

Abnormally Dangerous Activities

Certain activities such as the use of explosives are so inherently dangerous that no amount of care can prevent the damage that will occur. The actor is generally liable.

Example 8.20:

TNT Company is hired to implode an old downtown building using dynamite. The blast causes a large cloud of dust and dirt to engulf a nearby building. TNT Company will be liable for the cleaning of the buildings.

Animals

Animals can create liability for the owner depending on what type of animal is involved and what state laws are available. If the animal is a **wild or feral animal,** such as a pet lion or tiger, the defendant can expect strict liability to be applied with few defenses. If the animal is a **domesticated animal**, such as a dog, it is presumed to be harmless unless the owner has knowledge of the **vicious propensity** of the animal. Vicious propensity has been coined as the "**one bite**" rule. Once the dog bites someone, vicious propensity is established and strict liability may apply. Otherwise, simple negligence rules apply.

An Unusual Case

Posting a "Beware of Dog" sign may be a double-edged sword. Does the sign show ordinary care to warn others, or is the sign an indication of knowledge of vicious propensity?

Joint and Several Liability

When two or more torfeasors are found liable for damages there is a situation of **joint and several liability. Joint liability** means each tortfeasor is responsible for paying his or her respective share of damages. **Several liability** means each tortfeasor is responsible for paying all of the damages. If one of two tortfeasors is **judgment proof**, or without ability to pay, then the other must cover all of the damages. It is up to the solvent defendant to seek **contribution** from the insolvent defendant. The plaintiff should not be the person who is responsible for the lack of funds of one tortfeasor.

Market Share Liability

Particularly in product liability litigation, it may be impossible to determine which of multiple defendant companies actually produced the defective product that injured the plaintiff. In this situation the court may rule for **market share liability**. Each company is responsible for the percentage of damages equal to that company's percentage of the total market of sales, or market share.

Example 8.21:

Company A, Company B, and Company C make a generic brand of a drug that has been found to be defective and unreasonably dangerous. Company A maintains a 60% share of the market, Company B has a 30% share, and Company C has a 10% share. Assuming a $1,000,000 award, Company A must pay $600,000, Company B will pay $300,000, and Company C is responsible for $100,000. If Company A and B are judgment proof then Company C must pay the full judgment.

SUMMARY PROCEEDING (8.7) – LIABILITY ISSUES WITH TORTS

Strict or absolute liability – liability without proof of fault

- Product liability – liability for defective and unreasonably dangerous product
- Abnormally dangerous activity – no amount of care reduces risks

(Continued)

Summary Proceeding (8.7) – (Continued)

Animals

Wild animals – absolute or strict liability for injuries caused

Domesticated animals – strict or absolute liability with vicious propensity

Joint and several liability – multiple tortfeasors

Joint – each tortfeasor responsible for respective share

Several – each tortfeasor responsible for full judgment

Contribution – solvent tortfeasor must collect from insolvent torfeasor

Market share liability – defendants responsible for amount equal to share of market in sales

Author's Note: Damages are available for all torts and just not negligence in situations in which the student is referred to Chapter 3. Again, the suggestion is made to refer to Chapter 3 for a refresher on the subject of legal and equitable remedies.

Conclusions of Law

Torts may originate in common law, may be derived from common law concepts, or may exist from recent case and statutory law. Torts can be intentional or nonintentional. Torts can cause injury to persons and property. Torts will continue to grow as a field of law as long as people continue to injure people and property.

The Latin Language

Sine qua non – *sin*-ih kwah non

Respondeat superior – ri-*spahn*-dee-at

Exercises – Chapter 8

True/False Correction Determine if the statement is true or false; if false, insert the correct word in the blank below the question for the term in bold to make the statement true.

_____ 1. The communication to a third party of a slanderous comment is **publication**.

____

_____ 2. Liability of two tortfeasors is considered **vicarious** liability.

____

_____ 3. Litigation by heirs of a tort victim for mental anguish is a **survival** action.

____

_____ 4. Violation of a statute is **gross negligence**.

____

_____ 5. Duty under negligence concepts is determined by **forseeability**.

____

_____ 6. A judicial officer will have a(n) **conditional** privilege against defamation.

____

_____ 7. Interference with the exclusive use of another's personal property is **malice.**

____

_____ 8. Making false statements for economic or monetary gain is **fraud**.

____

_____ 9. A solvent tortfeasor seeking payment from an insolvent tortfeasor is **conversion.**

____

_____ 10. Acting despite knowledge of an obvious danger is **affirmative fraud**.

____

_____ 11. A customer who browses through your store is a **licensee**.

____

_____ 12. The desire to produce the result of injury is **intent**.

____

Definitions Insert the correct legal term in the blank above the definition.

1. ______________________________

The common law concept preventing lawsuits against a government

2. ______________________________

The failure to act or not act when a legal obligation is present

3. ______________________________

The action for the filing of a baseless criminal action, which results in acquittal

4. ______________________________

The "thing speaks for itself"

5. ______________________________

Examples: swimming pools and trampolines

6. ______________________________

Activity that is intentional but not with intent to harm

7. ______________________________

A form of liability without a showing of fault or negligence

8. ______________________________

The legal concept for intentionally and wrongfully confining a person

9. ______________________________

An action to recover personal property held by a law enforcement official

10. ______________________________

The federal statute that allows individuals to sue the U.S. Government for torts

11. ______________________________

The person who commits a tort

12. ______________________________

The exercise of dominion and control over another's personal property

13. ______________________________

A false oral statement injuring another's reputation

14. ______________________________

An agreement by a victim to let a tortfeasor act and injure the victim

15. ______________________________

The interference with another's use and enjoyment of land

Matching/Word Association Match the term in the right column with the best corresponding term in the left column.

_____ 1.	punitive	A.	defective product
_____ 2.	abuse of process	B.	"but for"
_____ 3.	outrage	C.	interference with social goal
_____ 4.	vicious propensity	D.	substantial factor
_____ 5.	respondeat superior	E.	unauthorized use of name
_____ 6.	product liability	F.	legal justification
_____ 7.	negligence per se	G.	legislative dispute resolution
_____ 8.	necessity	H.	trespass defense
_____ 9.	legal causation	I.	defense of property
_____ 10.	intervening negligence	J.	"one bite" rule
_____ 11.	mistake	K.	malice
_____ 12.	sine qua non	L.	groundless civil action
_____ 13.	privilege	M.	incorrect assumptions
_____ 14.	truth	N.	punishment
_____ 15.	reasonable force	O.	insurance company
_____ 16.	invasion of privacy	P.	intentional infliction of distress
_____ 17.	libel	Q.	forseeability
_____ 18.	contributory negligence	R.	master-servant
_____ 19.	direct action suit	S.	printed defamation
_____ 20.	premises liability	T.	defamation defense
_____ 21.	proximate cause	U.	slip and fall cases
_____ 22.	public nuisance	V.	superseding negligence
_____ 23.	gross negligence	W.	shocks the conscience
_____ 24.	claims commission	X.	bar to negligence action
_____ 25.	public figure	Y.	violation of law

List/Fill in the Blank List two types of defamation:

1. ______________________________

2. ______________________________

List the four elements to prove negligence in order:

1. ______________________________

2. ______________________________

3. ______________________________

4. ______________________________

List four types of nuisances:

1. ______________________________

2. ______________________________

3. ______________________________

4. ______________________________

List a defense to the action of nuisance:

1. ______________________________

List the status of the three parties who may be a plaintiff in a premises liability suit:

1. ______________________________

2. ______________________________

3. ______________________________

Section IV

Business Law

Chapter 9

Agency Relationships

Opening Statements

Agency relationships are relationships in which one party represents another party and are usually business relationships. To be more legally precise, an **agent** acts on behalf of a **principal**. Most important with this relationship is the issue of vicarious liability, which was discussed in Chapter 8 on Torts. The agent's acts can bind the principal to liability to third parties with whom the agent deals, especially in the areas of Torts and Contracts. Agency relationships derive from the common law concept of Master-Servant and fall within the doctrine of Respondeat Superior.

Parties to an Agency Relationship

The two parties to an **agency relationship** are the **principal**, who is the superior, and the **agent**, who is the subordinate.

A Different Case

The words *principal* and *principle* have completely different meanings. A principal is the superior or primary party in an agency relationship. A principle is a concept such as a principle of law.

Types of Agents and Agencies

General Agent

A **general agent** can conduct all acts that the principal can conduct and a **general agency** exists.

Limited Agent

A **limited**, or **special agent**, can only conduct specific acts connected to the principal and a **limited** or **special agency** exists.

Example 9.1:

A real estate agent would be a limited agent. The only act the real estate agent can conduct is the finding of a buyer for a home.

Universal Agent

A **universal agent** can conduct any act on behalf of the principal that can lawfully be delegated and a **universal agency** exists.

An Agent Coupled with an Interest

An **agent coupled (or vested) with an interest** has an interest in the subject matter of the agency relationship. There is an **agency coupled with an interest** and cannot be terminated without the agent's interest being satisfied.

Example 9.2:

If the agent loans the principal money to conduct the activities of the agency, then the agent is coupled with an interest.

An Independent Agent

An **independent agent** can represent several principals at the same time. It is most frequently seen in the insurance industry and the agent is sometimes called a **broker.**

A Summary Proceeding (9.1) – Types of Agents

General agent – can do anything and everything a principal can do
Special agent – authorized to act on behalf of a principal for a limited reason
Universal agent – can act in any lawful purpose that can be delegated
Agent coupled with an interest – agent has an interest in the subject matter of the agency
Independent agent – an agent with more than one principal

Creation of an Agency Relationship

Express Creation

An **express agency** is one that is created by oral or written statements. If the subject matter of the agency is such that must be in writing, such as real estate activities, the agency relationship must be established by a written document. Otherwise, agencies can be created by oral agreement. A well-known document that creates an agency is a **power of attorney**. In this situation, the agent is called an **attorney in fact**.

Durable Power of Attorney

At common law, an agency ended when the principal become incompetent. But this was the time at which a principal needed an agent the most. Statutory law created the **durable power of attorney**, which either survives the incompetency or springs at the time of the incompetency. If the agency survives or continues after the incompetency, it is a **surviving power of attorney**. If the agency begins at the incompetency, it is a **springing power of attorney**.

Implied Creation

If the agency relationship is inferred from the conduct of the parties, it is said to be an **implied agency** or **agency by implication**. Court will determine if this agency exists on a case-by-case basis and may look to the historical dealings of the parties.

Agency by Ratification

Agency by ratification is created after the event or activity of the agent when an agency did not exist. The principal must fully ratify all of the agent's actions, and the agent must disclose all of his or her actions.

Example 9.3:

Adam is not an agent for Peter, but Adam knows that Peter is desperately seeking to buy a certain painting. Adam sees the painting at a gallery and signs a contract on behalf of Peter to buy the painting. Peter reviews the painting and contract and agrees to Adam's actions and agrees to pay for the painting. Peter is now the principal and Adam is now the agent, as an **agency by ratification** has been established.

Agency by Estoppel

An **agency by estoppel estops** or **bars** the principal from claiming an agency exists. Two conditions usually exist for the estoppel to occur. The third party detrimentally relies on an act of the alleged agent because the principal has acted or failed to act in such a way that leads the third party to believe an agency exists.

Example 9.4:

Peter has fired his long-time agent, Adam, but does not notify Third Party of the termination. Adam convinces Third Party, with whom Adam has dealt many times, to sign a contract with Adam on behalf of Peter that Peter will loan Third Party money for his new business. Third Party contracts with Supplier for equipment for his new business. Peter cannot deny the agency because he should have notified Third Party of the termination.

A SUMMARY PROCEEDING (9.2) – CREATING AN AGENCY RELATIONSHIP

- Express Creation – agency relationship stated orally or in writing
  - Power of Attorney – attorney in fact is agent
    - Durable power of attorney – agency does not terminate at disability of principal
      - Surviving clause – agency survives disability of principal
      - Springing clause – agency begins at disability of principal
- Implied agency – created by conduct of parties
- Agency by ratification – created after agent acts by approval of principal
- Agency by estoppel – created by law when third party detrimentally relies on agent acts

Authority of Agents

Actual Authority

Actual authority is self explanatory as to a definition, but there are two categories of actual authority. **Express authority** is that which is stated orally or in writing. **Implied authority** is the authority not stated but necessary to complete express authority.

Example 9.5:

Client signs an engagement letter with Attorney to sue for an automobile accident. Even though the engagement letter doesn't specifically state that Attorney can investigate the wreck, that is something that would be necessary before the Attorney files the action. Attorney would have implied authority to instigate and express authority to sue.

Apparent Authority

Apparent authority sounds very similar to the agency by estoppel situation. In the estoppel situation, no agency existed but was being created by law. Here the agency exists, but the agent is exceeding his authority. The third party must detrimentally rely on the agent's actions, and there must be some action or inaction on the part of the principal that leads the third party to believe the agent has authority. This has been a problem situation in the banking industry and has been called "**lender's liability**."

Example 9.6:

Bank sends Loan Officer to meet with Customer about a loan. Loan officer has actual authority to make a loan up to $50,000 without committee approval. Loan Officer agrees to make Customer a $100,000 loan, and the Customer begins ordering supplies expecting the full loan. The bank is bound under the concept of apparent authority.

A Summary Proceeding (9.3) – Authority of an Agent

Actual authority
- Express – stated orally or in writing
- Implied – necessary to complete express authority

Apparent authority – actions of the principal that lead third party to believe agent has authority

Duties of an Agent

Once established as an agent, the agent is considered a **fiduciary**. A fiduciary is defined as one who must act in the best interest of another according to the terms of the agreement. It is important to note that although agency agreements are contracts, they are interpreted according to agency law. If the agent acts improperly, it is not said to be a breach of contract – it is said to be a **breach of fiduciary duty**.

Obedience

An agent must be **obedient**. This term comes mainly from the common law concept of Master-Servant, which is archaic. It is better said that the agent must **perform** under the terms of the agency.

Reasonable Performance

All agents must perform in a reasonable fashion. This duty brings in the concept of negligence under tort law. The agent must act as a reasonable or prudent agent would act under the same or similar circumstance.

Disclosure and Accounting

The agent must keep the principal advised as to the agent's actions. All knowledge of the agent is **imputed** to the principal. **Imputed knowledge** means that all knowledge of the agent is presumed to be knowledge of the principal. The agent should also **account** to the principal for sums expended on behalf of the principal.

Loyalty

There are two areas of **loyalty** that frequently arise with agency relationships. The first is a **conflict of interest**. An agent cannot represent two principals whose interests may be adverse. The second is **self-dealing**. The agent must act for the benefit of the principal, not for his or her own benefit.

Example 9.7:

Principal hires Agent to locate a certain antique car that is in operating condition and agrees to pay Agent a 5% commission. The Agent finds a Seller of that specific antique car, but the car does not run. Agent then signs an agreement with Seller to sell the car for a 5% commission. Agent then sells the car to Principal and collects two commissions.

Duties of a Principal

A principal must act according to established principles of law as well. Agents and principals both have duties as well as rights under an agency relationship.

Duty to Compensate

The principal must **compensate** the agent for his work. The compensation may be in the form of a commission, a salary, or a wage.

A Different Case

If an agent shares in the profits of the principal, he or she may no longer just be an agent. He or she may become a partner and incur additional liabilities. These issues will be discussed in Appendix 10A on Other Business Organizations.

Duty to Reimburse

Unless otherwise agreed on, the principal must **reimburse** the agent for any out-of-pocket expenses the agent incurs while acting on behalf of the principal.

Duty to Indemnify

The principal must also **indemnify** the agent against losses the agent may sustain. If the agent were sued in his capacity as agent, then the principal is required to cover the agent's losses.

Duty not to Compete

An agent takes his or her position with the intention of financial gain. If the principal conducts the activities from which the agent would benefit, the principal has violated his duty **not to compete.**

> *Example 9.8:*
>
> If you list your house with a real estate agent and then begin to show your house to friends to find a buyer on your own, you are competing with your own agent. Most real estate agency relationships specifically state that you will still be liable to pay a commission to the agent for the buyer you find.

Duty to Provide Safe Working Conditions

This is quite self-explanatory, but principals have been known to provide unsafe automobiles, tools, and yard equipment.

A Summary Proceeding (9.4) – Duties of Agent and Principal

Agent – fiduciary duty to act in best interest of principal
- Obedience – agent must perform as instructed
- Reasonable performance – agent must use ordinary care
- Disclose – provide information of activities to principal
- Account – provide information of use of principal's money
- Loyalty of agent
  - No conflict of interest – cannot serve another principal with adverse interest
  - No self dealing – agent cannot act for his or own benefit

Principal
- Must compensate agent by wage, salary, or commission
- Must reimburse agent for expenses
- Must indemnify agent for losses
- Must not to compete with agent
- Must provide safe working conditions

Liability of Principal to Third Parties

Contract Liability

A principal may or may not be liable to a third party with whom the agent has signed a contract. Liability depends on the issue of disclosure:

1. If the agent discloses the existence of the agency relationship and the identity of the principal, then the principal is generally liable for the agent's acts. This is known as a **fully disclosed agency relationship**.
2. If the agent discloses the existence of the agency relationship but not the identity of the principal, then the principal is generally liable. This is a **partially disclosed agency relationship**.
3. If the agent fails to disclose the existence of the agency or the identity of the principal, the agent is generally liable to the third party. This is an **undisclosed agency relationship**.

Tort Liability

If the agent's negligence causes injury to another, that negligence becomes **imputed negligence**. It becomes the negligence of the principal if the agent was acting **within the scope of his or her authority or employment**. Problems arise when agents go on a **frolic or detour**. If the agent is on a frolic or detour outside the scope of his or her authority, the agent is on his or her own and the principal is not liable. What constitutes a frolic and detour is a question of fact. It also presents sticky situations regarding the "deep pocket" concept.

Example 9.9:

Hospital owns and operates its own ambulance service. The ambulance is sent out on an emergency run for a possible heart attack patient. On the way back to the hospital, with the patient in the back of the ambulance, the Driver stops at a pizza parlor to order a pizza to go. The patient dies before arriving at the hospital.

A Summary Proceeding (9.5) – Vicarious Liability of Principal

Contract liability

- Principal liable if agent discloses agency and identification of principal
- Principal liable if agent discloses agency but not identification of principal
- Agent liable if agent discloses neither agency nor identification of principal

Tort liability

- Principal is liable if agent within scope of authority or employment
- Agent liable if on a frolic and detour

Terminating an Agency Relationship

For the most part, agency relationships are ended by **mutual agreement** of the parties. With limited or special agencies, **accomplishment of purpose** will end the agency. An agency can also end by **lapse of time**, whereby the agent fails to act. Finally, an agency can be terminated by **operation of law**, similar to the ending of a contract. Death of a party, destruction of the subject matter of the agency, and bankruptcy of a party will terminate the agency. Note at this point that it is important for the principal to notify third parties with whom the agent has dealt or the issue of agency by estoppel may arise.

Other Agency-Related Issues

Consignment

A **consignment** is a business agency in which the owner of goods entrusts another to sell the good. The owner is called a **consignor** and the seller is the **consignee.** The consignee is generally not considered an agent except for the sale.

Employees

Employees clearly can be agents and authorized to act on behalf of a business. Generally, a business will designate who does or does not have the authority to act and specify what authority exists. Employees still can create agency relationships by estoppel even though no express agency exists.

Independent Contractors

Independent contractors are those individuals or businesses that maintain control over the business situation, as opposed to an employer who maintains control over an employee. Generally, parties who hire independent contractors are not liable for the contractor's torts, but can, in some cases, be liable for the contracts of the independent contractor.

A Summary Proceeding (9.6) – Terminating an Agency and Other Issues

- Termination of Agency
  - Mutual agreement of both parties
  - Accomplishment of purpose
  - Lapse of reasonable time
  - Operation of law – death, disability, destruction of subject matter, and bankruptcy
  - Notice to third parties to avoid agency by estoppel
- Consignment – Consignor entrusts good to consignee for sale
- Employee – can be agent
- Independent contractor – maintains control over work; not an agent for tort liability

Conclusions of Law

Agency law can be tied directly to contract and property law, and that is why it is part of the Common Law section of this text. Agency law will also be tied directly to Business Organizations, which is the topic of the next chapter.

Exercises – Chapter 9

True-False Correction Determine if the statement is true or false; if false, insert the correct term in the blank below the question for the word in bold to make the statement true.

_____ 1. An **express** agency is stated orally or in writing.

____

_____ 2. The entrusting of goods to another for the sale of the goods is **reimbursement**.

____

_____ 3. Authority necessary to carry out express authority is **apparent** authority.

____

_____ 4. A person who maintains control over the work to be performed is an **employee**.

____

_____ 5. An agency that terminates after a reasonable time is said to **expire**.

____

_____ 6. An agent that represents several principals is an **universal** agent.

____

Definitions Insert the correct legal term in the blank above the definition.

1. ____

   An agency created by conduct of the parties

2. ____

   The disclosure of only the agency relationship but not the identity of the principal

3. ____

   A document creating an agency that survives the disability of the principal

4. ____

   An agency created by the principal after the agent acts

5. ____

   Information known by the agent that is presumed to be known by the principal

6. ____

   The Latin term for "vicarious liability"

Word Association-Matching Match the term in the left column with the best corresponding term in the right column.

_____ 1.	loyalty	A.	bar
_____ 2.	estoppel	B.	reimbursement for losses
_____ 3.	fiduciary	C.	durable
_____ 4.	power of attorney	D.	detrimental reliance on agent
_____ 5.	disclosure	E.	agent
_____ 6.	frolic and detour	F.	bankruptcy
_____ 7.	indemnification	G.	self dealing
_____ 8.	apparent authority	H.	outside scope of authority
_____ 9.	principal	I.	superior
_____ 10.	termination of agency	J.	accounting

Multiple choice Insert the correct answer in the blank provided.

_____ 1. An agent making a loan to a principal for the agency activities creates a

a. limited agency
b. agency coupled with an interest
c. both of the above
d. neither of the above

_____ 2. An agent who fails to perform has

a. been disobedient
b. has breached fiduciary duty
c. both of the above
d. neither of the above

_____ 3. A limited agent who has performed is terminated by

a. mutual agreement
b. accomplishment of purpose
c. both of the above
d. neither of the above

_____ 4. An agent who fails to communicate the agency and identity of the principal is a

a. undisclosed agent
b. personally liable
c. both of the above
d. neither of the above

_____ 5. A power of attorney that takes effect on disability has a

a. springing clause
b. survival clause
c. both of the above
d. neither of the above

Chapter 10

Business Organizations – Corporations

Opening Statements

Businesses are the foundation of the American system of economics. Corporations are the dominant form of business in the United States, and the most legally complex of all forms of business. A **corporation** is a separate legal and taxable entity. It is a **person**, albeit an artificial one, under the provisions of the U.S. Constitution except for the provisions of the Fifth Amendment regarding self-incrimination. It can sue and be sued. It can speak through **business records**. Corporations exist under statutory law and must strictly comply with all statutes in their formation and potentially perpetual existence. Other forms of business organization may be more common than corporations, but all other forms of business cannot come close to matching the revenues generated by corporations, or the legal work. Major corporations maintain **"in-house" counsel** and those legal departments can rival the size of many medium-sized law firms.

Types of Corporations

Public vs. Private

A **public corporation** is one whose stock is owned by the general public. Anyone can buy or sell the stock and become an owner of the corporation. Other terms for public corporations are **publicly held corporations** and **publicly traded corporations.** A **private corporation** is one whose stock is owned by a few individuals, usually a family. Private corporations are also called **close corporations** or **closely held corporations**.

Domestic vs. Foreign

A **domestic corporation** is one that is incorporated under the laws of a particular state. It is said to be **domiciled** within that state. It does not necessarily have to carry on business in its **state of incorporation.** A **foreign corporation** is one that is incorporated in a state other than in which it is **doing business**.

Parent vs. Subsidiary

A **parent corporation** is one that owns other corporations. A **subsidiary corporation** is owned by a parent corporation. A **wholly owned subsidiary** would be a corporation whose total outstanding stock is owned by a parent corporation.

Subchapter C vs. Subchapter S

A **Subchapter C corporation** is one that is organized as a separate taxable entity and can have an unlimited number of owners called *shareholders*. It is sometimes called a **C-Corp**. A **Subchapter S corporation** has a limited number of owners and is not taxed as a separate entity. It is taxed like a partnership with a pass-through of revenues and expenses to the owners. It is frequently called an **S-Corp**. The term *Subchapter* refers to sections of the Internal Revenue Code.

Profit vs. Nonprofit

A **for-profit corporation** is self-explanatory, as is the term *nonprofit*. **Nonprofit corporations** are established for benevolent reasons such as education or religion. Nonprofit corporations can be exempt from taxation, but only if an exemption is granted by the Internal Revenue Service.

Professional Corporations and Associations

A **Professional Corporation (P.C.)** is generally a single professional, such as a doctor, who wishes to incorporate for tax and liability reasons. A **Professional Association (P.A.)** is a group of Professional Corporations. Although still seen occasionally, this form of business organization is dwindling as there are newer forms of organization for groups of professionals.

De jure vs. De facto

A corporation that has complied with all statutory requirements for corporations is a **de jure corporation**, or a **corporation by law.** A **de facto corporation** is one that has not complied with statutory compliance, but by its conduct is **in fact** a corporation.

A Summary Proceeding (10.1) – Types of Corporations

Public/Publicly held – stock owned by the general public
Private/Close/Closely held – stock generally owned by family

Domestic – incorporated under the laws of its domiciliary state
Foreign – incorporated in a state other than state in which it is doing business

Parent – owns subsidiary corporations
Subsidiary – owned by parent corporation

Subchapter C – separate taxable entity with unlimited owners
Subchapter S – taxed as a partnership with limited owners

For-Profit – self-explanatory
Nonprofit – organized for benevolent purposes; may be exempt from taxation

P.C. – Professional Corporation – one-person corporation for a professional

P.A. – Professional Association – collection of Professional Corporations

De jure – corporation organized under statutory law
De facto – corporation not compliant with statutory law but acts like corporation

Formation of a Corporation

Organizational Meeting

It is not uncommon for those who wish to form a corporation to meet and discuss the aspects of incorporating. These individuals are called **organizers, promoters**, and **incorporators**. At this point, records, such as **minutes** of meetings, should be kept. These records are the **business records** that "speak" for the corporation because the corporation is an artificial, not a real, person.

Articles of Incorporation

The organizers will now prepare a document, called the **Articles of Incorporation**, to establish the existence of the corporation. Several issues must be addressed within this document:

1. Purpose of the corporation – A corporation should list its specific **purpose** and then state that it be allowed to conduct any other purpose allowed by law. Acting outside

of the stated purpose or purposes of the corporation is said to be **ultra vires** and is generally considered a violation of law, creating liability for the business.

2. Classes of stock – A corporation sells **stock,** which is an ownership interest in the company to finance its activities. It may sell **common stock, preferred stock, voting stock,** and **nonvoting stock.** A corporation must also list the total number of shares of stock that will be available for ownership, known as **authorized shares.**
3. Agent for service of process – Because a corporation is an artificial person, a real person must be named as the person who will receive service of process when a corporation is sued. Frequently, a foreign corporation will appoint the **Secretary of State** as **agent for service of process.**

The articles of incorporation must be filed with the Secretary of State of its domiciliary state. Once the articles are filed, the Secretary of State will issue the corporation a **charter** authorizing the corporation to do business. Corporations must also register with the Secretary of State in any state in which it plans to do business.

By-Laws

The next document a corporation must prepare is the **by-laws.** By-laws set forth the structure and operating guidelines for a corporation. They may contain such things as the number of **directors,** the times when directors shall meet, the **shareholder meeting** procedures, a list of **officers** authorized to act on behalf of the corporation, and the authority each officer shall have.

Resolutions

Each officer should have documented evidence of his or her authority to act on behalf of a corporation when so acting. The Secretary of the Board of Directors can issue to that officer a document called a **resolution** of the board of directors stating the officer's position and authority. Attached to the resolution should be a copy of the **minutes** of the board meeting electing the officer and an excerpt of the by-laws stating that officer's authority to determine if the officer is within the scope of his or her authority or employment.

A Summary Proceeding (10.2) – Formation of a Corporation

Organizers/promoters/incorporators meeting – keep business records

Prepare Articles of Incorporation

- Define purpose of corporation
- Identify classes of stock
- Appoint agent for service of process
- File with Secretary of State
- Receive charter

Prepare by-laws – structure of corporation

- Identify officers
- Establish authority of officers

Resolutions – provided by Secretary to Board to identify agents of corporation

Financing a Corporation

One distinct advantage of a corporation is that it can issue **securities** to obtain funds with which to operate. Securities law is a high-liability field of law and is practiced by only a few large law firms. The most commonly issued securities are **stocks** and **bonds**.

Stock

Stock is an ownership interest in a corporation. It is **intangible personal property** represented by a **certificate** of shares. An investor can buy **shares** of stock and is called a **shareholder**. A shareholder has the right to receive **dividends**, or earnings, if the board of directors **declares** a dividend. A shareholder usually has the right to vote on the major issues of a corporation, including electing the members of the board of directors, once a year at a **shareholder meeting**. Because most shareholders don't attend annual shareholder meetings, their shares are usually voted by **proxy**, or an individual designated to vote the shares for them.

The two primary classes of stock are **common stock** and **preferred stock**. Common shareholders are the true level of owners and are considered general creditors if the company files bankruptcy. Preferred shareholders receive preference as to the payment of fixed dividend amounts and are one step higher in the creditor classifications in bankruptcy.

A corporation can **issue** as many shares of stock as are authorized in the articles of incorporation. If the issued shares are held by the general public, the shares are called **outstanding**. If the issued shares are held by the corporation, the shares are considered **treasury stock**.

Bonds

Bonds are a debt instrument of a corporation. In fact, a bond is a promissory note of the corporation; it is an agreement of the corporation to pay back a loan from the public investor. Bondholders receive **interest** as earnings on their loan. Interest on a bond is due without any declaration by the board of directors.

Regulation of Securities

Securities are regulated by both federal and state administrative agencies. The **Securities and Exchange Commission (S.E.C.)** issues federal regulations and monitors the issuance and trading of securities. Each state agency regulating securities issues rules that are nicknamed **blue sky laws**.

One of the primary purposes of securities regulation is to provide for **registration** of securities. Another is to provide for **disclosure** of financial information so an investor can make an informed choice as to investments. The primary disclosure document is called a **prospectus**. In addition to regulating the issuance of securities, federal law regulates the trading, or buying and selling, of securities through regulation of brokers. This is accomplished by the **National Association of Securities Dealers** (N.A.S.D.).

Issuance of Securities

When a corporation wishes to "go public" and sell securities to the general population they will structure an **initial public offering**, or **IPO**. The corporation will hire an **underwriter**, who is a large brokerage firm, to buy and resell the securities to their customers. This is the **primary market** for securities issuance, whereas the **secondary markets** are where existing shareholders buy and sell outstanding stock. Examples of a secondary market are the **New York Stock Exchange** and **NASDAQ**, which stands for the **National Association of Securities Dealers Automated Quotation** system.

An Unusual Case

The world of underwriting securities can be quite colorful. A preliminary or draft prospectus is called a **red herring.** State securities laws are called **blue sky laws.** If an initial public offering is so successful that it sells immediately, the underwriter can request a **green shoe,** which is a 10% increase in the amount of stock offered in the IPO.

A Summary Proceeding (10.3) – Financing a Corporation

Securities
- Stocks – owners of corporation; receive dividends; vote at annual meeting
- Bonds – debts of corporation; holders receive interest

Securities Regulation
- Federal – Securities and Exchange Commission
- State – blue sky laws
- Prospectus – financial disclosures

Issuance of Securities
- Initial public offering – primary market created by underwriters
- Secondary market – New York Stock Exchange

Liabilities of Corporate Personnel

A main reason for establishing a corporation is for the limitation of liability of individuals connected with the corporation. A corporation can sue and be sued and provides a shield of immunity for its shareholders, directors, and officers.

Shareholders

Under the "deep pocket" theory, it is presumed that the corporation has more assets to satisfy a judgment against it. That is not necessarily the case, especially with one-person corporations. Some individuals use the corporate shield simply to protect all assets that are held as personal assets as opposed to corporate assets. If it can be shown that this shareholder did not act as a corporation, a lawsuit can be filed directly against the offending owner by **piercing the corporate veil.** The law will not let a wrongdoer use the corporate structure as a sham or artifice to avoid liability.

Directors

Directors are considered **fiduciaries** of the corporation and should act in the best interests of the corporation for the benefit of the owners: the shareholders who elect the members of the board. Directors may make mistakes, or they may simply be derelict in their duties by not attending meetings and analyzing corporate activities. If this **breach of fiduciary duty** causes shareholders to suffer a loss, they may file a **shareholder derivative action** against the directors. Here, the shareholders do not seek personal awards, but seek the award for the corporation.

Courts are reluctant to "second guess" members of a board of directors in many situations. Some jurisdictions follow the **business judgment rule** to prevent courts from making business decisions on behalf of corporations. These courts look for fraud and gross mismanagement to hold against directors.

Officers

Officers, who are elected by the board of directors, are considered **agents** of the corporation and liability, or **vicarious liability**, is established under agency law. If the officer is inside the scope of his or her authority or employment with a tort situation, the corporation may be held liable. If the officer fully discloses his employer and his capacity, the corporation is responsible for the contracts the agent signs with third parties.

Dissolution of a Corporation

Although corporations have perpetual existence, that existence may voluntarily terminate for various reasons. A corporation may decide to voluntarily **dissolve** or go out of business. The corporation will file **Articles of Dissolution** with the Secretary of State. It will then **wind up** its affairs, **liquidate** its assets, and **distribute** the proceeds of the liquidation to its investors. Corporations may also find themselves in dire financial straits, with the only option being bankruptcy.

Occasionally a corporation will suffer an **involuntary dissolution**. Here, the corporation may be forced into bankruptcy by the decision of its creditors. This will be discussed in a later chapter on bankruptcy. The corporation may have its **charter revoked** by the Attorney General of its domiciliary state for ultra vires activities, or if the corporation is found to be **not in good standing** for failure to pay corporate franchise fees.

A SUMMARY PROCEEDING (10.4) – CORPORATE PERSONNEL LIABILITY AND DISSOLUTION

Shareholders – plaintiff may pierce the corporate veil and sue shareholders personally

Directors – may be sued by shareholders in a derivative action suit for breach of fiduciary duty

Officers – vicarious liability rules of agency law apply

(Continued)

A Summary Proceeding (10.4) – (Continued)

Dissolution of Corporation

Voluntary – File Articles of Dissolution; wind up affairs; liquidate and distribute to owners

File voluntary bankruptcy

Involuntary – Creditors for involuntary bankruptcy

Attorney General revokes charter,

Conclusions of Law

Corporations are extremely complex entities, but they are by no means the only form of business organization. Many smaller forms of business organization exist and will be discussed in Appendix 10A.

The Latin Language

De jure – day jur-ee

De facto – day *fak*-toh

Ultra vires – *ul*-trah *vi*-rees

Appendix 10A

Other Business Organizations

Opening Statements

Although corporations are the most legally complicated of all business formations, they are not the most common; sole proprietorships hold that position. Partnerships are dwindling in popularity, and limited liability companies are growing in popularity. Franchises are a unique form of business organization that needs discussion, whereas cooperatives and syndicates are formed for very specific reasons.

Sole Proprietorships

Anyone can "hang out a shingle," so to speak. One person can go into business for him or herself with ease. Assuming the proprietor has the necessary qualifications such as professional licenses, there is very little legal complexity to forming a one-person business. At most, the proprietor will have to file a **fictitious name certificate** with the Secretary of State. A fictitious name certificate is also called a **trade name certificate** or an **assumed name certificate**. The proprietor is listed as "**doing business as**" or d/b/a the trade name.

Example 10A.1:

Jim Smith opens a business named Jim Smith Plumbing. This business requires no filing of a fictitious name certificate because it uses Jim Smith's name in the name of the business. If Jim had called his business Speedy Plumbing, then a fictitious name certificate identifying Jim Smith as the owner should be filed.

Although the legal aspects of beginning a sole proprietorship are quite easy, the legal liabilities of such a business can be great. The owner is the business and the owner's personal assets are at risk in any lawsuit. There are no shields of liability similar to a corporation.

Partnerships

Partnerships are classified as either **general partnerships** or **limited partnerships** and, just like corporations, are governed by state statutory law.

General Partnerships

A **general partnership** is two or more persons carrying on a business as co-owners for profit. Note that the business must be ongoing in nature and not just a single business event, which would be a **joint venture**.

General partnerships can be formed in three ways:

1. **Formation** by **express** written or oral statements. If formed by written statement, **Articles of Partnership** can be drafted defining the relationship of the parties as to control of the business, as well as division of profits and losses. Without a written

document the state code, which may be the **Uniform Partnership Act, (U.P.A.)** or the **Revised Uniform Partnership Act (R.U.P.A.)** will control.

2. There may be **implied formation by conduct** of the parties. Courts will look to the activities of the parties from past or current acts to infer the existence of a partnership.
3. **A partnership by estoppel** exists where one individual allows another to act as a partner and a third party detrimentally relies on the actions of the "partner." The court will bar the other "partner" from claiming a partnership exists.

Each general partner is an **agent** of each other general partner and owes **fiduciary duty** to the partnership and the other partners. This agency relationship between partners also brings vicarious liability into play. All general partners are vicariously liable for all acts of all other general partners. This liability extends to the personal assets of each general partner if the partnership assets are unable to satisfy the obligations of the partnership.

General partnerships can be terminated by **dissolution**, winding up, liquidation of partnership assets, and distribution of proceeds to each partner. Each time a new partner is added or one withdraws from the business, dissolution actually occurs and a new partnership continues in business.

Limited Partnerships

Limited partnerships contain at least one general partner to operate the business and at least one **limited partner** who contributes financing to the business. A limited partnership must be in writing and filed with an appropriate government office, usually the Secretary of State. Limited partners cannot participate in the operation of the business and cannot have their name in the partnership name. In return for being silent in the business, limited partners are not liable for partnership activities. Their liability is limited to their contribution. Limited partnerships are controlled by the **Uniform Limited Partnership Act (U.L.P.A.)** or the **Revised Uniform Limited Partnership Act, (R.U.L.P.A.)** depending on state adoption. Limited partnerships also terminate by the dissolution process.

Limited Liability Companies

A business organization that provides the greatest amount of immunity from individual liability is the **limited liability company**. Formation begins with **articles of organization** prepared by the organizers and filed with the Secretary of State. An **operating agreement** similar to by-laws is signed by each **member** of the company. Members have equal status in the company and are specifically shielded from personal liability similar to a member of a nonprofit. **L.L.C.s**, as they are called, have **continuity of existence**. They need not be re-formed to add or delete members like a partnership must. State statutory law specifically controls L.L.C.s.

Franchises

An immensely popular form of business organization, especially for retail outlets, is the **franchise**. A **franchisor** grants a **franchisee** the right to sell specific goods and services.

Fees vary for this arrangement, but normally a lump sum initial fee or an annual fee known as a *royalty*, or both, is paid by the franchisee to the franchisor. Both the franchisee and the franchisor are usually corporations, but they act as independent businesses. Franchise law is found in federal statutes and regulated by the **Federal Trade Commission (F.T.C.)**.

Cooperatives

Cooperatives, which may be incorporated or **unincorporated associations,** are organizations formed for the economic benefit of the members. Cooperatives are nonprofit corporations under most state laws.

Syndicates

A **syndicate** is a group of people who join together to finance a specific project. They are frequently seen in the securities industry, when brokers sell initial public offerings.

A Summary Proceeding (10A.1) – Other Business Organizations

- Sole Proprietorships – one-person business with high legal liability as to personal assets
- Partnerships
  - General – two or more carrying on business for profit
    - Formation – express, implied by conduct and by estoppel
    - Fiduciary duty – all general partners are agents
    - High legal liability – personal assets at risk
  - Limited – limited partners are contributors of financing
    - Formation – by written document filed with governmental office
    - Liability – limited partners' liability limited to contribution
    - Management – limited partners cannot manage or have name in business
- Joint Venture – general partnership for limited business activity
- Limited Liability Companies
  - Formation – articles of organization and operating agreement
  - Members – shielded from all personal liability
- Franchises – franchisor grants rights to franchisee to sell product or service
- Cooperatives – nonprofit organizations for economic benefit of members
- Syndicates – association of persons to provide for financing

Conclusions of Law

Business organizations are utilized and created for one primary reason: to shield the individuals of the business from liabilities of the business. As long as there are lawyers attempting to impose liability, there will be lawyers attempting to establish immunity from personal liability through the creation of new business formations.

Exercises – Chapter 10 and Appendix 10A

True-False Correction Determine if the statement is true or false; if false, insert the correct term in the blank below the question for the word in bold to make the statement true.

_____ 1. A corporation can be a **person** under the U.S. Constitution.

____

_____ 2. Common stocks can be sold on the **secondary** markets.

____

_____ 3. A corporation that owns other corporations is a **subsidiary** corporation.

____

_____ 4. A corporation that strictly complies with statutes is a **de facto** corporation.

____

_____ 5. A corporation formed for benevolent reasons is a **for-profit** corporation.

____

_____ 6. A financial disclosure document for sale of common stock is a **proxy.**

____

_____ 7. The document evidencing a corporate officer's authority to act is a **security**.

____

_____ 8. A partner whose liability may extend to personal assets is a **limited** partner.

____

_____ 9. A **franchisor** prepares and files Articles of Incorporation.

____

_____ 10. Bondholders of a corporation receive **dividends** as earnings.

____

Definitions Insert the correct legal term in the blank above the definition.

1. ____

   Stock that is issued by a corporation but is not outstanding

2. ____

   The term for attorneys that are hired by and work for a corporation

3. ____

   The term for all states' securities laws

4. ____

   The business entity that sells another business entity the right to sell retail goods

5. ____

   A business organization formed for the economic benefit of its members

6. ____

   A general partnership for a single business activity

7. ____

   A corporation with a limited number of owners that is taxed as a partnership

8. ____

   A meeting of the owners of a corporation

9. ____

   The term for the total number of shares of stock allowed by articles of incorporation

10. ____

    A document filed to terminate the existence of a corporation

11. ____

    A stockbroker who sells originally issued shares of a corporation

12. ____

    A business formed solely for the obtaining of financing

Matching/Word Association Match the term in the left column with the best corresponding term in the right column

_____ 1.	domicile	A.	organizer
_____ 2.	promoter	B.	Secretary of State
_____ 3.	foreign corporation	C.	unauthorized act of corporation
_____ 4.	estoppel	D.	dividend
_____ 5.	ultra vires	E.	shareholder lawsuit
_____ 6.	LLC	F.	bar
_____ 7.	corporate director	G.	closely held
_____ 8.	trade name	H.	agent
_____ 9.	common stock	I.	document of corporate existence
_____ 10.	business records	J.	pierce the corporate veil
_____ 11.	derivative action	K.	state of incorporation
_____ 12.	agent for service of process	L.	vote
_____ 13.	securities	M.	directors' defense
_____ 14.	green shoe	N.	articles of organization
_____ 15.	corporate officer	O.	additional stock issuance
_____ 16.	proxy	P.	doing business
_____ 17.	private corporation	Q.	minutes of meetings
_____ 18.	charter	R.	assumed name
_____ 19.	business judgment rule	S.	stocks and bonds
_____ 20.	shareholder liability	T.	fiduciary

Identification Fully identify the abbreviation/acronym listed.

1. PC: ______________________________
2. SEC: ______________________________
3. IPO: ______________________________
4. UPA: ______________________________
5. NYSE: ______________________________
6. RULPA: ______________________________
7. FTC: ______________________________
8. LLC: ______________________________
9. NASD: ______________________________
10. ULPA: ______________________________
11. PA: ______________________________
12. S-Corp.: ______________________________

Chapter 11

Commercial Law – The Uniform Commercial Code

Opening Statements

Since the 1950s, all states have adopted at least a portion, if not all, of The **Uniform Commercial Code (UCC).** The **UCC** is a model statute that has brought uniformity to several areas of commercial law, especially areas of specific types of contracts. The UCC is divided into **Articles,** three of which will be discussed in this chapter.

ARTICLE 2 – THE SALE OF GOODS

Definitions

Goods

Goods are considered to be movable, tangible personal property. The term *goods* does not include money, investment securities, or land. Article 2 covers the sale of goods, not services. Contracts for services are covered by common law or statutory law.

Sale

A **sale** is the transfer of title to goods for a price. By this definition, gifts are not covered by the UCC because no value is given for a gift. The seller must have title to the goods and cannot transfer title to stolen goods. A lease of goods is not considered a sale.

Merchants

The UCC applies to the sale of goods by **merchants**. A merchant is one who regularly deals in the goods being sold, who by occupation has expertise in the transaction, or employs one who has skill about the goods. A merchant must always deal in **good faith**.

Example 11.1:

Car Buyer buys a used car from a used car dealer. The UCC would cover this sale. If Car Buyer buys a used car from an individual, the UCC does not apply.

The Sale

On a sale, a seller must deliver **conforming goods,** or goods that meet the buyer's specifications. If the goods are nonconforming, the buyer may **reject** the goods, accept the goods, or accept in part and reject in part. On delivery of nonconforming goods and **rejection** there is not a breach of contract as there would be under common law, but rather, the seller now has a reasonable time, and the duty, to **cure** and deliver conforming goods.

The buyer must **accept and pay** for conforming goods on **delivery**. Delivery occurs at the sellers' place of business. The buyer will be able to reject any nonconforming goods determined by a later **inspection** after payment.

Example 11.2:

Buyer pays for a refrigerator at Discount Store. Discount Store delivers the refrigerator at its rear loading dock. Buyer takes the refrigerator home, removes the carton, and discovers it to be the wrong color. Buyer may reject and return the refrigerator, and seller must deliver the conforming color within a reasonable time.

Warranties

The UCC firmly introduced the concept of statutory warranties, both express and implied. Before the UCC, common law did **imply** a **warranty of safety** with goods and products; other than that, the prevailing concept was **caveat emptor,** or "let the buyer beware." A **warranty** is a representation or statement by a merchant that a good conforms to certain standards.

Warranty of Title

Under the UCC, a seller **warrants** that he or she is passing **good title** and will defend the title against all claims. Even if the seller cannot pass title to stolen goods, he or she is responsible to the buyer if the goods are in fact stolen.

Express Warranties

An **express warranty** is a merchant's oral or written promise, guarantee, or representation that a product conforms to a certain standard.

Example 11.3:

Merchant displays a model of a printer and allows Customer to print various complex colors. Merchant has made a representation that the printer will print complex colors.

Implied Warranties

An **implied warranty of merchantability** exists with every sale made by a merchant. *Merchantable* means that a product has a quality comparable to that in the industry. The product should perform as expected.

An **implied warranty of fitness for particular purpose** arises when a buyer relies on the skill of the seller to select a product. The buyer must have informed the seller as to his or her particular needs.

Example 11.4:

Buyer informs Seller that he needs a chainsaw that will cut hardwoods as opposed to just softwoods. Seller directs buyer to a line of chain saws that Seller claims will cut all hardwoods.

Warranty Disclaimer

Some merchants may wish to disclaim the existence of warranties connected to their product. This is particularly true with used goods such as cars. Generally, the term "AS IS" can be **conspicuously displayed** to limit the application of warranties. Warranties and **warranty disclaimers** can apply to **third parties** who are users of the product.

A Summary Proceeding (11.1) – Article 2 Sale of Goods

Definitions
- Goods – movable, tangible personal property
- Sale – transfer of title to goods for a price
- Merchant – one who regularly deals in goods being sold

The Sale
- Seller to deliver conforming goods
- Buyer can inspect, accept, or reject
- Seller can cure delivery of nonconforming goods
- Buyer must accept and pay for conforming goods
- Payment must be made on delivery
- Delivery occurs at seller's place of business

Warranties
- Common law – implied warranty of safety
- Uniform Commercial Code
  - Warranty of title – seller must defend against stolen property claim
  - Express warranty – seller's oral or written statement as to quality of product
  - Implied warranties
    - Merchantability – product performs as expected
    - Fitness for particular purpose – skill of seller used to select product
- Warranty disclaimer – Conspicuous display of "as is"

ARTICLE 3 – NEGOTIABLE INSTRUMENTS (COMMERCIAL PAPER)

Types of Negotiable Instruments

Drafts

A **draft** is a written order to pay. Three parties are involved in a draft: the **drawer** who orders the **drawee** to pay the **payee**.

Example 11.5:

Insurance Company sends a draft payable through First National Bank to Owner of Damaged Car and Repair Shop as payees. Insurance Company is the drawer who is drawing on their account at First National Bank, the drawee.

An Unusual Case

Drafts are payable "through" a bank, whereas checks are payable "at" a bank. Drafts require special attention before being paid. The insurance company may wish to review the endorsements of the draft to make sure the Owner of the Damaged Car has in fact repaired the car, which would be shown by the endorsement of a repair shop. In a worst-case scenario, the insurance company may wish to have the repair bill attached to the draft before payment on the draft occurs. Checks do not require such review or documents.

Drafts can be **sight drafts**, which are payable on "sight" by the bank, or they can be **time drafts** which are payable on a specific future date.

Checks

Checks are drafts drawn on a bank and are payable on demand or on sight by the bank. This means that a **post-dated check** can be paid by a drawee bank on the check's arrival at the drawee bank. The drawee bank has no duty to wait until the date on the check before paying.

Cashiers' Checks

Cashiers' checks are checks drawn on a bank's checking account and are signed by the cashier of the bank who is the person responsible for the bank's checking account. Here, the bank is both drawer and drawee. A stop payment can be placed on a cashiers' check, but only pursuant to bank policies.

Certified Checks

A **certified check** is a check of a customer that the drawee bank will **honor** in advance. Banks rarely issue certified checks, because you cannot stop payment on a certified check. Once a check is honored by a bank, it must be paid.

Notes

Notes, or **promissory notes**, as they are more frequently called, are **promises to pay**. The person who promises to pay and signs a note is called a **maker**. The person who receives the note and the promise to pay is the payee. Most promissory notes are demand notes.

Certificates of Deposit

A **certificate of deposit** is a promise of a bank to pay the depositor of money a certain sum of money in the future. The bank is the maker and the depositor is the payee.

A Summary Proceeding (11.2) – Types of Negotiable Instruments

Draft – an order by a drawer to the drawee to pay a payee

- Sight draft – payable on sight by the drawee
- Time draft – payable at a specific future date

(Continued)

A Summary Proceeding (11.2) – (Continued)

Check – a draft drawn on a bank and payable on demand

Cashiers' check – a check drawn on a bank's checking account

Certified check – a check that is honored in advance of issuance

Promissory note – a promise to pay made by a maker

Certificate of deposit – a promise of a bank to pay a depositor for sums deposited

The Concept of Negotiability

Negotiability means that a negotiable instrument can be transferred from one party to another. Transfer can occur by **delivery** of a **bearer instrument**, an instrument that does not specify the payee or by **endorsement** of **order instrument** by the payee. Before transfer occurs, the negotiable instrument must be "**perfectly formed.**"

Formation of a Negotiable Instrument

A negotiable instrument is a **formal contract** and must meet the following requirements:

1. It must be **written.**
2. It must be payable to **order** or **bearer.**
3. It must be an **unconditional promise** or **order to pay.**
4. It must contain a **sum certain.**
5. It must be **payable on demand** or at a **specific future date.**
6. It must be signed by the **maker** or the **drawer.**

Just a few explanatory notes are needed to fully understand the six requirements for formation of a negotiable instrument. Some may surprise you:

1. Although a negotiable instrument must be in writing, it need not be on paper unless it is a check drawn on a bank. Stories abound regarding taxpayers who have sketched a check on the back of their shirt and mailed it to the Internal Revenue Service on April 15.
2. The section at the bottom left-hand corner of a check designated "For" can cause problems. Placing a condition to payment of the check such as "house painting if I like it when finished" creates a condition and prevents the check from being a negotiable instrument.
3. The reason a drawee bank makes you fill out a dollar amount on a check as well as a written amount is to determine the sum certain to pay.
4. A check should not be made payable at a specific future date. It is payable on demand and therefore should never be post-dated.

Endorsement

Negotiable instruments that are order instruments, or made payable to a specific payee, must be **endorsed** (also spelled **indorsed**) by the payee for negotiation or transfer to occur. The payee is the **endorser** and the person to whom the instrument is transferred is the **endorsee.** There are four ways to endorse a negotiable instrument:

1. **Blank endorsement** – The payee signs the check or note exactly as his or her name appears in the order or promise.
2. **Special endorsement** – The payee signs the check or note by making the note or check payable to another specific payee.
3. **Restrictive endorsement** – The payee signs the check or note with instructions such as "for deposit only."
4. **Qualified endorsement** – The payee signs the check or note with the term "without recourse," which means the payee cannot be liable for the check or note if it is not good.

Holder in Due Course

To receive the greatest protection under the UCC, a **holder**, or possessor of the negotiable instrument, who wishes to collect or be paid on the check or note must be a **holder in due course.** This status will protect the holder from certain defenses the drawer or maker may have when refusing to pay on the instrument. To be a holder in due course, three requirements must be met:

1. The holder must have given **value** for the instrument, not received it as a gift;
2. The holder must have taken the instrument in **good faith in a commercially reasonable transaction**; and
3. The holder must not have any notice of the instrument being **defective**.

An example can best sum up the concepts of negotiable instruments, negotiability, endorsements, and holders in due course and why a person should be careful when taking an endorsed check as payment or cashing a check.

Example 11.6:

Homeowner hires Painter to paint his house while he is away on vacation. When Homeowner returns on a Friday, the Painter has finished painting the house. Homeowner signs and gives Painter a check dated that Friday for $3,000 for house painting. Painter goes down the street to a friend of his, who is Homeowner's Neighbor. Painter asks Neighbor to cash the check for him and endorses it in blank to Neighbor. Neighbor has no problems cashing the check because Neighbor knows Homeowner is good for the check and has known Painter for years to be a great housepainter. Neighbor deposits the check in her account on Monday and it is returned with a stop payment designation. Neighbor goes to Homeowner and notices that Homeowner's freshly painted house has faded badly; when presenting the check to Homeowner, Neighbor finds out that Painter used cheap whitewash instead of paint. Homeowner

Example 11.6: (cont'd)

refuses to pay Neighbor for the check. Under the UCC Neighbor should win litigation against Homeowner because she is a holder in due course of a negotiable instrument. Neighbor is not part of the breach of contract dispute between Homeowner and Painter and should not suffer the loss, Homeowner should. The check is a separate legal document from the contract dispute.

A Summary Proceeding (11.3) – The Concept of Negotiability

- Negotiability – transfer of a negotiable instrument
  - Bearer instrument – transferred by delivery
  - Order instrument – transferred by endorsement
- Perfectly formed negotiable instrument
  - Must be in writing
  - Must be signed by maker or drawer
  - Must be payable to order or bearer
  - Must be unconditional order or promise to pay
  - Must be certain sum
  - Must be payable on demand or future date
- Endorsements
  - Blank – signed by payee as name appears in instrument
  - Special – signed to the order of indorsee
  - Restrictive – for deposit only
  - Qualified – without recourse
- Holder in due course
  - Must give value for instrument
  - Must take in good faith
  - Must not have notice of defects in instrument

ARTICLE 9 – SECURED TRANSACTIONS

In commercial transactions, credit may be necessary for a buyer of goods to complete the purchase. **Creditors**, those who loan money or extend credit, such as banks, prefer to be **secured creditors**. *Secured* means the loan to the borrower, known as the **debtor**, has **collateral** pledged to support the repayment to the creditor if the debtor **defaults**, or fails to pay. Without a pledge of collateral by the borrower, the credit is considered **unsecured**. The UCC has guidelines for the activities involved with **secured transactions**.

Establishing a Secured Transaction

Security Agreements

The creditor will have the debtor sign an agreement, known as a **security agreement**, pledging tangible personal property as collateral. The security agreement creates a **security interest** in the property in favor of the creditor. On the execution of the agreement and a transfer of value (i.e., credit) to the debtor, the legal process of **attachment** creates a **lien** in the hands of the creditor.

Collateral

Collateral is generally tangible personal property. Frequently, the property being pledged as collateral consists of the goods being purchased. Other times the property may be business property, such as equipment or inventory.

Perfection of Security Interest

For the creditor to establish his or her priority as a creditor he or she must **perfect** the interest. This can be done in one of three ways:

1. The creditor can file a **financing statement** identifying the debtor and property pledged with the appropriate government official usually the Secretary of State. This filing is notice to the world that the creditor is first in line to use the collateral for repayment of the loan;
2. The creditor can take **possession** of the collateral for safekeeping. This is usually seen in pawnshop loans; or
3. The creditor can establish a **Purchase Money Security Interest** through the agreement signed by the customer.

Example 11.7:

Discount Store sells a refrigerator to Customer and finances the purchase for the customer. It would be impractical for a national discount chain to file a financing statement every time an item was sold on credit, and even more impractical for Discount Store to keep the refrigerator until Customer pays off the loan. The Purchase Money Security Interest Agreement gives Discount Store superior rights to the refrigerator if the debtor defaults.

Default and Foreclosure

If the debtor fails to pay, or **defaults,** the creditor may initiate **foreclosure** proceedings. The first step in foreclosure is **repossession** of the collateral. The UCC allows the creditor to use "**self-help repossession**" if the peace is not breached.

Example 11.8:

Car Dealer sells a car to Car Buyer on credit and Car Buyer defaults. Car Dealer sends a repossession man to recover the car. If the Car Buyer sees the "repo" man attempting to take his or her car and objects, the "repo" man must leave because the peace has been breached.

After repossession the creditor may sell the property at a **commercially reasonable sale,** which may be a private sale or at public auction, and apply the proceeds toward the outstanding loan of the debtor. If the proceeds of the sale are insufficient to cover the loan, there is a **deficiency** and the debtor is still liable for that amount.

Liens by Operation of Law

Two other liens can be established without agreement of the debtor or involvement with the UCC. The first is a **mechanics and materialmens' lien**. Any unpaid contractor who works on real estate can file a mechanics and materialmens' lien against the property. This creates a cloud on the title that must be cured before a sale can occur. In most states the land can be sold to satisfy the debt.

The second type of automatic lien on property is the **possessory lien**. It is also called an **artisan's lien,** a **bailee's lien,** and a **garagemens' lien**.

Example 11.9:

Car Owner takes his car to Repair Shop. When Car Owner returns for the car, he cannot afford to pay the repair bill. Repair Shop is in possession of the car and may keep the car until the bill is paid or force the sale of the car to satisfy the debt.

A Summary Proceeding (11.4) – Secured Transactions and Other Liens

Secured Transaction
- Security agreement create security interest
- Attachment creates lien on collateral in favor of creditor
- Collateral – tangible personal property
- Perfection of security interest
  - Filing of financing statement with government official
  - Possession of collateral by creditor
  - Purchase money security interest
- Default – failure of debtor to pay

(Continued)

A SUMMARY PROCEEDING (11.4) – (CONTINUED)

Repossession – self-help repossession without breach of peace

Sale of property – proceeds applied to debt; debtor liable for deficiency

Liens by Operation of Law

Mechanics and materialmens' lien – contractor lien on real estate

Possessory lien – garagemens', bailees', or artisan's lien

Conclusions of Law

Without the UCC, national retail chains and interstate banks would have to sort through 50 sets of state codes for at least three separate areas of law. This would add enormous costs to the consumer for goods and limit the ability of consumers and businesses to obtain credit.

Appendix 11A

Bankruptcy Law

Opening Statements

Bankruptcy laws are specifically authorized under the **U.S. Constitution** Article 1, Section 8. Congress is empowered to establish uniform laws on the subject of bankruptcies throughout the United States. **Bankruptcy courts** are therefore federal courts and have **limited, exclusive jurisdiction** over bankruptcies. Congress has enacted the **Bankruptcy Code,** which is divided by **chapters.**

Bankruptcy laws have been called **"fresh start"** laws and are infinitely better than the medieval concept of **debtors' prisons.** Most individual bankruptcies are due to the loss of employment or medical expenses, whereas most business bankruptcies are due to poor management. A **bankrupt** is one who is unable to pay his, her, or its debts as they come due.

Chapter 7

Chapter 7 bankruptcy is available to both individuals and businesses. It is also called **straight bankruptcy** or **liquidation bankruptcy** because the **debtor,** also known as the **insolvent** or **bankrupt,** will have to liquidate assets to pay **creditors.** It is the most well-known form of bankruptcy.

The Bankruptcy Proceeding

Petition

Debtors can file **voluntary bankruptcy,** or creditors can file an **involuntary bankruptcy** for the debtor. The **petition for bankruptcy** must contain the following:

1. A **list of assets** of the debtor;
2. A **list of creditors** and **amounts owed;**
3. A statement of **current income and expenses** of the debtor; and
4. A statement of **financial affairs** of the debtor.

Automatic Stay

With the filing of the petition all creditors are barred from collection activities. Assets of the debtor are frozen under the **automatic stay.**

Bankruptcy Trustee

A **trustee** will be appointed to call a **creditors' meeting** and review the **proof of claim** forms submitted by the creditors. The trustee will also proceed to collect the estate of the debtor. Trustees have extensive powers when collecting assets under the concept of avoiding

preference payments. Any payments made by the debtor within 90 days of the filing of the petition can be voided by the trustee, and the creditor will have to deliver monies received to the trustee.

Exempt Property

Certain property of the debtor is not subject to liquidation by the trustee. This **exempt property** is determined by the Bankruptcy Code or by **state exemption laws**. The primary exempt property is the **homestead** of the debtor or a specified amount of the equity in the homestead held by the debtor. Other miscellaneous exemptions exist for automobiles, jewelry, and personal items.

Priority of Creditors

Historically debtors have far fewer assets than debts, and the proceeds of the liquidated assets are therefore distributed in a particular order. **Secured creditors**, those who have collateral pledged in a security agreement (See Chapter 11, Secured Transactions), are first on the list. This priority position, a position even higher than the **costs of the bankruptcy administration**, shows the importance of secured transactions. The secured creditor can even obtain the collateral for his or her benefit through a process of **adequate protection**. Other **priority creditor claims** are wages of employees, child support, and taxes. Last on the list are **general**, or **unsecured creditors**. Rarely do general creditors receive any payment of their claims.

Discharge

After distribution of the liquidation proceeds, the individual debtor is **discharged** as to the unpaid debts. Discharge is an extinguishment of the unpaid debts, but not necessarily forever.

An Unusual Case

Care should be taken when drafting the will of an individual who has been discharged from bankruptcy. Language in the will authorizing a personal representative to pay debts and claims of the decedent may revive debts discharged by bankruptcy.

Not all debts are dischargeable; some are **nondischargeable** and must still be paid by the debtor. The two most well known nondischargeable debts are **student loans** and **child support** payments. Other nondischargeable debts include debts incurred immediately before bankruptcy, back taxes, alimony, and fines due to a government.

A Summary Proceeding (11A.1) – Chapter 7 Bankruptcy

- Petition for bankruptcy filed voluntarily by debtor or involuntarily by creditors
- Contents of petition
  - List of assets of debtor
  - List of creditors and amounts due

(Continued)

A Summary Proceeding (11A.1) – (Continued)

Statement of income and expenses of debtor
Statement of financial affairs of debtor
Automatic stay – assets of debtor frozen; all collections by creditors end
Trustee in bankruptcy appointed
Creditor committee meeting for review of claims
Collection of assets of debtor less exempt properties
Liquidation of nonexempt properties
Distribution of proceeds of liquidation to creditors by priority
Discharge of individual debtor

Chapter 11

Chapter 11 bankruptcy is reserved for businesses. This type of bankruptcy has been called **business reorganization** bankruptcy because it allows the business to continue under the review of the Bankruptcy Court.

There are several differences between a Chapter 7 and a Chapter 11 bankruptcy. The obvious one is that the business continues without a liquidation of assets. There is also no trustee appointed in a Chapter 11 bankruptcy. Instead, the Bankruptcy Court will appoint a **debtor in possession,** who has the same fiduciary duties to the creditors that a trustee would have. A similarity with Chapter 7 is the automatic stay that halts creditors' collection activity.

The debtor in possession will convene a **creditors' committee** meeting to formulate a **plan of reorganization**. Two-thirds of the creditors must agree to the plan or the court will implement a "**cram down,**" forcing a plan on the creditors. Creditors stand in similar priority to the Chapter 7 priority. The plan will last for 5 to 7 years. Hopefully, the business will survive as an ongoing, profitable business.

Chapter 13

Chapter 13 bankruptcy is available for individuals and sole proprietorships because sole proprietorships are legally individuals. Like Chapter 11 bankruptcy, it is not a liquidation-type bankruptcy. It has been called **wage-earner rehabilitation.** One requirement is that the debtor must have a regular income because Chapter 13 bankruptcy also adopts a plan, called a **confirmation**, to pay creditors over a period of time (usually 3 years, with a maximum of 5).

The trustee in a Chapter 13 bankruptcy does not collect and liquidate assets of the debtor, but rather, collects the debtor's income for payments to the creditors and monitors the debtor's financial position. There is no discharge unless the Chapter 13 plan is unsuccessful and the debtor files for Chapter 7 bankruptcy.

Under recent changes to the bankruptcy laws, debtors with income in excess of a certain amount must file Chapter 13 before to filing Chapter 7. This has eliminated abuse of the bankruptcy laws by those who attempt to discharge debts when payment is possible.

A SUMMARY PROCEEDING (11A.2) – CHAPTERS 11 AND 13 BANKRUPTCY

Chapter 11 – Business Reorganization

- Automatic stay in effect
- Debtor in Possession appointed – no trustee
- Creditor Committee approves 5- to 7-year reorganization plan or court orders cram down

Chapter 13 – Wage-Earner Rehabilitation

- Automatic stay in effect
- Trustee appointed to collect debtor's income and pay on confirmation plan to creditors
- Plan lasts 3 to 5 years with no discharge

Conclusions of Law

Bankruptcy exists for the protection of those who cannot pay their debts, but it should be the last resort. A bankruptcy stays on a credit record for 10 years and prohibits a second filing for 6 years.

Exercises – Chapter 11

True-False Correction Determine if the statement is true or false; if false, insert the correct term in the blank below the statement for the word in bold to make the statement true.

_____ 1. The Uniform Commercial Code is broken down into **sections.**

____

_____ 2. An amount still due on a note after sale of collateral is called a **default**.

____

_____ 3. A creditor who has no collateral on a loan is an **unsecured** creditor.

____

_____ 4. Under common law, products came with an implied warranty of **safety**.

____

_____ 5. A check drawn on a bank's checking account is a **certified** check.

____

_____ 6. Delivery of goods occurs at the **buyer's** place of business.

____

_____ 7. A certificate of deposit includes a(n) **order** to pay.

____

_____ 8. A representation that a good conforms to a certain standard is a **warranty**.

____

_____ 9. A statement that a good conforms to a certain standard is an **implied** warranty.

____

_____ 10. Failure to pay a note creates a **debtor**.

____

Definitions Insert the correct legal term in the blank above the definition.

1. ______________________________

An exchange of tangible products for a price

2. ______________________________

A signature of a payee on a negotiable instrument

3. ______________________________

A negotiable instrument which has been honored in advance by a bank

4. ______________________________

The cashing of a check

5. ______________________________

The party to whom a draft is payable

6. ______________________________

The party who orders a draft to be paid

7. ______________________________

The party on whom a draft is drawn

8. ______________________________

A warranty arising when a buyer relies on the skill of the seller

9. ______________________________

Perfection of a security interest without possession or filing of documents

10. ______________________________

A negotiable instrument containing a promise to pay by a bank

Matching/Word Association Match the term in the left column with the best corresponding term in the right column.

_____	1. merchant	A. on demand
_____	2. nonconforming goods	B. perfection by filing
_____	3. delivery	C. negotiable instrument
_____	4. payee	D. artisan's lien
_____	5. sight draft	E. possessor of note
_____	6. maker	F. guaranty
_____	7. bearer	G. good faith
_____	8. formal contract	H. lender
_____	9. holder	I. endorser
_____	10. foreclosure	J. draft on bank
_____	11. possessory lien	K. repossession
_____	12. public auction	L. lien
_____	13. attachment	M. collateral
_____	14. disclaimer	N. seller's place of business
_____	15. creditor	O. industry standards
_____	16. financing statement	P. promise to pay
_____	17. check	Q. as is
_____	18. merchantability	R. rejection
_____	19. pledge	S. commercially reasonable sale
_____	20. warranty	T. transfer by delivery

Fill in the Blank List the six requirements for negotiable instrument formation:

1. ______________________________

2. ______________________________

3. ______________________________

4. ______________________________

5. ______________________________

6. ______________________________

List four types of endorsements and briefly define or give an example of each:

1.	______________	A.	______________
2.	______________	B.	______________
3.	______________	C.	______________
4.	______________	D.	______________

List the three requirements to be a holder in due course:

1. ______________________________

2. ______________________________

3. ______________________________

Appendix 11A – Exercises

Matching/Word Association Match the term in the left column with the best corresponding term in the right column.

_____	1. Bankruptcy court	A. secured creditor
_____	2. automatic stay	B. proof of claim
_____	3. priority creditor	C. Chapter 13 plan
_____	4. will	D. exempt property
_____	5. confirmation	E. exclusive jurisdiction
_____	6. cram down	F. Chapter 7
_____	7. discharge	G. contents of petition
_____	8. creditor petition	H. court ordered plan
_____	9. trustee	I. United States Constitution
_____	10. debtor in possession	J. involuntary bankruptcy
_____	11. homestead	K. debtor's assets frozen
_____	12. list of creditors	L. void
_____	13. creditor claim	M. debt extinguishment
_____	14. preference payment	N. fiduciary
_____	15. bankruptcy laws	O. revival of debts

List/Fill in the Blank List four nondischargeable debts in bankruptcy:

1. ______________________________

2. ______________________________

3. ______________________________

4. ______________________________

List the four requirements of the contents of a petition in bankruptcy:

1. ______________________________

2. ______________________________

3. ______________________________

4. ______________________________

List another name for the following types of bankruptcies:

Chapter 7: ______________________________

Chapter 11: ______________________________

Chapter 13: ______________________________

List two types of bankruptcy petitions:

1. ______________________________

2. ______________________________

List two other terms for the term **bankrupt**:

1. ______________________________

2. ______________________________

Section V

Law and the Family

Chapter 12

Domestic Relations

Opening Statements

The area of **domestic relations,** also known as **family law,** primarily addresses **marriage, divorce,** and children. Although some of its roots are in common law, domestic relations has become state statutory law. Some of family law has its background in religion, and moral issues have become frequent in domestic relations. Sexual activity between spouses is implicit in family law, and topics regarding sex are covered here as well. Even constitutional law has entered the law of the family more than once.

Marriage

Premarital Activities

Cohabitation

In some jurisdictions **cohabitation** or "living together" forms the basis for **common law marriage.** If the parties have the intent to be husband and wife and openly act as such, a court can recognize a marriage to have existed on "divorce" or estate proceedings.

An Unusual Case

The U.S. Census Bureau has grappled with categorizing persons of the opposite sex sharing living quarters. The solution was the acronym POSSLQ and a new term was created.

Contracts

With the increase in second marriage, in which both spouses may have accumulated wealth, the use of **prenuptial** or **antenuptial agreements** has expanded greatly in recent years. These agreements are basically a waiver of a spouse's right to receive what would normally be received pursuant to divorce/property settlement laws or inheritance laws.

Engagement

The question about engagement centers around the ring given to the female. Is it a **gift,** which is considered **irrevocable,** and to be kept by the female if the engagement is broken? Some courts have resolved the issue by saying the ring is a "conditional gift," the condition being the marriage, which must occur for the ring to be kept, while others have said the gift is not **complete** until the marriage occurs.

The Marriage

Marriage has been said to be a contract between a man and a woman; some states even recognize a **covenant marriage,** which is a marriage based on an actual written contract between the husband and wife that defines the duties and responsibilities of each party. Others have said that a marriage is a **partnership** and consider all property of the marriage as being owned half and half. In any event, the state can and does regulate the marriage process through civil law.

Licensing

States regulate who can get married through the **licensure** procedure. Primarily the state, through a county official, wants to determine if both parties have the **capacity to consent** to the marriage. **Minors** do not have the capacity to marry without permission of the parents.

Some states still require blood tests to determine if any transmissible diseases are present. Others require a waiting period after the issuance of the **marriage license** and the actual marriage. Records of the marriage will be useful for obtaining benefits under state and federal programs.

Solemnization

Most marriages are **solemnized** with a **ceremony** and can be called a **ceremonial marriage.** Ceremonies can be conducted by ordained ministers, judges, and justices of the peace. Those conducted by judges and justices are frequently called **civil ceremonies.** Some states require no ceremony at all and allow the parties to merely state their intent to a judge or justice of the peace and obtain a signature on the license. The executed license is then returned to the issuing official, whereupon a **marriage certificate** is issued.

An Unusual Case

It is possible to get married and not attend the ceremony. At common law, a **proxy marriage** could occur in which a stand-in could assume the position of a party. Some states still allow for this.

Consummation

To **consummate a marriage** means to engage in sexual intercourse. Because the marriage itself was the historical sanction for sexual activity, **consummation** is the completing act of marriage. Once consummated, the partners have now become **spouses** and are in **wedlock.** The male spouse is the **husband** and the female spouse is the **wife.** The spouses are now **tenants by the entirety** for ownership of property.

A Summary Proceeding (12.1) – Premarital Activities and Marriage

- Cohabitation – Forms the basis for common law marriage
- Contracts
    - Prenuptial or antenuptial agreements waiving property rights upon divorce or death
    - Covenant marriage – Written contract defining duties and rights of spouses
- Engagement – Ring considered a conditional or uncompleted gift
- Marriage
    - Regulated by state through licensing those with capacity to consent
    - Solemnization by ceremonial marriage
    - Issuance of Marriage Certificate
    - Consummation of marriage to become husband and wife

Dissolution of Marriage

Separation

Spouses may decide to begin the termination of a marriage by **separating from bed and board.** This decision may be reduced to writing in a **separation agreement.** This is an interim agreement until formal **dissolution** by **annulment** or **divorce** occurs. Frequently seen in these agreements are clauses of **maintenance** or **spousal support,** which are clauses specifying monies to be paid by one spouse to a dependent spouse.

Annulment

An **annulment** is a process to review the validity of the marriage. To annul a marriage means to declare it **void ab initio,** or void from the beginning. It is a judicial decision that the marriage never existed due to some defect.

Grounds for Annulment

State statutes are very specific as to which marriages can be annulled. Several examples are as follows:

1. **Non-age** – one of the spouses was a minor at the time of the marriage
2. **Bigamy/polygamy** – one of the spouses was married to another at the time of the marriage
3. **Incest** – the spouses were too closely related by blood
4. **Mental incompetence** – one spouse was a ward or otherwise diminished in capacity
5. **Fraud** – false statements as to chastity, fertility, or intent to marry

Results of an Annulment

If the marriage never existed and children were born while the marriage allegedly existed, the children will not become **illegitimate** as a result of the marriage. Annulment will not allow for **alimony,** however, because alimony is based on the existence of a marriage.

Divorce

Divorce is by far the most common method for dissolving a marriage. Divorce is rarely the contentious issue in dissolution of marriage, however. Property settlements and child custody/child support issues take up far more of a court's time.

Jurisdiction

A marriage is a matter, a thing, or a **res.** Therefore, a court must have **in rem jurisdiction** over a marriage. In rem jurisdiction is established by **residency** of one of the partners in the state in which the divorce is sought. Divorce is an **equitable proceeding** in most states.

Grounds

Many **grounds** exist for the granting of a divorce. **Adultery** and **physical** and **mental cruelty** exist in most state codes that require grounds to be established. **Abandonment** or **desertion** of the marriage exists when the parties have remained separate from bed and board for a specified length of time, usually 1 to 2 years. Other states have a lax standard for grounds such as **general indignities.**

Some states have eliminated grounds completely and have implemented **no-fault** divorce statutes. If one party alleges **irreconcilable differences** between the parties, or that the marriage is **irretrievably broken,** then a divorce can be granted.

Defenses

Should the defendant or respondent wish to contest the divorce, there are several ways to do so. First would be **recrimination,** which is claiming that the filing party committed the acts giving rise to grounds for divorce and is barred from proceeding. Next would be **reconciliation** or **condonation,** or that the parties have resolved their differences and no grounds exist. Finally could be **connivance** and **collusion,** in which the parties agreed on the grounds for divorce without the grounds actually existing or agreed on the acts giving rise to the grounds for divorce, respectively. The party who wins the action is generally granted a **decree.**

A SUMMARY PROCEEDING (12.2) – DISSOLUTION OF MARRIAGE

Separation – Spouses separate from bed and board

Annulment – Declaration that a marriage never existed

- Grounds – Non-age, mental incompetency, bigamy, incest, and fraud

Divorce

- Jurisdiction – In rem jurisdiction based on residency
- Grounds – Adultery, physical and mental cruelty, abandonment, and general indignities
- No Fault – Showing of irreconcilable differences or irretrievably broken marriage
- Defenses – Recrimination, reconciliation, condonation, collusion, or connivance

Property Settlements

A **property settlement** is a **post-nuptial agreement** and should be in writing. It may be mutually agreed on, determined by state law, or ordered by the court.

Equitable Distribution

The common law principle of **equitable distribution** has the court decide what is fair between the parties. Although a court looks at the properties as a whole for this decision, it will pay particular attention to the concepts of **marital property** and **separate property.** Marital property is that which was acquired during the marriage, whereas separate property may have been brought into the marriage by one partner or acquired by one partner through gift or inheritance.

Community Property

Community property states usually declare that all marital property is owned fifty-fifty as tenants in common and will be distributed as such. Separate property remains with the separate owner. The lines between separate and marital property can be blurry.

Example 12.1:

Husband enters a marriage with 100 shares of stock worth $1 per share, or a total of $100. After 20 years of marriage, the 100 shares of stock are now worth $1,000 per share, or a total of $100,000. Is the increase in value community property, or are the 100 shares of stock separate property?

Alimony

Alimony was based on the assurance that a dependent spouse would be provided with sufficient income to maintain a style of living to which she had become accustomed. Today, however, permanent alimony is not common. **Temporary,** or **rehabilitative alimony,** would provide short-term periodic payments until the dependent spouse could establish a livable income, possibly by returning to college. **Lump sum alimony,** especially when one spouse has paid for the other spouse's education, is also seen.

An Unusual Case

Palimony, or payments to a long-term live-in companion, is often confused with the concept of alimony. In reality, the initial case of palimony involves a breach of implied contract action, not a dissolution of a marriage action.

Children

The rights and duties of parents take up most of the time in a divorce action and become the central, if not the most contentious issue.

Child Custody

Child custody issues are determined according to the **best interests of the child.** One corollary rule is that a **child of tender years** should be in the custody of the mother. The general results of child custody are usually **sole custody** with **visitation** rights of the noncustodial parent; **joint custody,** in which each parent has a voice in major decisions affecting the child; and **divided custody,** in which the child lives with each parent for specified times.

Childnapping is a situation in which the noncustodial parent takes a child to another jurisdiction and attempts to change the custodial orders based on the new state determining the best interests of the child. The **Uniform Child Custody Jurisdiction Act** has addressed this issue.

Child Support

There is no question that parents have the **duty to support** a child. Under more recent constitutional law decisions this is an equal duty between the spouses, but the amount of support contributed by each may differ. Both parents must provide complete financial information to the court for a determination of amounts due from each. The problem becomes one of balancing the **needs of the child** versus **ability of the parent to pay.** Pursuant to federal legislation all states now have guidelines for determining child support, and they vary dramatically.

Enforcement of child support payments is a major issue. When a parent has not made support payments, he or she is **in arrears.** Uniform laws have allowed for expedited procedures of collection in states in which the nonpaying parent resides. Federal regulations provide for collection through wage withholding and tax refund withholding.

An Unusual Case

Some states allow for more drastic measures than just garnishment of wages or attachment of personal property for collection of a judgment or decree for child support. Some states classify a parent in arrears as a debtor and allow for a body attachment order to satisfy the debt. The nonpaying parent will have his or her body "attached" as though it were personal property and placed in jail with only a cash bond equal to the amount due being allowed for release.

A Summary Proceeding (12.3) – Property Settlements and Children

- Property Settlements
  - Equitable distribution – Court decides what is fair
  - Community property – Marital property divided equally
- Alimony
  - Temporary or Rehabilitative – Periodic until dependent spouse increases living standards
  - Lump Sum – Granted to spouse who provided educational income
- Child Custody
  - Best interests of the child rule
  - Tender years doctrine – Mother receives custody of infant and young children
  - Types of custody

(Continued)

A SUMMARY PROCEEDING (12.3) – (CONTINUED)

Sole custody with visitation
Joint custody on major issues affecting child
Divided custody for alternating periods of time
Child Support
Parents have equal duty of support
Support determined by balancing needs of child vs. ability of parent to pay
Arrears – Enforcement procedures vary

OTHER FAMILY ISSUES

Adoption

Adoption is the legal process during which the relationship between a child and his or her **natural** or **biological parents** is severed and a new relationship is established between the child and the **adoptive parents.** All rights and duties of the natural parents in relation to the child end completely. Courts generally have a preference toward certain adults being the adoptive parents. Blood relatives are given first consideration with an **orphan. Foster parents** are also given consideration. Courts will also consider a **step-parent** as a viable candidate for adoptive parent when the noncustodial natural parent is absent.

Paternity

Children are frequently born out of wedlock without knowledge of the father's identity. These children are known as **bastards, illegitimate children,** and **nonmarital children.** Determining who the father is may result in a **paternity action,** an **affiliation action,** or a **bastardy action.** DNA, or deoxyribonucleic acid tests are quite conclusive as to fatherhood and impose on the man the duty to support the child.

An Unusual Case

If a child is born to a man and woman who are husband and wife, the husband is conclusively presumed to be the father even if he isn't. If this father divorces the mother, he is still responsible for child support even if the natural father is determined by DNA testing. Some states are beginning to reconsider this long-standing common law rule.

Surrogacy

Having a woman bring a child to term for another person is called **surrogate motherhood.** The arrangement, in which one woman carries the fertilized egg of another man and woman, is usually pursuant to a **surrogacy contract.** Moral objections to such a relationship, which is an enforceable contract, have led many states to heavily regulate such contracts.

Emancipation

Occasionally, it is necessary for a court to remove the legal limitations placed on a minor and declare the minor to be an adult through the concept of **emancipation.** Some states allow for this in marriages of minors approved by parents.

Family Law Tort Issues

Alienation of Affection

At common law, but very rarely seen in this day and age, is the concept of **alienation of affection.** The most basic description of this civil cause of action is "someone stole your spouse away from you." Yes, it is possible to sue someone for luring a spouse's affections away. Another strange family law cause of action is to sue that person who lured your spouse away for **criminal conversation,** or, having sexual relations with your spouse.

Loss of Consortium

Not so uncommon is the claim for damages for **loss of consortium.** Consortium is the physical love and affection, including sex, that one spouse provides another.

Example 12.2:

Defendant causes an automobile accident that leaves Husband paralyzed from the waist down, thereby eliminating sexual intercourse with Wife. Defendant is responsible for damages for loss of consortium.

A SUMMARY PROCEEDING (12.4) – OTHER FAMILY ISSUES

Adoption – Severing a parental relationship and establishing a new parental relationship

Paternity – Establishing the father of a child; also known as an affiliation or bastardy proceeding

Surrogacy – A contract to bear a child for another

(Continued)

A SUMMARY PROCEEDING (12.4) – (CONTINUED)

Emancipation – Judicial removal of the limitations placed on a minor

Family Tort Issues

- Alienation of affection – Luring another's spouse away from the marriage
- Criminal conversation – Having sexual relations with another's spouse
- Loss of consortium – Damages for loss of physical love and affection

Conclusions of Law

Family law is very intense because of the close personal relationships that exist. Family law, above most other areas of law, changes with the times. Social issues, values, and morals change and family law will too.

THE LATIN LANGUAGE

void ab initio – void ab ih – *nih* – shi -o

Exercises – Chapter 12

True-False Correction Determine if the statement is true or false; if false, insert the correct term in the blank below the question for the word in bold to make the statement true.

_____ 1. A marriage ceremony is considered **consummation** of the marriage.

____

_____ 2. Residency establishes **in personam** jurisdiction for dissolution of a marriage.

____

_____ 3. A property settlement on divorce is a **prenuptial** agreement.

____

_____ 4. State regulation of marriages includes **licensure.**

____

_____ 5. A final order granting a divorce is a **judgment.**

____

_____ 6. Incestuous marriages are **valid.**

____

_____ 7. **Recrimination** bars a petitioner from proceeding with a divorce action.

____

_____ 8. An engagement ring may be considered a **completed** gift.

____

_____ 9. A contract to bear a child for another couple is a **covenant** contract.

____

_____ 10. Removing a minor's legal limitations is **child support.**

____

Definitions Insert the correct legal term in the blank above the definition.

1. ______________________________

Marriage to two persons

2. ______________________________

The civil action for sexual relations with another's spouse

3. ______________________________

A marriage performed by a justice of the peace or judge

4. ______________________________

Spousal support for a dependent spouse in a separation agreement

5. ______________________________

The primary rule for determining child custody

6. ______________________________

A joint tenancy with right of survivorship between husband and wife

7. ______________________________

A child born out of wedlock

8. ______________________________

Damages awarded for the loss of sexual ability

9. ______________________________

The general term for termination of a marriage

10. ______________________________

The concept of falling behind with child support payments

Matching/Word Association Match the term in the left column with the best corresponding term in the right column.

_____	1. domestic relations	A. wedlock
_____	2. common law marriage	B. biological parents
_____	3. minors	C. ceremony
_____	4. solemnization	D. desertion
_____	5. needs of child	E. adoption
_____	6. paternity	F. family law
_____	7. marriage	G. spousal support
_____	8. prenuptial agreement	H. bed and board
_____	9. natural parents	I. wife
_____	10. reconciliation	J. affiliation
_____	11. irreconcilable differences	K. no-fault divorce
_____	12. alimony	L. waiver of property rights
_____	13. annulment	M. collusion
_____	14. abandonment	N. nonage
_____	15. marital property	O. sexual intercourse
_____	16. separation	P. void ab initio
_____	17. connivance	Q. cohabitation
_____	18. consummation	R. community property
_____	19. spouse	S. condonation
_____	20. orphan	T. ability to pay

List/Fill in the Blank List five grounds for annulment and give a brief description or example of each:

1. ______________________ A. ______________________

2. ______________________ B. ______________________

3. ______________________ C. ______________________

4. ______________________ D. ______________________

5. ______________________ E. ______________________

List three individuals who can perform a marriage ceremony:

1. ____

2. ____

3. ____

List four defenses to divorce and give a brief description of each:

1. ______________________ A. ______________________

2. ______________________ B. ______________________

3. ______________________ C. ______________________

4. ______________________ D. ______________________

List three terms for the court proceeding to determine the natural father of a child:

1. ____

2. ____

3. ____

Chapter 13

Wills, Estates, and Trusts

Opening Statements

Most attorneys and legal authors tend to group wills, estates, and trusts with property law. In fact, some law schools teach the topic with property courses. Admittedly, wills, estates, and trusts achieve the purpose of property management and disposition, but one cannot argue that the death of a family member, the aging of a parent, the financial support of a widow, or a child's education are not family issues.

Wills, estates, and trusts are governed by state law and tend to be extremely state specific. Although the **Uniform Probate Code (UPC)** was established in 1969, only 16 states have chosen to adopt it. With the exception of Florida, Minnesota, and Michigan, the adopting states tend to be rural or less populated. Only slight reference to the UPC will occur in this chapter.

The Last Will And Testament

A **will** is more properly termed a **last will and testament.** A will provides for the disposition of real property, whereas a **testament** provides for the disposition of personal property. A will is the most important **estate-planning** tool. Estate planning is designed to manage, maintain, and dispose of assets at death while protecting family interests and preserving financial interests. The right to write a will is generally statutory in nature, and strict compliance with statutes is paramount.

Testamentary Capacity

The person making a will is referred to as a **testator,** if male, and a **testatrix,** if female. This person must have **testamentary capacity** or, in other words, be of **sound and disposing mind** when executing a will.

Intent

The testator must **intend** to make a will and have **knowledge** that the document being prepared and executed is a will. The rule for interpreting the provisions of a will is to determine the intent of the testator. If the testator is under undue influence or duress, then intent may not be present and the will may be subject to contest and declared invalid.

Example 13.1:

Home Care Nurse has been attending to Elderly Testator for several years. As Testator has aged and become more mentally and physically infirm, Nurse has increased her discussions about her financial woes and how Testator's children are so financially comfortable. At Testator's death, a recently executed will leaving all of his estate to Nurse appears. Undue influence should be suspected.

Bounty

Testators should be generally aware of their **bounty,** or what they own. It is not necessary for the testator to be able to recite his possessions from memory, but a list prepared by the testator before execution is good evidence of knowledge of bounty.

Objects of the Bounty

In the interview with the testator, the paralegal should direct the discussion to the family members of the testator. Spouses, children, grandchildren, siblings, as well as parents should be noted. Then the conversation should center on the **objects of the bounty.** Testators generally provide for family members. Complete deviations from this norm should be discussed with the testator.

An Unusual Case

Care should be taken when interviewing a testator to assure confidentiality. Family members should not be present during the interview. More than once has a testator needed to admit the existence of an extramarital child.

Freedom from Delusions or External Influences

This is another extremely sensitive area of discussion. **Delusions** are just not a situation of the testator "hearing voices," but things such as memory lapses during the discussion or constant drifting into reminiscing may alert the paralegal to a mental condition. Even with existing mental conditions it is still possible to have testamentary capacity for execution of a will during a **lucid interval.**

Age

Most states specifically state the **age** at which a person can have the capacity to execute a will. Eighteen is the most common age, but exceptions exist especially for married minors and military personnel.

Types of Wills

Executed Wills

An **executed** will is usually drafted by an attorney and is signed by the testator and the witnesses during a small ceremony. A notary public will be present to complete the process. The process is the practice of law and should have an attorney present to ensure compliance with state statutes.

A Different Case

An executed will is one that has been signed by the testator and witnesses. An executed contract is one that has been performed.

Holographic Wills

A will that is substantially or completely in the handwriting of the testator and is signed at its end is a **holographic will.** There need not be any witnesses or notary public present at the execution. Not all states allow holographic wills.

Nuncupative Wills

A very few states allow for **nuncupative wills,** which are oral wills. These wills are limited to the disposition of personal property and may be limited in use to military personnel at times of war or testators on their "death bed" with witnesses present.

Joint Wills

A **joint will** is one will for two people, who are usually husband and wife. Care should be taken not to draft the will so as to make it **irrevocable** after one party dies by requiring changes to the will being made on both parties' consent.

Mutual or Reciprocal Wills

Frequently a husband and wife will write separate wills that have identical provisions. These are known as **mutual** or **reciprocal wills.**

Example 13.2:

Husband executes a will that says that all of his estate goes to his wife if he dies first, and if she dies first then the estate goes equally to the children. Wife executes a will that says that all of her estate goes to her husband if she dies first, and if he dies first the estate goes equally to the children.

Living Will

A **living will** is not a will for purposes of distributing property at death. A living will is an **advance directive** that allows the testator the option of refusing medical treatment in the case of imminent death from a terminal illness. Living wills are usually executed with a **health care proxy,** which appoints an individual who will decide what medical treatment may be provided.

Codicils

A **codicil** is an amendment to a will. It should be executed with the same formalities as a will. It is possible for an executed will to have a holographic codicil and vice versa.

A Summary Proceeding (13.1) – Testamentary Capacity and Types of Wills

Testamentary Capacity

- Know you are making a will and intend to do so
- Know your bounty
- Know the objects of your bounty
- Be free from delusions

Types of Wills

- Executed – Will signed by testator and witnesses
- Holographic – Will written in handwriting of testator and signed at end
- Nuncupative will – Oral will disposing of personal property
- Joint will – One will for two persons

(Continued)

A Summary Proceeding (13.1) – (Continued)

Mutual/Reciprocal will – Wills of husband and wife with similar provisions
Living will – Advance directive as to medical care
Codicil – Amendment to a will

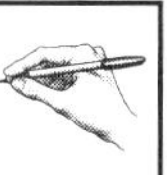

Will Clauses

Although most states do not have model wills, many wills follow a similar format. The following are some of the basic clauses within a will.

Exordium Clause

The **exordium** clause is the opening of the will. It will include the identity of the testator, the **publication** of the will, jurisdictional information for probate proceedings, and a **revocation** of all former wills and codicils.

Example 13.3:

I, Thomas Testator, of Pulaski County, Arkansas, being of sound and disposing mind and over the age of 18, do hereby make, publish, and declare this to be my Last Will and Testament, hereby revoking all former wills and codicils made by me.

Dispositive Provisions

Dispositions of real estate are called **devises.** The testator is the **devisor** and the recipient is the **devisee.** Devises of real estate can be **specific** and identify the particular piece of property to be devised, or the gift can be **general** such as "all of my real estate."

A disposition of personal property is called a **bequest** if the gift is tangible personal property, and a **legacy,** or a **pecuniary bequest,** if the gift is money. The testator is called a **legator** and is said to **bequeath** property to a **legatee.** Bequests can be specific or general. A legacy can be a **demonstrative legacy** if the money is designated to come from a particular fund. Many states allow the testator to attach a separate writing to a will disposing of tangible personal property; this attachment allows the testator to change the disposition without the constant need for a codicil. The attachment is **incorporated by reference** in the will.

Ademption and Lapse

Specific devises and bequests can **adeem** if the property is not found in the estate. If the property has already been given to the heir, it is a situation of **ademption by satisfaction.** If the property cannot be found, it is a situation of **ademption by extinction.**

If a beneficiary does not survive the testator, then that property is said to **lapse** and passes according to the **residuary clause.** Some states have adopted **anti-lapse statutes,** which state that the **issue (lineal descendants)** of the beneficiary receive the property. The testator can stop the lapse by using the term **per stirpes,** which means property given to a child who **predeceases** the testator automatically goes to the issue of that child. The testator could also use the term **per capita,** which means that the property would go to the other children.

The Residuary Clause

The final dispositive provision of a will is the **residuary clause,** which disposes of all property not disposed of by devise or bequest. If no residuary clause exists, the testator dies **intestate,** or without a will, as to that property and state law will govern the disposition of that property.

Nomination of Fiduciaries

The testator needs to choose who will act on his or her behalf after death. Several categories of **fiduciaries** will be discussed later, but it is important to note that the testator **nominates,** or suggests, who shall serve and the probate court will **appoint** the representatives.

Miscellaneous Clauses

Certain clauses may be necessary depending on the testator. Such things as trusts, which will be discussed later, tax provisions, depending on the size of the estate, and provisions for disinheritance may be necessary. A testator cannot disinherit a spouse, but can disinherit a child. Mentioning the disinherited child prevents the child from claiming **pretermitted heir,** or forgotten heir, status to contest the will. The testator can also use an **in terrorem clause** or **no contest clause,** which states if the disinherited heir contests the will then that heir's portion goes to the residuary.

Testimonium Clause

The **testimonium clause** is also called the **signature clause** where the testator **affixes** his signature.

Attestation Clause

This is where the witnesses **attest** to seeing the testator execute the will and **subscribe** their signatures to the will.

Self-Proof Clause

Because it is necessary for witnesses to testify to prove a will before it is admitted to court, and because it is unlikely that the witnesses will be available at the testator's death, a short paragraph similar to an **affidavit** can be executed with the will. A notary can administer an oath to the witnesses and acknowledge their signatures so the will can "prove itself."

Fiduciaries

Executors

The testator should nominate someone to administer and close his estate. If this person is a male, he is called an **executor**; if a female, she is called an **executrix.** If the court appoints the nominated individual, he or she will be issued **Letters Testamentary,** which are documents evidencing the authority to act on behalf of the estate. The testator should also consider nominating an **alternate** or **successor executor** if the first nominee declines or is unable to serve.

Administrators

If the testator fails to nominate an executor, if no nominee can serve, or if there is no will present, the court will appoint an **administrator** or an **administratrix.** These individuals will receive **Letters of Administration.**

Personal Representatives

The UPC has done away with the various titles given to those who administer estates and uses the term **Personal Representative** to denote those who receive **Letters of Authority.**

Guardians

If minor children are heirs, then **guardians** must be chosen. A **guardian of the person** will care for the day-to-day living needs of the child. A **guardian of the estate or property** will manage the property left to the minor child. Many states have adopted the **Uniform Transfer to Minors Act (UTTMA),** which allows the testator to choose who shall serve as **custodian** of the account holding the minor's inheritance. A custodian need not report to the court as a guardian must. Guardians will receive **Letters of Guardianship,** but custodians need no court-provided documentation to act.

Trustees

If the testator wishes to establish a trust within the will for the benefit of his heirs, a **trustee** needs to be nominated. The trustee will be imposed with the responsibility to manage the property for the benefit of the heirs.

Bonds and Sureties

All fiduciaries may be required to post a **bond** equal or greater to the amount of assets in the estate or the amount of assets they will manage. The court will decide if a bond or **surety** is necessary, even if the testator **waives the requirement of bonds and sureties** in the will. Normally bank trust departments will receive the waiver, but individuals may not.

Fiduciary Powers

Most states have statutes that grant general powers to all fiduciaries. These statutes should be **incorporated by reference** into a will to give the representatives the authority to act in various situations.

A Summary Proceeding (13.2) – Will Clauses and Fiduciaries

Will Clauses

- Exordium – Identifies testator, publishes will, establishes jurisdiction, and revokes prior wills
- Dispositive provisions
  - Bequest – Gift of tangible personal property
  - Legacy – Pecuniary bequest or gift of money
  - Devise – Gift of personal property
    - Ademption of specific bequests
    - Lapse to residuary without antilapse statute
- Residuary clause – Disposes of property not disposed of by devise or bequest
- Nomination of fiduciaries – Executor, guardians, and trustees
- Miscellaneous – Tax payments, trusts, and disinheritance clauses
- Testimonium clause – Signature of the testator
- Attestation clause – Signature of witnesses
- Self-proof clause – Affidavit of witnesses as testimony to prove will
- Fiduciaries
  - Executor/Executrix – Nominated in will and appointed by court
  - Administrator/Administratrix – Appointed by court
  - Personal representative – UPC
  - Guardians
    - Of the person – Cares for child
    - Of the property – Manages property left to child
- Custodian – Determined under Uniform Transfer to Minors Act
- Bonds of fiduciaries – Waived in will, determined by court
- Powers of fiduciaries – State statutes incorporated by reference

Decedents' Estates

When an individual dies, he or she is referred to as the **decedent.** Depending on how the decedent's property was held during life, separately or jointly, an estate proceeding may be necessary. The first consideration is whether or not the decedent had a complete and valid will. If he did, he is said to have died **testate**; if not, the decedent died **intestate** and **intestacy** laws will apply to determine the distribution of property. These laws are also referred to as the **laws of descent and distribution.** *Descent* refers to the passing of real property and *distribution* refers to the passing of personal property. Other than that major distinction, the actual estate proceedings are the same.

Intestacy

As mentioned before, the lack of a residuary clause in a will may create the need for the application of state intestacy laws. An executed will may not be valid for several reasons, which will be discussed in will contests. When a person dies without instructions as to who should receive his or her property, the state law has specific rules for distribution. A more complete definition of intestacy is dying without a complete and/or valid will.

Protection of the Surviving Spouse

The first spousal protection is usually the **homestead.** Surviving spouses can generally keep the primary family residence and land, regardless of amount involved, at least for life. Some states limit the homestead exemption to a specified amount of the value of the homestead. States differ as to whether this is a statutory or constitutional protection.

Next is the complicated issue of **dower** for a wife and **curtesy** for a husband. Dower and curtesy are fractional interests in **separate,** as opposed to **joint,** property of the decedent. Depending on whether or not the property is real or personal, the surviving spouse usually receives one-third to one-half of the property **for life** or **in fee.**

Finally, most states allow some property or cash allowance to the surviving spouse. Theses **statutory allowances** or **statutory exemptions** are very limited in amount. The UPC limits the amount to $3,500.

Determination of Heirs

Kinship is first defined by **consanguinity** or blood relationship. Secondary to consanguinity is **affinity,** or martial relationships. Consanguine relationships are then divided into **lineal** and **collateral** relationships. **Lineal ascendants** would be parents and grandparents. **Lineal descendants** would be children and grandchildren, also known as **issue. Collateral** heirs would be sisters and brothers.

Although states differ dramatically, first in line as **heirs at law** are usually the lineal descendants, also known as **issue. Adopted children** share the same as **natural children,** as do **illegitimate children** and **children of the half blood.** Grandchildren take a child's share **per stirpes** if the child has predeceased the decedent.

If no lineal descendants are present the next heirs in line are usually the lineal ascendants, such as parents and grandparents. Some states place the spouse as an heir after the issue. Collateral heirs are usually next. Collateral heirs frequently receive property **per capita** if a sibling has predeceased the decedent.

Rarely are there no blood relation heirs that can be found; in this case, some states look to **affinity heirs** if the decedent was married at the time of his or her spouse's death. If no heirs at all can be found the property then **escheats** to the government.

A Summary Proceeding (13.3) – Intestacy

Intestacy – Dying without a complete and valid will

Protection of Spouse

- Homestead – Right to primary residence or value thereof
- Dower/Curtesy – Surviving spouse receives fractional interest in separate property
- Statutory allowance – Spouse may receive limited amount of property or cash of estate

Determination of heirs

- Consanguinity – Blood relations
- Affinity – Marital relations
- Lineal descendants – Children and grandchildren; known as *issue*
- Lineal ascendants – Parents and grandparents
- Collateral heirs – Brothers and sisters
- Escheat to government with no heirs found

Probate Proceedings

Probate is the process of administering and closing **the estate** of the decedent. The first decision to make is whether or not probate proceedings are necessary. If all property was held by the decedent in a **joint tenancy with right of survivorship** or **tenancy by the entirety,** then the property passes automatically to the surviving tenant by operation of law. If the property passes by contract, such as an insurance policy, then no probate is necessary.

Probate proceedings are in rem proceedings. The court is addressing the matter of an estate. Probate is also within equitable jurisdiction and will have no juries. Most probate proceedings, unless contested, are ex parte. There are several common steps to probate.

Petition for Probate

Any **proponent** of a will or interested party, such as an heir, can **petition to admit a will** to probate. A **self-proving will** should be admitted easily. A **holographic will** may need the testimony of two or three witnesses testifying as to the decedent's handwriting. The petition will also request the court to appoint a personal representative such as an executor or administrator. The process will also include **giving notice** of the proceeding to **heirs** and **creditors** of the decedent.

At this point, a respondent to the petition can enter and possibly **contest** the will. **Grounds** for contest of a will can include **improper execution, undue influence, duress, unsound mind,** or **another will. Pretermitted heirs,** including a spouse if a spouse is omitted from a will, may at this time elect to **take against a will** or take a **forced** or **elective share** equal to what he or she would have received in an intestacy proceeding. Once the will, if any, is proved the court will proceed to appoint a personal representative and issue letters.

Inventory

The personal representative should collect and **inventory** the assets of the decedent's estate. This inventory should be filed with the court and is usually due within 30 to 60 days after opening the estate. If the decedent has real property in another state, then an **ancillary probate proceeding** will be opened in that state.

Payment of Claims and Expenses

The personal representative should collect all debts of the decedent as well as claims against the estate. Creditors have a specified length of time from the publication of notice to make claims for amounts due. The time frame is frequently 3 to 6 months and is referred to as the **period of non-claim.** Expenses of last illness and funeral expenses up to specified amounts frequently can be paid without court order.

Preparation, Filing, and Payment of Taxes

Up to six tax returns may be necessary to prepare and file on behalf of a decedent. **Final** federal and state **individual income tax returns** are necessary. If the estate earns income while open, it must file federal and state **fiduciary income tax returns.** Finally, if the estate is large enough, federal and state **estate tax returns** may be necessary. Some states also have **inheritance taxes** imposed on the beneficiaries of an estate.

An Unusual Case

In 2009, the top estate tax rate will be 45% and the amount exempted from taxation will be $3.5 million. In 2010, there will be no estate tax at all. In 2011, the top estate tax rate will be 55% but only $1 million will be exempt.

Accountings

The personal representative must account to the court and all heirs at least once a year and immediately before the final closing of the estate. An **accounting** should reflect all charges to the personal representative, which includes all amounts received since the inventory as well as credits for all amounts paid from the estate, including the fees of the personal representative and the attorney for the estate. Some states allow the heirs to waive the notices of these filings.

Distribution and Discharge

Based on the net amounts, the personal representative is charged with a **distribution** to the heirs at law in an intestacy proceeding or to the heirs under the will. The personal representative should collect receipts for distributions and present them to the court for an order of **discharge.**

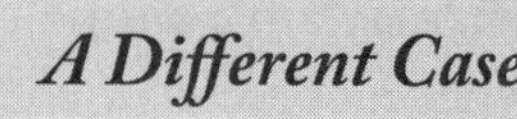

A Different Case

Many states allow for a small estate proceeding that possibly can be completed in a few days. If the estate, exclusive of real estate, is less than a certain amount, usually $10,000 to $50,000, an interested party can present an affidavit to the court of the size of the estate and that no claims are outstanding and an order can be issued transferring personal property to the heirs.

A Summary Proceeding (13.4) – Probate Proceedings

Probate Court – In rem jurisdiction, court of equity

Petition for Probate

- Prove and admit will, appoint personal representative, give notice to heirs and creditors
- Inventory of estate filed with court
- Claims against estate and expenses of last illness paid
- Final income tax, fiduciary income tax, and estate tax returns prepared and filed
- Accounting filed with court and heirs unless waived
- Property distributed and personal representative discharged

Trusts

Parties to a Trust

Grantor

The **grantor** is the party who establishes the trust. A grantor is also known as a **settler, donor,** and **trustor.** The grantor's assets will become the assets of the trust.

Trustee

The **trustee** is the party who takes legal title to the trust property and will manage the trust assets. The trustee can be the grantor, a separate individual, or a corporate trustee such as a bank. Even if the trust document fails to name a trustee, one can be appointed by the court. A trustee is a fiduciary and imposed with some of the highest duties known to law.

Beneficiary

The **beneficiary,** or **cestui que trust,** is the party or parties for whom the trust is established. There must be a beneficiary named in the trust creation. The trustee manages the trust for the sole benefit of the beneficiaries. Beneficiaries can include the grantor.

Creation of a Trust

Declaration of Trust

A grantor can expressly declare a trust to exist. In a **declaration of a trust** the grantor becomes the trustee, which is a separate legal capacity from the grantor's individual capacity. The legal title to the trust assets remains with the grantor, as trustee, and the beneficial title to the trust assets is with the beneficiary.

Conveyance in Trust

The grantor can expressly convey or make a grant of assets to a trust. With a **conveyance in trust** the grantor and the trustee are separate entities. Again, there is a separation of legal title and beneficial title.

Implied Trusts

Constructive Trusts

A **constructive trust** may be established by operation of law to prevent unjust enrichment through wrongdoing.

> *Example 13.4:*
>
> Wife murders Husband to inherit Husband's wealth. If the state does not have a **slayer statute** preventing the Wife from inheriting the property, a constructive trust exists for the remaining heirs of Husband. Wife now holds legal title only for the benefit of the remaining heirs.

Resulting Trusts

A **resulting trust** is created by the intentions or conduct of the parties.

> *Example 13.5:*
>
> Father buys and makes payments on a house for Daughter, placing the house in her name. Daughter attempts to sell the house to pay gambling debts. A resulting trust is created for the benefit of Father.

Trust Documents

A document establishing a trust is called an **agreement** or an **indenture.**

Trust Property

Real property and personal property of all types can be placed in a trust. The trust property is called the **trust fund, res, principal, corpus,** and **estate.**

A Summary Proceeding (13.5) – Trusts

Parties to a trust

Grantor – Establishes trust by declaration or conveyance; separates legal and equitable title; also known as trustor, settler, donor

Trustee – Receives legal title to property; manages property for beneficiary

Beneficiary – Receives equitable title or benefit of trust

Trust document – Called trust agreement or trust indenture

Trust property – All personal and real property transferred to trust; also called trust res, trust principal, trust corpus, trust fund, and trust estate

Types of Trusts

Living Trust vs. Testamentary Trust

A trust established during the life of a grantor is a **living trust** also known as an **inter vivos trust.** A trust established under the terms of a will is called a **testamentary trust.** Care should be taken with the language creating a testamentary trust. There should be clear direction in the will for a trust to exist. **Precatory** language, such as "I wish for my brother to use this gift for my sister's needs," is ambiguous and may not create a trust.

Revocable vs. Irrevocable Trust

A **revocable trust** is one that can be revoked or amended by the grantor during life. An **irrevocable trust** is one that cannot be revoked or amended by the grantor. Once a grantor of a revocable living trust dies, the trust becomes irrevocable. Irrevocable trusts created during the life of the grantor have **estate** and **gift tax** considerations.

Spendthrift Trusts

A **spendthrift** is an individual who cannot control his or her spending. Clauses can be inserted in a trust to make the trust a **spendthrift trust** to protect the beneficiary as well as the trust assets. These clauses protect against **creditor attachment,** beneficiary **alienation,** or sale, of the trust assets, and beneficiary **assignment,** or pledge, of the trust assets as collateral for loans.

Discretionary Trusts

Discretionary trusts give the trustee control over disbursing the principal and income of the trust as the trustee deems necessary. These trusts are also called **sprinkling** or **spray** trusts. When a trustee does disburse principal, he or she is said to **encroach** on or **invade** the principal.

An Unusual Case

The spendthrift concept can be combined with the sprinkling concept to create a **wasting trust.** The grantor may allow for a disbursement of one-third of the principal of the trust when the beneficiary reaches age 30, one-half of the principal at age 40, and the remaining principal when the beneficiary reaches age 50.

Pour Over Trust

A grantor can link a will to a living trust. The terms of the will can "pour over" into the living trust any assets not previously conveyed to the trust. Some call this arrangement a **pour over will,** as opposed to a **pour over trust.**

Charitable Trusts

A grantor can, by will or during his or her life, establish a **charitable trust.** A charitable trust is set up to benefit public and benevolent purposes that will be charitable, tax-exempt organizations that the trustee chooses. This type of trust is sometimes called a **public trust** and is usually monitored by the Attorney General of the state. Charitable trusts have the unique characteristic of being perpetual in nature, in that the trust never **vests** in the hands of any party. Normally, such a trust would violate the **rule against perpetuities.** Even if a specific recipient of a charitable trust ceases to exist, courts can apply the **doctrine of cy pres** to continue the charitable trust.

Totten Trusts

A **Totten Trust** is a trust of personal property in which the title to the property is in the name of grantor, but distributed to another person at the death of the grantor. These trusts are most frequently seen in **payable on death** bank accounts.

Marital Deduction Trusts

A **marital deduction trust** is a trust used for estate planning purposes because of its tax advantages. A marital deduction trust can be established by a will or within a living trust. The tax advantage is the fact that all gifts to a spouse are **deductible** from the **gross estate** of the grantor-decedent, no matter how large the gift.

Life Insurance Trusts

Another estate planning device is the **irrevocable life insurance trust.** Placing a life insurance policy into an irrevocable trust when the life insurance policy has no cash value allows a testator to avoid gift taxes and estate taxes when the death proceeds are collected.

A Summary Proceeding (13.6) – Types of Trusts

Living trust – Created during life of grantor, also known as inter vivos trust

Testamentary trust – Created under the terms of a will

Revocable trust – Trust that can be amended and revoked by grantor

Irrevocable trust – Trust that cannot be amended or revoked by grantor

Spendthrift trust – Clauses to protect beneficiary and assets of trust from excessive spending

Discretionary trust – Allows trustee to encroach on principal of trust

Pour over trust – Links a trust with a will

Charitable trust – Perpetual trust for public and benevolent purposes

Totten trust – Trust of personal property; bank payable of death accounts

Marital deduction trust – Trust for surviving spouse entitled to deduction from gross estate

Life insurance trust – Estate and tax planning device to remove assets from gross estate

Conclusions of Law

Wills, estates, and trusts are very detailed areas of law. Many attorneys will acquire a masters' degree in law (L.L.M) specializing in taxation before concentrating in the field. It is, however, an area of law that will always be present because it has often been said, "There are two things you can be sure of: death and taxes."

The Latin Language

cy pres – sigh pray

inter vivos – inter *vee*-vos

Exercises – Chapter 13

True/False Correction Determine if the statement is true or false; if false, insert the correct term in the blank below the question for the term in bold to make the statement true.

_____ 1. The assets of the testator can be called **bounty.**

____

_____ 2. An administrator is issued **Letters Testamentary.**

____

_____ 3. Property not found in an estate or with the heir has adeemed by **satisfaction.**

____

_____ 4. A testator who disposes of land is a **legator.**

____

_____ 5. A person caring for the day-to-day needs of a minor is a guardian of the **person.**

____

_____ 6. A person who dies without a will is said to die **testate.**

____

_____ 7. A probate proceeding is an in **personam** proceeding.

____

_____ 8. A trust beneficiary who sells trust assets is said to **assign** property.

____

_____ 9. A legacy paid from a particular fund is a **specific** legacy.

____

_____ 10. A trustee is **appointed** under the terms of a will.

____

Definitions Insert the correct legal term in the blank above the definition.

1. ______________________________

The management and disposition of assets to protect family and financial interests

2. ______________________________

An heir who has been forgotten or omitted from a will

3. ______________________________

The primary residence the surviving spouse may be able to keep

4. ______________________________

The formation of a trust by transferring legal title to property to a separate trustee

5. ______________________________

The interest possessed by a surviving wife in separate property of the decedent

6. ______________________________

The legal relationship established by blood

7. ______________________________

The legal relationship of a brother or sister

8. ______________________________

The doctrine allowing a charitable trust to continue if a specific charity ceases to exist

9. ______________________________

An implied trust formed by the intent and the conduct of the parties

10. ______________________________

The introductory paragraph of a will establishing jurisdiction and identity of testator

Word Association/Matching Match the term in the left column with the best corresponding term in the right column.

_____ 1. Totten Trust	A.	affidavit
_____ 2. self-proof clause	B.	creditor attachment
_____ 3. issue	C.	constructive trust
_____ 4. slayer statute	D.	specific bequest
_____ 5. accounting	E.	oral
_____ 6. delusions	F.	Letters of Authority
_____ 7. nuncupative	G.	handwritten
_____ 8. testimonium clause	H.	predeceased child
_____ 9. personal representative	I.	surety
_____ 10. lapse	J.	husband
_____ 11. beneficiary	K.	charges and credits
_____ 12. custodian	L.	lucid interval
_____ 13. spendthrift	M.	successor
_____ 14. subscription	N.	cestui que trust
_____ 15. fiduciary bond	O.	advance directive
_____ 16. curtesy	P.	payable on death account
_____ 17. health care proxy	Q.	Uniform Transfer to Minors Act
_____ 18. ademption	R.	witness signature
_____ 19. alternate	S.	signature clause
_____ 20. holographic	T.	children and grandchildren

Synonyms List a synonym for the word provided (there may be more than one).

1. testamentary capacity: ______
2. mutual will: ______
3. legacy: ______
4. guardian of the estate: ______
5. intestacy laws: ______
6. statutory allowances: ______
7. forced share: ______
8. grantor: ______
9. trust res: ______
10. trust agreement: ______
11. living trust: ______
12. sprinkling trust: ______
13. encroach: ______
14. pour over trust: ______
15. no contest clause: ______

Section VI

Law and the Government

Chapter 14

Constitutional Law

Opening Statements

The **U.S. Constitution** is the supreme law of the land. The **U.S. Supreme Court** is the ultimate interpreter of the Constitution. The Constitution is written in general language, which requires constant and sometimes changing interpretations of its meaning. During the latter half of the twentieth century, the Supreme Court exercised what many legal scholars described as **judicial activism** as opposed to **judicial restraint**. Judicial activism is generally considered legislation from the bench, or where the court tends to make the law instead of merely interpreting the law. Judicial restraint has also been connected to the term **strict constructionist,** which refers to a judge who will limit construction of the clauses in the Constitution to their plain and historical meaning. In any event, the Constitution says whatever the Supreme Court tells us it says. Here, the Constitution is studied through its two primary divisions: the Articles and the Amendments.

Articles

The first three Articles of the Constitution establish the three branches of our federal government. They are the **Congress,** the **Presidency,** and the **Judiciary** also known as the **legislative** branch, the **executive** branch, and the **judicial** branch. The doctrine of **separation of powers** has evolved from the specific powers of each branch listed in Articles I, II, and III and establishes a system of checks and balances of the power bestowed on the federal government.

Article I

Congress

The Constitution establishes a **Congress** with two chambers: an upper chamber known as the **Senate,** and a lower chamber known as the **House of Representatives**. A legislative body having two chambers is said to be **bicameral,** as opposed to **unicameral,** which means single chambered. Nebraska is the only state in the nation with a unicameral **legislature**. The purpose of a legislature is to **enact** or make laws. The powers of Congress lie within Section 8 of Article I. Some of the more important powers are listed in the following sections.

The Commerce Clause

One of the most powerful clauses is referred to as the **Interstate Commerce Clause,** which allows Congress to regulate commerce among the several states. Commerce solely within a state's borders is considered **intrastate commerce** and is regulated by the state. Almost everything that has come before the Supreme Court has been declared to be interstate commerce.

Example 14.1:

Restaurant decided that the 1964 Civil Rights Act did not apply to local restaurants, and therefore Restaurant could deny minorities the right to enter for a meal. The Supreme Court decided that serving interstate travelers or buying food products delivered from other states made the restaurant a part of interstate commerce.

A Different Case

In 1922, the Supreme Court decided that baseball was a "local show" and not part of interstate commerce, despite the crossing of state lines by teams. Since then, all cases before the Supreme Court have upheld the decision as precedent, claiming judicial restraint, and that Congress should decide whether baseball is interstate commerce.

The Necessary and Proper Clause

The Supreme Court has also decided that the enumerated powers, those listed in Article I, Section 8 do not limit Congress from making laws that are **necessary and proper** to complete their authority under Section 8. The definition of "necessary and proper," however, is for the Supreme Court to decide.

Taxation

Article I, Section 8 also gives Congress the power to **lay and collect taxes.** This has also been interpreted by the Supreme Court to be an extensive power. In fact, the United States can collect income taxes on illegal activities.

> ***An Unusual Case***
>
> Although movies and television shows would lead one to believe that Eliot Ness and The Untouchables were successful in bringing Al Capone to justice, it was actually Frank Wilson, an IRS agent, who made the case against Capone for income tax evasion.

Article II

The Presidency

The **President** and **Vice President** are elected by **electors,** or the electoral college, not by a popular vote. The President can be removed from office by **impeachment** of the House of Representatives and trial by the Senate. The executive branch enforces the law.

Powers of the President

The powers of the President are actually quite limited. The President is the **Commander in Chief** of the armed forces, but cannot declare war; only Congress can **declare war.** The President has the power to **make treaties** and **appoint** various federal officials subject to **confirmation** by the Congress. The President has the power to grant **reprieves and pardons** for federal offenses. The President must report to Congress periodically with a **State of the Union** address.

> ***An Unusual Case***
>
> The veto power of the President is not found in Article II; it is found in Section 7 of Article I, with the discussion of submission of legislative bills to be presented to the President by Congress.

Article III

The Judiciary

The judicial branch consists of one **Supreme Court** and such **inferior courts** as Congress shall establish. One specific constitutionally derived court established by Congress is the **Bankruptcy Court,** pursuant to Article I, Section 8 of the Constitution. Other than jurisdictional issues, issues of trials for crimes, and the issue of treason, the courts are given no specific duties or powers.

Article IV

The two most well known clauses of Article IV of the Constitution are the **full faith and credit clause** and the **privileges and immunities clause**.

Example 14.2:

If Husband obtains a no-fault divorce in Missouri and moves to Arkansas. Arkansas must give full faith and credit to the judicial proceedings in Missouri, even though Arkansas does not allow for no-fault divorces under its laws. Otherwise, Husband would be a bigamist in Arkansas if he remarried.

Example 14.3:

If Licensed Driver from Kansas is driving through Oklahoma and Oklahoma allows Licensed Drivers from Oklahoma to drive on its roads, Licensed Driver from Kansas must be afforded the privilege of driving in Oklahoma.

Articles V, VI, and VII

Amendments to the Constitution

Article V gives Congress the right, by two-thirds vote of both houses, to **submit amendments** to the Constitution to the states, which can **ratify** the amendment by three-fourths vote. Article V also gives Congress the right, on application by two-thirds of the states, to call a **constitutional convention,** which can amend the Constitution by three-fourths vote.

The Supremacy Clause

Article VI clearly states that all laws of the United States, including treaties, shall be **the supreme law of the land.**

Ratification of the Constitution

Article VII required nine of the original thirteen states to **ratify** the Constitution by state conventions before it would be adopted.

A Summary Proceeding (14.1) – Articles of the U.S. Constitution

Articles establish the structure and powers of the U.S. government:

Article I – Congress consists of bicameral legislature – Senate and House of Representatives

- Commerce clause – Congress regulates interstate commerce
- Necessary and proper clause – Congress enacts laws necessary and proper to achieve enumerated powers
- Taxation – Extensive authority to lay and collect taxes

Article II – The Presidency – President and Vice President elected by Electors

- Limited Powers – Make treaties, appoint federal officials, grant pardons, report to Congress
- Veto Power – established under Article I
- Impeachment by Congress for removal

Article III – The Judiciary – consists of a Supreme Court and inferior courts

Article IV – Established full faith and credit clause and privileges and immunities clause

Article V – Procedure for amending Constitution

Article VI – Supremacy clause – established federal law and Constitution as supreme law of the land

Article VII – Established nine state requirement for ratification of Constitution

Amendments

The **amendments** to the Constitution have been enacted primarily to establish individual liberties and further to refine the structure of the government. The first ten amendments were termed the **Bill of Rights.** A total of 27 amendments have been made to the Constitution. A few of the more litigated amendments that have not been discussed previously are discussed here.

Amendment I

Religion

The "**establishment clause**" prevents Congress from making a law respecting the establishment of a religion. A law respects the establishment of a religion when it has a **nonsecular purpose,** when it **endorses** a religion, including endorsement by **coercion,** and when it creates an **entanglement** of religion and government. Religious freedom is also protected by Amendment I.

Speech

Amendment I also prevents Congress from abridging the **freedom of speech**. Protected speech under the Constitution includes **political speech, commercial speech,** and **professional speech. Unprotected speech** includes speech that creates a **clear and present danger,** as well as **obscenity** and defamation.

Example 14.4:

Yelling "fire" in a crowded theater would be speech that creates a clear and present danger.

Amendment V

Due Process

The Fifth Amendment prevents the federal government from depriving any **person** from **life, liberty,** and **property** without **due process** of law. A person can be a U.S. citizen or a non-citizen. Due process is generally considered **fundamental fairness** and will be discussed more thoroughly under the Fourteenth Amendment.

Eminent Domain

Although clearly a property issue, the **taking** of private property has recently become more of a constitutional issue interpreting the clause **public use**. If a government takes private property for public use, the owner must receive **just compensation**.

Example 14.5:

City exercises eminent domain to purchase private property on a riverfront for sale to a commercial developer for hotels and malls. Is the taking of property from one private owner to sell to another private owner for the purpose of increasing property tax values considered public use? The Supreme Court has said yes.

Amendment VII

The right to a **trial by jury** in federal civil cases is established by Amendment VII. If the **value in controversy** exceeds $20 and involves a **common law cause of action,** there is the right to a trial by jury.

Amendment XIV

Second only to Amendment IV litigation would be issues under the **due process clause** and the **equal protection clause** of the Fourteenth Amendment. The Fourteenth Amendment applies to the state governments when there is an attempt to restrict individual liberties. The doctrine of **selective incorporation** applies almost all of the Bill of Rights to the states.

Due Process

Due process is divided into to two parts: **procedural due process,** which involves notice and opportunity to be heard in legal matters, and **substantive due process,** which involves the fundamental fairness of the law itself. It is the substantive due process concept that leads some to allege that the Supreme Court has usurped the power of the legislatures by exercising judicial activism and creating law.

Equal Protection

The **equal protection** clause of the Fourteenth Amendment states that no state shall deny to any person the equal protection of the laws. The student will see, however, that even the most basic of rights such as equal protection are not absolute.

A SUMMARY PROCEEDING (14.2) – AMENDMENTS TO THE U.S. CONSTITUTION

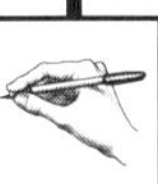

Amendment I

Religion – Establishment clause prevents congressional act respecting establishment of religion

Speech – Includes protected speech and unprotected speech considerations

Amendment V

Due Process Clause – Prevents federal government from depriving persons of life, liberty, and property

Eminent Domain – Prevents taking of private property without just compensation

Amendment VII – Establishes right to trial by jury in federal civil cases

Amendment XIV – Provides for due process and equal protection as against state governments

Selective Incorporation – Applies Bill of Rights to persons as against state governments

The Constitutionality Of Laws

When a government enacts a law that restricts individual liberties, the courts, and eventually the Supreme Court, must pass on the constitutionality of the law. The courts will use a test, depending on the right involved, to balance the rights of the individual versus the power of the government. Two rules must be remembered when applying constitutional law:

1. No right is absolute. All rights can be restricted by a government.
2. The person restricting rights must act with **color of authority,** which means the person must be an agent of the government and acting on behalf of the government.

Categories of Rights

Fundamental Rights

Those rights which are enumerated in the Constitution are considered **fundamental rights**. Examples would be the right to a speedy trial, the freedom of speech and religion, and the right to be free from unreasonable searches and seizures.

Non-Fundamental Rights

All other rights are to be considered nonfundamental. Examples would be property and business interests.

Economic and Social Rights

Some rights, called **social** or **economic** rights, have been established as fundamental rights by case law even though the right is not specifically enumerated in the Constitution. These include the **right to privacy** and an **abortion,** as well as the right of **marriage.** These rights fall within the doctrine that such rights are **"implicit in the concepts of ordered liberty"** under the liberty concept of the Due Process clause of the Fourteenth Amendment or the **penumbra doctrine** of the Fourth, Fifth, and Ninth Amendments.

Tests for Constitutionality of Laws

The Strict Scrutiny Test

If a fundamental or enumerated right is infringed on, the courts will apply the **strict scrutiny** test. Within this test the government will have to show a **compelling state interest** for the restriction and that the law is **narrowly tailored** to achieve that interest.

Example 14.6:

College applies the concept of affirmative action, which favors minorities in the admission process. This violates the equal protection clause. However, if the college can show that **diversity** is a compelling reason for the program and that the favoritism is applied only in individual comparisons between students, as opposed to a **preference by class,** the program will be upheld.

An Unusual Case

Abortion has been defined as a fundamental right but does not receive the strict scrutiny test. The **undue burden test** for abortion requires the plaintiff to prove that the abortion restriction puts an undue burden of the exercising of a right to an abortion.

The Rational Basis Test

If governmental action impedes a business or property interest, the government must show a **rational basis** for the law. To meet this test, the government must show that the restriction was **reasonable** and served a **legitimate state interest**.

Example 14.7:

City enacts a zoning plan that restricts commercial activity within a residential neighborhood. The city has a legitimate interest in preserving the safety, peace, and quiet of neighborhoods by preventing business traffic. The prohibitions are reasonable in that they only extend to residential areas with other areas being classified as commercial areas.

The Void for Vagueness Test

If a law is so broad or vague that a reasonable person cannot determine nor have notice that their conduct violates the law, the law must be stricken as **void for vagueness**.

Example 14.8:

City passes an ordinance prohibiting car prowling. Whereas one individual could slowly drive the streets of a neighborhood checking driveways to see if residents' cars are gone, indicating an empty house, another individual may just be lost and trying to find a specific house to visit a new friend.

A Summary Proceeding (14.3) – Testing Constitutionality of Laws

Application rules

- No right is absolute; color of authority must be present

Categories of rights

- Fundamental rights – enumerated in the Constitution
- Nonfundamental rights – property and business interest
- Social/Economic rights – established by case law

Tests for constitutionality

- Strict scrutiny – government shows compelling interest and narrow tailoring of law
- Rational basis – reasonable restriction with legitimate state interest
- Undue burden – applied in abortion cases
- Void for vagueness – reasonable person cannot determine violation of law

Conclusions of Law

Constitutional law is the cornerstone of American law. Not only must it balance the powers of the government from within, it must balance the rights of the individuals as against government actions. It must also balance the need for consistency within the law, with the need for change of the law to correlate to societal changes. It is the most talked-about law for the fewest number of cases decided.

Exercises – Chapter 14

True/False Correction Determine if the statement is true or false; if false, insert the correct term in the blank below the question for the term in bold to make the statement true.

_____ 1. The **Bankruptcy Court** is the final arbiter of the United States Constitution.

____

_____ 2. Commerce within one state is considered **interstate** commerce.

____

_____ 3. The President is elected by **popular vote**.

____

_____ 4. Eminent domain requires a payment of **just compensation**.

____

_____ 5. The branch of the government responsible for enacting laws is the **judiciary.**

____

Definitions Insert the correct legal term in the blank above the definition.

1. ____

   The type of legislature with only one chamber

2. ____

   The reason for which a government may implement eminent domain

3. ____

   The doctrine of applying the Bill of Rights to the states

4. ____

   The doctrine determining the fairness of the law itself

5. ____

   The doctrine that makes yelling "fire" in a crowded theater unprotected speech

Matching/Word Association Match the term in the left column with the best corresponding term in the right column.

_____ 1.	U.S. Constitution	A. eminent domain
_____ 2.	bicameral	B. grants pardons
_____ 3.	U.S. Supreme Court	C. federal government legislature
_____ 4.	enumerated rights	D. undue burden test
_____ 5.	obscenity	E. establishment clause
_____ 6.	taking	F. fundamental rights
_____ 7.	due process	G. State of the Union address
_____ 8.	abortion	H. rational basis test
_____ 9.	Senate	I. Constitutional court
_____ 10.	judicial restraint	J. compelling state interest
_____ 11.	zoning	K. fundamental fairness
_____ 12.	religion	L. strict constructionist
_____ 13.	amendment	M. supreme law of land
_____ 14.	Presidential power	N. nonprotected speech
_____ 15.	diversity	O. constitutional convention
_____ 16.	federal civil trial	P. upper chamber
_____ 17.	Congress	Q. first ten amendments
_____ 18.	Bill of Rights	R. opportunity to be heard
_____ 19.	Presidential duty	S. two-chambered
_____ 20.	procedural due process	T. common law cause of action

Chapter 15

Administrative Law

Opening Statements

Administrative law is the law that governs **administrative agencies** of a government, as those agencies regulate aspects of our lives. Administrative law is procedural in nature as opposed to the substantive law of **regulations** enacted by the agencies. Administrative agencies carry out laws passed by the state legislatures as well as the federal government. It would be impossible for the legislatures, chief executive officers, and courts to address the almost infinite number of legal situations that arise in our ever-growing society. The statutes, rules, and cases that exist in the field of administrative law put a check on the power of the government to control our everyday lives. Without these checks administrative agencies, which are operated by appointed officials as opposed to elected officials, would have no one or nothing to which to answer. Agencies are also referred to as a **board,** a **commission,** a **department,** a **bureau,** a **service,** and an **administration.**

Examples of Administrative Agencies

To better understand administrative law, a list of commonly known agencies is appropriate.

Agency	Acronym	Government
Equal Employment Opportunity Commission	EEOC	Federal
Federal Bureau of Investigation	FBI	Federal
Occupational Safety and Health Administration	OSHA	Federal
Department of Labor	DOL	Federal/State
Securities and Exchange Commission	SEC	Federal
Environmental Protection Agency	EPA	Federal
Federal Deposit Insurance Corporation	FDIC	Federal
Social Security Administration	SSA	Federal
Food and Drug Administration	FDA	Federal
Public Service Commission	PSC	State
Federal Trade Commission	FTC	Federal
Office of the Comptroller of Currency	OCC	Federal

Creation of an Agency

Agencies are created by a legislative act known as an **enabling statute.** This act **delegates authority** to the agency to make, enforce, and interpret the law. An agency has legislative authority, executive authority, and judicial authority within the limits of the enabling statute.

Rulemaking

Agencies create rules and **regulations** by the process of **promulgation.**

Types of Rules

1. Substantive rules – These are laws that carry the same force and effect of legislative laws known as *statutes.* Regulations are not a lesser form of law.

2. Procedural rules – These are rules that define the internal structure and operation of an agency and are governed by the **Administrative Procedure Act (APA),** which applies to all federal agencies and has been adopted by several states.
3. Interpretive rules – These are the rules for interpreting the substantive rules.

Rulemaking Procedures

Informal procedures allow the agency to draft the regulations and then provide notice to the public of the regulations and allow comments from the public. **Formal procedures** would require that the agency also hold public hearings with a vote of the appointed officials creating the regulations.

Publication of Regulations

Federal regulations are first published in the **Federal Register** when the agency utilizes informal procedures for rulemaking. Once the regulation has become final, it is published in the **Code of Federal Regulations** by topic.

A Summary Proceeding (15.1) – Creation and Activities of Agencies

Agencies also known as boards, commissions, departments, bureaus, services, administrations

Enabling statute – Delegation of authority to agency by legislature
- Legislative, executive, and judicial authority

Rulemaking – Promulgation of regulations
- Substantive rules
- Procedural rules – APA
- Interpretive rules

Rulemaking Procedures
- Informal procedures – Comments from interested parties
- Formal procedures – Public hearings and votes

Publication of Regulations
- Federal Register – Chronological order
- Code of Federal Regulations – Topical order

Enforcement Procedures

Routine Enforcement

Many enforcement activities of an administrative agency are **routine** in nature. Taking applications and issuing permits and licenses are the day-to-day functions of much of the agency. The process of issuing a license is known as **licensure.**

Example 15.1:

Teenager goes to the Office of Drivers' Services to make an application for a Learners' Permit to take a drivers' education course. After completion of the course, Teenager may now apply and be tested for a drivers' license.

Investigative Powers

Self-Monitoring

Businesses are frequently required to **self-monitor** compliance with regulations and self-report, including violations of regulations, to an administrative agency. Businesses must admit a violation of the law because they do not have protection under the Fifth Amendment to the U.S. Constitution against self-incrimination.

Example 15.2:

National Bank must send quarterly "call reports" to federal agencies that regulate the industry. These agencies include the Federal Reserve Bank, the Federal Deposit Insurance Corporation, and the Office of the Comptroller of Currency. These call reports include a complete set of financial statements including income statements, balance sheets, and cash flow statements.

Direct Observation

Agencies have the right to inspect businesses. Most frequently the agency will notify the business of a planned **inspection** or **examination,** but the agency can make unannounced visits to obtain information. Constitutional issues such as a warrant for a search or seizure are relaxed as to the application to a business.

Subpoena Powers

A **subpoena** is a formal legal request to appear and testify or provide documents to the agency. Unless the business wishes to quash the issuance of a subpoena, the business must comply. Agencies can also seek subpoenas to obtain information about the businesses' customers.

Enforcement Penalties

Agencies have the power to seek civil or criminal actions against violators for their misconduct. More often, however, agencies implement **sanctions,** or penalties, against an individual or business for violation of regulations. Sanctions may include suspension of a license, permit, or rights, cease-and-desist orders, or regulatory fines.

A SUMMARY PROCEEDING (15.2) – ENFORCEMENT POWERS OF AGENCIES

Routine Enforcement – Applications, tests, permits, and licensure

Investigative powers
- Self-Monitoring by companies
- Direct observation – Examinations and inspections
- Subpoena power

Enforcement Penalties
- Civil and criminal actions
- Sanctions
  - Suspension of licenses, rights, and permits
  - Cease and desist orders
  - Regulatory fines

Judicial Functions of an Agency

Agencies can use discretion to use formal procedures known as an **administrative hearing** or an **adjudicatory hearing** to implement an **administrative remedy.** A **hearing officer or hearing examiner,** also known as an **Administrative Law Judge (ALJ),** will conduct a formal process of reviewing the violation and determining the remedy. In some instances, a panel of hearing officers may be convened. Hearings can also be held for decisions of the agency as to routine activities as well if a person is dissatisfied with a decision as to benefits, such as a license, denied by the agency. All agencies should have procedural rules established for the hearing and appeals process.

Judicial Review of Administrative Agency Decisions

Jurisdiction

Most enabling statutes will declare the court that will have **jurisdiction** over the subject matter of agency decisions. Enabling statutes may also deny the **reviewability** of an agency decision.

Case in Controversy

In addition to the requirements that a party have **standing** (i.e., be the one who is aggrieved) and **ripeness** (i.e., an actual injury), the reviewability of agency decisions must also consider **exhaustion of remedies.** Agencies usually will have an internal appeals process for routine and discretionary decisions of the agency. The aggrieved party must complete the appeals process for the decision of the agency to be final and create the harm.

Scope of Judicial Review

Because an administrative agency is the government, or at least a person acting on behalf of the government with color of authority, constitutional questions arise. The Due Process Clause of the Fifth and Fourteenth Amendments to the U.S. Constitution apply to the federal and state governments, respectively.

Procedural Due Process

Any party aggrieved by an administrative agency action must be given **notice** of the action or charges against them. The party is entitled to the **opportunity to be heard** or in some cases a **hearing** if constitutionally protected interests are being deprived.

A Different Case

Sometimes the notice of an administrative hearing is called *judicial notice.* This should not be confused with the concept of judicial notice when a court accepts evidence as a fact without proof.

Substantive Due Process

An agency decision must be based on **substantial evidence.** Substantial evidence is that which is sufficient to keep the decision from being **arbitrary and capricious.** A decision that is arbitrary and capricious is said to be an **abuse of discretion** by the agency. An excellent case that relates to substantive due process, college students, and the administrative agency process is provided in the Case Analysis.

A Summary Proceeding (15.3) – Judicial Aspects of an Agency

- Administrative/Adjudicatory Hearings
  - Hearing examiner, hearing officer, Administrative Law Judge (ALJ)
  - Administrative remedy
- Judicial Review of Administrative Agencies
  - Jurisdiction and reviewability
  - Case in controversy
    - Standing of aggrieved party

(Continued)

A SUMMARY PROCEEDING (15.3) – (CONTINUED)

Ripeness of issue

Finality of harm – Exhaustion of remedies

Scope of Judicial Review

Fifth and Fourteenth Amendments to U.S. Constitution

Procedural due process

Notice and opportunity to be heard

Substantive due process

Substantial evidence

Arbitrary and capricious remedy

Abuse of discretion

Control of Administrative Agencies

Although enabling statutes, the APA, and case law provide sources of law to regulate the regulators, other ways of controlling the potential for abuse of power by the government exist.

Appropriations

Agencies rely on congressional **appropriations.** Congress and state legislatures control the "purse strings" of allocation funds for agency budgets. Even though administrative officials do not report to the electorate, they do report to elected officials.

Sunshine Laws

Administrative agencies cannot act in secret. Agencies generally have to open their meetings to the public under **sunshine** or **open meeting laws.** Announcements of board and commission meetings must be made, and minutes of meeting should always be kept.

Freedom of Information Act

The records of the activities of agencies are also subject to public review under the **Freedom of Information Act.** Requests by the public or the media allow for a check on the activities of the agency.

A SUMMARY PROCEEDING (15.4) – CONTROL OF ADMINISTRATIVE AGENCIES

Enabling Statute, APA, case law

Congressional appropriations

Sunshine Laws – Open meeting laws

Freedom of Information Act

Conclusions of Law

The government is everywhere and is endowed with tremendous power. The law places a limit as to how powerful the government can actually be. Administrative law is one of the fastest growing areas of law and will continue to be so as long as our nation and government continue to grow.

Exercises – Chapter 15

Matching/Word Association Match the term in the left column with the best corresponding term in the right column.

_____	1. administrative law	A. routine activity
_____	2. enabling statute	B. procedural rules
_____	3. inspection	C. cease and desist order
_____	4. licensure	D. delegation of authority
_____	5. administrative hearing	E. aggrieved party
_____	6. sanction	F. public hearing
_____	7. exhaustion of remedies	G. arbitrary and capricious
_____	8. formal rulemaking	H. adjudicatory hearing
_____	9. sunshine laws	I. administrative notice
_____	10. abuse of discretion	J. public comments
_____	11. standing	K. regulatory law
_____	12. promulgation	L. open meetings
_____	13. A.P.A.	M. ripeness
_____	14. judicial notice	N. rulemaking
_____	15. informal rulemaking	O. examination

List/Fill in the Blank List four other terms or designations of an administrative agency:

1. ________________________________

2. ________________________________

3. ________________________________

4. ________________________________

List three sanctions an administrative agency can impose:

1. ________________________________

2. ________________________________

3. ________________________________

Fully identify the following acronyms:

1. SEC: ________________________________

2. APA: ________________________________

3. EEOC: ________________________________

4. CFR: ________________________________

5. FDIC: ________________________________

6. FOIA: ________________________________

7. EPA: ________________________________

8. DOL: ________________________________

9. OSHA: ________________________________

10. PSC: ________________________________

Section VII

Law and the Legal Professional

Chapter 16

The Legal Professional and the Law Office

Opening Statements

Even the law office will have its own unique language. Senior partners, associates, case reporters, and legal administrators are just a few of the terms the legal professional will encounter when entering the legal workforce. From solo practitioner offices to corporate legal departments, the "terminology" environment will be pretty much the same.

The Firm

The Solo Practitioner

In an environment with only one attorney, the legal professional will be much more than just a legal assistant. He or she may very well be the complete support staff. This means he or she will be the **receptionist, legal secretary, paralegal payroll clerk, librarian,** and **office manager.**

The Small Firm

Not only does the number of lawyers increase in a two- to ten-attorney firm, but the number of support staff increases even more. There could very well be an office manager who serves as the **accounting officer** and librarian, but a separate receptionist may be present. Each lawyer may have his own legal secretary and/or paralegal, which may result in the position of **senior paralegal** or even **managing paralegal** being available. The lawyers may be **partners** and share in the profits or **associates** who work for a salary and hope to be a partner one day.

The Mid-Sized Firm

As the firm grows to a size of 10 to 40 attorneys, two things will be evident in the organizational structure. Management functions will increase, and departmentalization will appear. At this level there will be a **management committee** composed of the more senior partners. A **managing partner** will be appointed. There will be junior partners and associates, as well as summer interns. The library will grow to need a separate librarian, with a support staff that also handles technology for the firm. The accounting department will be created as a separate function. Paralegals may all report to one managing paralegal, whereas secretaries and **file clerks** report to an **operations or support staff supervisor.**

The Large Firm

Firms have no limit to size. Larger metropolitan areas may have 100 + attorneys in one office location and satellite offices across the region or country. A full corporate structure will become evident, especially with departmentalization. Attorneys will begin working in a particular specialty or division such as the **corporate division,** the **litigation division,** the **tax division,** or the **real estate division,** depending on the specialization of the firm. Each division will have its own managing partner. The number of nonlawyers, secretaries, paralegals, and clerks may outnumber the lawyers by two to one or more.

The Corporate Law Office

Corporations have legal departments with what is referred to as "**in-house**" counsel. Usually the senior or managing lawyer is referred to as **General Counsel,** and in larger legal departments may serve as Secretary to the Board of Directors. There will also be positions of **associate general counsel, assistant general counsel,** or **deputy general counsel.** Many corporate legal departments work solely within the corporation and do not make appearances in court. Frequently, **"outside" counsel** will be used for litigation.

Types of Practices

Although many solo practitioners will claim to be in the general practice of law, many will tell you that their practice concentrates on two or three areas. Many willingly limit their practice to certain types of cases, and some even specialize. Specialty practices, even for the larger firms, include, but are in no way limited to, **personal injury** law, **employment and labor** law, **tax** law, **bankruptcy** law, **real estate** law, **elder** law, and **patent, trademark, and copyright** law.

A SUMMARY PROCEEDING (16.1) – FIRMS AND PRACTICES

Solo practitioner – One attorney and one paralegal who acts as secretary, receptionist, office manager, payroll clerk and librarian

Small firm – Separation of functions of support staff including accounting officer and librarian, with possible managing paralegal

Mid-sized firm – Organizational structure becomes evident with managing committees and managing Partner

Large firm – Departmentalization based on specialty of attorneys

Corporate law – General counsel who serves as Secretary of Board; use of outside counsel for litigation

Types of practice – General practice, practice with concentrations, practices limited to specialty area and specialty practices

ETHICS

Whether the firm has one or 121 lawyers, **ethics** are the same. Defining ethics is a problem in and of itself. What is moral or right or wrong is frequently a judgment call. Consequently, legal associations for attorneys and paralegals have drafted model codes for guidance. **Professional responsibility** or **professional conduct** is addressed in these codes. The unique problem with ethics of paralegals and secretaries is that no state currently licenses either individual. A violation of ethics could cost the paralegal/secretary his or her job, could subject the attorney to sanctions, or could lead to the paralegal's/secretary's expulsion from a fraternal association, but it cannot cost the paralegal/secretary a state license he or she does not have.

Unauthorized Practice of Law

Several areas of activity, especially by a paralegal, are commonly accepted as the unauthorized practice of law.

Giving Legal Advice

Rendering an opinion of any type as to the merits of a legal issue or fact situation presented to the paralegal by a client can be considered the unauthorized practice of law. Recommending that a person take or not take any course of action can be viewed as legal advice. Simply telling someone that they don't need an attorney for a particular situation is also legal advice.

Court Appearances

Only an attorney should **appear in court** on behalf of the client. Problems arise when the paralegal appears in court on behalf of the attorney to inform the court of the attorney's inability to appear. Some administrative agencies, however, allow nonlawyers to act as an advocate for another person.

Drafting of Documents

Paralegals can **draft documents** for the attorney, but not for the client. All documents prepared by the paralegal in the course of their employment, including those that are simply filling in the blanks of a prototype form, should be reviewed by the attorney before presentation to the client. Even some attorneys can be found to be engaged in the unauthorized practice of law with this activity.

Example 16.1:

Trust Officer, who is an attorney, prepares a simple will for a client that appoints the Trust Officer's bank as executor. Trust Officer has engaged in the unauthorized practice of law. Trust Officer can act on behalf of the bank, but cannot act on behalf of an individual customer.

Legal Relationships and Fees

A paralegal cannot establish the **legal relationship** between an attorney and a client, nor should the paralegal determine what **fees,** if any, are to be placed on any case. Only an attorney can perform these acts.

Conflicts of Interest

Although a paralegal cannot represent one party to an action, much less both parties to an action, a paralegal can be faced with a **conflict of interest** situation.

Example 16.2:

Paralegal works for Attorney Adams, who represents Plaintiff A. Paralegal takes a new job with Attorney Baker, who represents Defendant against Plaintiff A. Paralegal may have a conflict of interest.

The paralegal in this situation should disclose to Attorney Baker his or her position, because the paralegal may be privy to **confidential information** about Plaintiff A. If that is the case, Attorney Baker must inform the client of the possible conflict and establish a "**Chinese Wall**" between the Paralegal and the case at hand. The paralegal should be separated from all aspects of the case.

Confidentiality

Just as the attorney is bound by **confidentiality** regarding **communications** with the client, so is the paralegal/secretary. Confidentiality also applies to **work product** of the attorney. Such things as information about a case from research by the attorney or paralegal or strategies for proceeding with a case are work product.

Solicitation

Although attorneys can **advertise** and do so with mailings that are part of an overall advertising/marketing plan to prospective clients, **individual solicitation** of clients is still prohibited. The paralegal/secretary should be careful to initiate the individual solicitation of clients.

Commingling

Any monies held for a client should never be **commingled** with the attorney's personal funds. Such activities are considered the most unethical of all. Attorneys are required to establish a separate **client trust account** for the separation of funds.

A Summary Proceeding (16.2) – Legal Ethics

Unauthorized practice of law

- Giving legal advice on merits of an issue
- Appearing in court on behalf of client
- Drafting of legal documents
- Establishing a legal relationship or fees

Conflict of Interest

- Paralegal with privy to information adverse to another party due to prior relationship
- Establish Chinese wall

Confidentiality

- Applies to communications with client and attorney work product

Solicitation

- Permits advertising but prohibits individual solicitation

Commingling

- Separation of clients' funds from personal funds of attorney; use of client trust account

The Law Library

Even if, or better yet, when, electronic information replaces libraries consisting of shelf after shelf of books, the basic knowledge of legal research material will still be necessary for the paralegal.

Primary Sources of Law

Primary sources of law are the law. Primary sources of law are **federal** and **state constitutions, statutes/codes** and **regulations, court decisions** and **common law cases, municipal ordinances,** and **court rules.**

The Reporter System

Each state, the U.S. Supreme Court, and the federal court system have an **official reporter** system. A **reporter** is one approved by the court for producing the official case opinions of that court. There is also a **national reporter system** composed of seven **regional reporters** for state cases.

Codes

Codes are issued by order of the legislature that enacts the bills, which become **statutes.** Some codes are annotated, which means each section of the code has footnotes citing cases that refer to that section of the code. Federal statutes are found in the **United States Code** or the **United States Code Annotated.**

Regulatory Law

Federal regulations are chronologically published in the **Federal Register.** They are published by topic in the **Code of Federal Regulations.**

Court Rules

Federal and state courts each have published rules to govern the litigation process. The federal courts use the **Federal Rules of Civil Procedure** and the **Federal Rules of Criminal Procedure.**

Secondary Sources of Law

Secondary sources of law are writings that attempt to explain the law. Secondary sources include **law reviews** and **law journals, legal dictionaries** and **encyclopedias,** and **restatements.**

Law Reviews and Journals

Law schools offer membership to the **Law Review** to students who rank in the upper portions of their class. These students write articles and review articles submitted by attorneys and professors for inclusion in a **Law Review** or **Law Journal.**

Dictionaries and Encyclopedias

Legal dictionaries and **encyclopedias** are self-explanatory. They cannot be all-encompassing as to terms or topics of law due to the sheer volume of law in our nation. They are excellent starting points for researching the law. A well known legal dictionary is **Black's Law Dictionary.** Two well-known encyclopedias are **Corpus Juris Secundum** and **American Jurisprudence 2nd.**

Restatements

Restatements were created to give uniformity across the states to certain areas of law, mostly the common law topics of torts, property, and contracts. Although much more precise than legal encyclopedias, they are still secondary sources of law.

Finding Tools

Without finding tools there would be no possible way to conduct research. Finding tools consist of indexes, digests, and citators.

Indexes

An **index** for a **code** is quite similar to an index for any other book. It is an alphabetical listing of terms at the end of the code, usually a separate volume or two, which refers you to the appropriate code section covering the topic. To use an index you must be well versed in topics of law and the specific terminology of that topic.

Digests

Digests are the saving grace to finding any case in point to the legal issue you are researching. A digest divides **topics** of law alphabetically and then numbers each topic. Within each topic are subtopics, which have a **keynote number.** Once you find the keynote number, you proceed to that section of the digest and find a listing and brief discussion of the precedent that addresses your issue. Digests exist for state reporters, federal reporters, regional reporters, and Supreme Court reporters.

Example 16.3:

Assume you are researching negligence. **Negligence** could be topic 304 in your regional reporter. Under topic 323 would be subtopics of negligence, which could be **keynote 16** for the concept of duty. Under keynote 16 there could be further subtopics, such as forseeability, which is **subtopic (3).** You would then proceed to **keynote 16(3)** under topic 323 in the appropriate volume of the digest and read the annotations of the issue you are researching. The annotation will cite the case you must research as possible precedent.

Citators

Once the precedent has been found, the paralegal must make sure the case is still valid precedent. This is where **citators** come in. Shepard's citations are the most well known. In a citatory, each reporter volume is listed numerically by volume number and page number to correspond with the case citation. Once you find your case you simply review all other subsequent cases that have cited your case to see what effect the subsequent case has on your case. The subsequent case could **follow, modify,** or **overrule** your case. Shepard's is so well known that attorneys ask if you have "Shepardized" the case instead of "have you updated the case?"

Citations

With such an enormous amount of resources available in law, the problem of referring to these sources has been solved by a uniform system of **citations.** Citations are simply abbreviations or acronyms of the full name of the reporter or code with volume and page number of the case or code section. Southwestern Reporter 3rd would be **S.W.3d** and United States Code Annotated would be **U.S.C.A.** A case in S.W.3d could be

155 S.W.3d 610. The paralegal will soon learn there is more than one reporter for most cases and **parallel citation** must be learned. Words such as **dismissed** becomes **D** and **certiorari denied** becomes **cert den.** A course on legal research and writing will provide the dozens of citations a paralegal must know.

The Case Brief

Once you have found your case in point that will be cited as precedent, the paralegal should **brief the case.** Briefing a case is the elementary step in legal writing. The more common method of analyzing and briefing a case is referred to as the **IRAC** method. After you have analyzed the caption of the case for its jurisdiction, the year of the case for its recent application, and the facts of the case to confirm it being in point, you are ready to discuss the Issues, the Rule of law that applies to the respective issue, the Application of the rule to the respective issue, and your Conclusions.

A Summary Proceeding (16.3) – The Law Library

- Primary sources of law
  - State and federal constitutions
  - State and federal statutes – reduced to codes, which may be annotated
  - Case law – reduced to reporters – state, federal, regional, and Supreme Court reporter systems
  - Regulations – found chronologically in Federal Register and topically in Code of Federal
- Regulations
  - Court Rules – established by each system of courts
- Secondary Sources of law – used to explain law
  - Law Reviews and Journals – published by law schools
  - Legal dictionaries and encyclopedia – alphabetical definitions and discussions of general law
  - Restatements – created for uniformity of common law
- Finding Tools
  - Index – alphabetized topics of law for codes
  - Digests – divisions of law by topics and keynote
  - Citators – used to update law to current case
- Citations
  - Uniform system of abbreviations and acronyms to identify sources of law

Technology

Imagine, if you can, that the year is 1976. The solo practitioner has a two-room office, one for him or herself and one for the secretary in the outer waiting area. The attorney is surrounded by bookshelves with the state code, the state reporter, the state digest, and several formbooks for the general practice of law. There might be a few select volumes of a legal dictionary governing the specific fields of law in which the attorney concentrates. Any additional research will require a stop by the county law library. Today's decision is whether to buy or lease a copy machine or continue to use the copy shop downstairs in the office building.

The secretary is pleased that she has a new electric, self-correcting typewriter, but is trying diligently to convince the attorney to purchase the copy machine so she can completely stop using carbon paper for copies. Rush documents have to rely on a company that just started advertising overnight delivery services.

The larger law firm has a copy machine and a new device called a "word processor." Each attorney can dictate into a small, hand-held tape recorder and drop the tape off at the word processing unit, which used to be the stenographic pool or secretarial pool. Soon the attorney will be able to dictate over the telephone and dispose of the tapes and tape recorder entirely. Fax machines are still 5 to 7 years away. Personal computers are 10 years away and the Internet is 20 years in the future.

Now, fast-forward some 30 years to approximately 2006.

The solo practitioner must decide whether his desktop computer has enough memory and disk space to accommodate two new **specialty programs** for **office management and case-litigation management,** something the larger law firms have had for a few years. The subscription to the **hourly fee legal research site** via the **Internet** is renewing this month, and a competing sales representative is scheduled for this afternoon. **Computer-Assisted Legal Research (CALR)** saves enormous amounts of time and the expense of a full library. Generic legal documents and even documents tailored to each state's law can be purchased at minimal cost per document online. The final decision is whether or not to replace the all-in-one color printer/copier/fax and scanning system with a newer, faster system.

Everything in the law office has changed and will continue to change. It is no longer enough that a paralegal/secretary simply be proficient at reading, writing, and typing; they must also be technologically efficient with software programs and Internet research.

A Summary Proceeding (16.4) – Technology

- Specialty software programs
    - Office management systems
    - Case management systems
    - Litigation management systems
- Computer-Assisted Legal Research – CALR via the Internet
- Customized legal documents via the Internet

Conclusions of Law

A law office is an office of professionals. Lawyers, paralegals, and legal secretaries are all specifically trained and either licensed or professionally certified. The work can be intense and the workload can be heavy. Deadlines occur not only daily, but sometimes hourly; however, the rewards, and not just financial ones, are available.

Exercises – Chapter 16

Matching/Word Association Match the term in the left column with the best corresponding term in the right column.

_____	1.	general counsel	A.	commingling
_____	2.	Chinese wall	B.	case brief
_____	3.	solicitation	C.	conflict of interest
_____	4.	client trust account	D.	digest
_____	5.	legal encyclopedia	E.	reporter
_____	6.	Law Review	F.	advertisements
_____	7.	Restatements	G.	unauthorized practice of law
_____	8.	Shepard's	H.	common law
_____	9.	primary source	I.	S.W.3d
_____	10.	work product	J.	in-house counsel
_____	11.	finding tool	K.	confidential
_____	12.	citation	L.	citatory
_____	13.	IRAC	M.	Corpus Juris Secundum
_____	14.	document drafting	N.	statutes
_____	15.	codes	O.	law school publication

List/Fill in the Blank List four areas of unauthorized practice of law for a paralegal:

1. ______________________________

2. ______________________________

3. ______________________________

4. ______________________________

List two areas of concern regarding confidentiality:

1. ______________________________

2. ______________________________

List three types of specialty legal software:

1. ______________________________

2. ______________________________

3. ______________________________

List three types of partners in a law firm:

1. ______________________________

2. ______________________________

3. ______________________________

List two specific sets of court rules:

1. ______________________________

2. ______________________________

Case Analysis

The following is a reprint of a case from the State of Arkansas. It involves college cheating and primarily relates to Administrative Law. However, the case also includes legal terms from many other areas of law. To stress the importance of identifying legal terms and the context in which they are used, the student should closely read the case. Exercises identifying all legal terms within the case and the field of law from which they come follow the case. Additional exercises involving concepts of law that have been provided in this text are also included.

LYON COLLEGE v. Melissa GRAY

999 S.W.2nd 213, 67 Ark. App. 323

Court of Appeals of Arkansas

Division II

Opinion Delivered September 29, 1999

1. **Motions – directed verdict – appellate review.** – A directed verdict is a challenge to the sufficiency of the evidence; on appeal the appellate court views the evidence in a light most favorable to the appellee.

2. **Colleges & universities – disciplinary proceedings – administration of.** – An educational institution, particularly a private one, must be given some discretion in the administration of its disciplinary proceedings; there is a general policy against interference by the courts in matters best left to the school.

3. **Colleges & Universities – academic decisions – judicial review of.** – The avenue for judicial review of the substance of academic decisions is narrow; a court has no power to interfere in the exercise of a state regulated university's discretion in the promulgation and implementation of disciplinary measures unless it is shown by clear and convincing evidence that the university abused its discretion; abuse of discretion may occur if the university fails to follow its own procedural guidelines or if its disciplinary decision is not based upon substantial evidence.

4. **Colleges & universities – conflicting evidence – question for university's disciplinary committee.** – Evidence in conflict presents a question of fact to be decided by the university's disciplinary committee.

5. **Colleges & universities – witness credibility – honor council's determination.** – Where review by the circuit court should have been confined to whether appellant's decision to sanction appellee was supported by substantial evidence, and the evidence before the council was conflicting and a matter of credibility determination, the honor council's decision to believe a roommate's testimony gave it substantial evidence to find appellee guilty of an honor code violation.

6. **Appeal and error – directed verdict should have been granted for appellant – jury's verdict reversed and dismissed.** Where there was no clear and convincing evidence of an abuse of discretion by appellant, once it was shown that appellant followed its own procedural guidelines and based its disciplinary decision on substantial evidence, judicial review of appellant's actions should have ceased, and the case should not have gone to the jury; a directed verdict should have been granted in favor of appellant; the jury's verdict was reversed and dismissed; appellee's attorney fee award was also reversed and dismissed.

Appeal from Independence Circuit Court; John Dan Kemp, Judge; reversed and dismissed.

Hughes & Luce, L.L.P., by Jim Hunter Birch, for appellant

Robert M. Abney, P.A., for appellee

Judith Rogers, Judge.

This appeal is brought from jury verdict awarding appellee Melissa Gray $20,644 on her breach of contract claim against appellant Lyon College. In 1995, while appellee was a student at Lyon, she was accused by the college's Honor Council of using improper information to prepare for a physics test. The council founder her guilty, and her conviction was upheld on appeal to the president of the college. As a result, she was suspended from the school for the remainder of the 1995-1996 academic year, given an "F" in her physics course, and given a "W" in her other courses. In 1996, she filed suit against the college, which resulted in the aforementioned jury verdict. Appellant contends on appeal that the trial court should have granted a directed verdict in its favor. We agree and reverse and dismiss the case.

Appellant is a private Presbyterian affiliated college located in Batesville. In 1995, it employed an Honor System which was set out in the student handbook. The system consisted of an Honor Code, an Honor Pledge, and the procedures for administering and enforcing the system. The Honor Code provided, among other things, that "we understand honor to include ... a commitment to abstain from all forms of cheating and plagiarism." In the Honor Pledge, students promised, among other things, to abstain from all fraud in academic work. The administering body of the system was the Honor Council, composed of twelve students. The council's duties included investigation of reports of possible Honor Code violations, conducting trials of those charged with violations, and imposing a penalty if an accused were found guilty. An accused was provided with written notice of an allegation of a code violation; written notification of actual charges; a student adviser as an assistant and advocate; a closed, recorded hearing; the opportunity to present witnesses at the hearing and to cross-examine other witnesses; an the right to appeal the council's decision to the president of the college.

On October 18, 1995, appellee was notified by the Honor Council that an investigation had begun "surrounding the possibility of an honor violation in your Physics class." Ten days later, she was informed that a trial would be conducted and that she was being charged with using "inappropriate information in preparation for the test administered on October 9 & 10." The dates referred to corresponded with a test given by physics professor Dr. John Sample. Dr. Sample gave his students the option of taking the exam, which was the second of the year, on either day. Appellee took the test on October 10 and scored 100. In her prior exam, she had scored a 29, with a 21 on the corresponding take-home test.

In studying for her October 10 exam, appellee looked at a copy of one of Professor Sample's exam for the previous year. As it turned out, the October 10 test and the previous year's test were identical. Within days after the test was taken the Honor council began an investigation. Although the use of the old test did not, in and of itself, constitute a code violation, the council explored the possibility that certain students had procured a copy of the old test after having received information that it and the current year's test were the same.

During appellee's trial before the Honor Council, she admitted that she had studied from the old exam. However, she denied any prior knowledge of the content of the test she took on October 10. Her testimony was contradicted by her roommate and sorority sister, Julie Roach. Roach testified that, on the evening of October 9, appellee informed her that the old test and the upcoming test were going to be the same. Roach saw appellee and appellee's boyfriend, Lynn Monroe, working through the problems on the old test. Further, she testified that, when she told appellee that having prior knowledge about the next day's test was probably cheating, appellee replied that she did not care, that her grades were low in physics, and that she could not afford not to study from the old test.

After the trial, the Council found appellee guilty of a code violation and imposed sanctions. Appellee immediately appealed the decision to Jon Griffith, President of the college. In her letter to him she stated that she had always maintained her innocence in the case and the trial had come down to "the accuser's word against my own." Griffith reviewed the evidence before the council and some additional evidence, including Dr. Sample's grade sheet which reflected that, on the corresponding take-home portion of the October 10 exam, appellee had scored a 51. Following his review, Griffith upheld the sanctions imposed by the council. Appellee withdrew from school, whereupon she lost approximately $15,000 in financial aid, the receipt of which had been dependent upon her academic performance. She subsequently enrolled at UA-Fayetteville.

On May 13, 1996, appellee filed the lawsuit that is the subject of this case. She alleged that the Honor System contained in her student handbook constituted a contract between herself and the college and that the college, by its unwarranted suspension, of her breached the contract. At trial, appellee testified, as she had before the Honor Council, that she was innocent of any misconduct. Upon being cross-examined, she admitted that the college had followed its procedures in its investigation and conduct of the trial. Further, she acknowledged that the Council had been presented with two different versions of what happened on the evening of October 9–hers and Julie Roach's – and that the Council was "pretty much" faced with the decision of which of them was telling the truth. Additionally, she admitted that it would constitute an Honor Code violation if a person studied for a test by using knowledge obtained from someone else regarding the content of the test. Appellee's testimony regarding her lack of culpability was corroborated by Lynn Monroe (who was also convicted of a code violation). However, John Griffith testified that he had not found appellee's story believable.

At the close of the appellee's case, appellant moved for a directed verdict, *inter alia*, on the grounds that, because the college had fully complied with it Honor System procedures and had based its decision on the credibility of the witnesses, the court system should not interfere with the college's decision. The trial judge took the matter under advisement and directed appellant to proceed with its case. At the close of all of the evidence, appellant renewed its motion for a directed verdict. The trial judge reserved a ruling but submitted the case to the jury. The jury returned with a general verdict in favor of appellee. Appellant filed a motion for judgment notwithstanding verdict based upon its earlier directed verdict arguments. The court did not act on the motion, and it was deemed denied after thirty days. This appeal followed.

A directed verdict is a challenge to the sufficiency of the evidence. *Sparks Regional Medical Ctr. v. Smith*, 63 Ark. App. 131, 976 S.W. 2nd 396 (1998). On appeal, we view the evidence in a light most favorable to the appellee. *Id.*

Virtually all courts recognize that an educational institution, particularly a private one, must be given some discretion in the administration of its disciplinary proceedings. *Slaughter v. Brigham Young Univ.*, 514 F. 2d 622 (10th Cir.) *cert. denied*, 423 U.S. 898 (1975); *Clayton v. Trustees of Princeton Univ.*, 608 F. Supp. 413 (D.N.J. 1985); *Blaine v. Savannah County Day School*, 228 Ga. App.224, 491 S.E. 2d 446 (1997); *Napolitano v. Trustees of Princeton Univ.*, 186 N.J. Super. 548, 453 A.2d 263 (1982). See also, *Annot., Breach-School Dismissal* 47 A.L.R. 5th 1 (1997). Likewise in Arkansas, we are reluctant to allow the judiciary to encroach upon the disciplinary proceedings of an education institution. In *Henderson State Univ. v. Spadoni*, 41 Ark. App 33, 848 S.W.2d 951 (1993), this court recognized there is a general policy against interference by the courts in matters best left to school authorities. In *Smith v. Denton*, 320 Ark. App. 253, 895 S.W.2d 550 (1995), our supreme court stated that "[t]he avenue for judicial review of the substance of academic decisions is narrow" and that a court "has no power to interfere in the exercise of a state regulated university's discretion in the promulgation and implementation of disciplinary measures unless it is shown by clear and convincing evidence that the university abused its discretion." Abuse of discretion may occur if the university fails to follow its own procedural guidelines or if its disciplinary decision is not based upon substantial evidence. *Slaughter v. Brigham Young Univ., supra; Napolitano v. Trustees of Princeton Univ., supra.*

Because we have no allegations of a procedural due process violation in this case, the circuit court review should have been confined to whether appellant's decision to sanction appellee was supported by substantial evidence. The evidence before the Honor Council, by appellee's own admission, was conflicting and a matter of a credibility determination. Despite appellee's testimony that she was innocent of any wrongdoing, Julie Roach provided evidence that appellee had prior knowledge of the content of the October 10 test. If the Council believed Miss Roach's testimony, as it apparently did, then it had substantial evidence to find appellee guilty of an Honor Code violation. Evidence in conflict presents a question of fact to be decided by the university's disciplinary committee. *Henderson State Univ. v. Spadoni, supra.*

Based on the forgoing, we hold that a directed verdict should have been granted in favor of the appellant. Even when the facts are viewed in a light most favorable to the appellee, there was no clear and convincing evidence of an abuse of discretion by appellant. Once it was shown that appellant followed its own procedural guidelines and based its disciplinary decision on substantial evidence, judicial review of appellant's actions should have ceased, and the case should not have gone to the jury. The jury's verdict is therefore reversed and dismissed. Consequently the appellee's attorney fee award is also reversed and dismissed.

Meads and Roaf, JJ., agree.

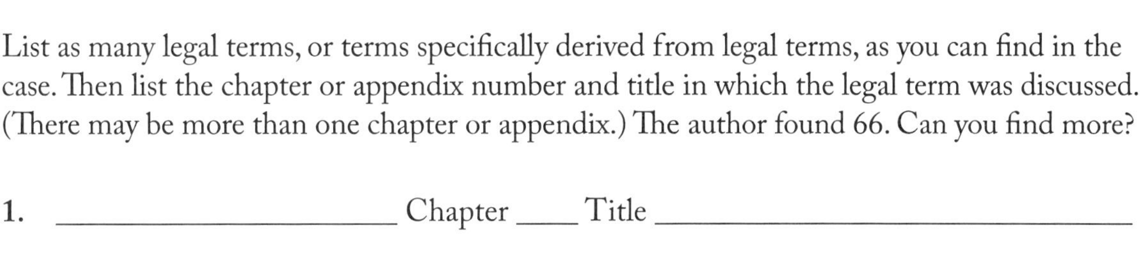

Exercises – Case Analysis

List as many legal terms, or terms specifically derived from legal terms, as you can find in the case. Then list the chapter or appendix number and title in which the legal term was discussed. (There may be more than one chapter or appendix.) The author found 66. Can you find more?

1. ____________________ Chapter ____ Title ____________________________

2. ____________________ Chapter ____ Title ____________________________

3. ____________________ Chapter ____ Title ____________________________

4. ____________________ Chapter ____ Title ____________________________

5. ____________________ Chapter ____ Title ____________________________

6. ____________________ Chapter ____ Title ____________________________

7. ____________________ Chapter ____ Title ____________________________

8. ____________________ Chapter ____ Title ____________________________

9. ____________________ Chapter ____ Title ____________________________

10. ____________________ Chapter ____ Title ____________________________

11. ____________________ Chapter ____ Title ____________________________

12. ____________________ Chapter ____ Title ____________________________

13. ____________________ Chapter ____ Title ____________________________

14. ____________________ Chapter ____ Title ____________________________

15. ____________________ Chapter ____ Title ____________________________

Exercises – Case Analysis (Continued)

16. ______________________ Chapter ___ Title ______________________________

17. ______________________ Chapter ___ Title ______________________________

18. ______________________ Chapter ___ Title ______________________________

19. ______________________ Chapter ___ Title ______________________________

20. ______________________ Chapter ___ Title ______________________________

21. ______________________ Chapter ___ Title ______________________________

22. ______________________ Chapter ___ Title ______________________________

23. ______________________ Chapter ___ Title ______________________________

24. ______________________ Chapter ___ Title ______________________________

25. ______________________ Chapter ___ Title ______________________________

26. ______________________ Chapter ___ Title ______________________________

27. ______________________ Chapter ___ Title ______________________________

28. ______________________ Chapter ___ Title ______________________________

29. ______________________ Chapter ___ Title ______________________________

30. ______________________ Chapter ___ Title ______________________________

31. ______________________ Chapter ___ Title ______________________________

32. ______________________ Chapter ___ Title ______________________________

Exercises – Case Analysis (Continued)

33. ________________________ Chapter ____ Title __________________________________

34. ________________________ Chapter ____ Title __________________________________

35. ________________________ Chapter ____ Title __________________________________

36. ________________________ Chapter ____ Title __________________________________

37. ________________________ Chapter ____ Title __________________________________

38. ________________________ Chapter ____ Title __________________________________

39. ________________________ Chapter ____ Title __________________________________

40. ________________________ Chapter ____ Title __________________________________

41. ________________________ Chapter ____ Title __________________________________

42. ________________________ Chapter ____ Title __________________________________

43. ________________________ Chapter ____ Title __________________________________

44. ________________________ Chapter ____ Title __________________________________

45. ________________________ Chapter ____ Title __________________________________

46. ________________________ Chapter ____ Title __________________________________

47. ________________________ Chapter ____ Title __________________________________

48. ________________________ Chapter ____ Title __________________________________

49. ________________________ Chapter ____ Title __________________________________

Exercises – Case Analysis (Continued)

50. ______________________ Chapter ____ Title ______________________________

51. ______________________ Chapter ____ Title ______________________________

52. ______________________ Chapter ____ Title ______________________________

53. ______________________ Chapter ____ Title ______________________________

54. ______________________ Chapter ____ Title ______________________________

55. ______________________ Chapter ____ Title ______________________________

56. ______________________ Chapter ____ Title ______________________________

57. ______________________ Chapter ____ Title ______________________________

58. ______________________ Chapter ____ Title ______________________________

59. ______________________ Chapter ____ Title ______________________________

60. ______________________ Chapter ____ Title ______________________________

61. ______________________ Chapter ____ Title ______________________________

62. ______________________ Chapter ____ Title ______________________________

63. ______________________ Chapter ____ Title ______________________________

64. ______________________ Chapter ____ Title ______________________________

65. ______________________ Chapter ____ Title ______________________________

66. ______________________ Chapter ____ Title ______________________________

Exercises – Case Analysis (Continued)

Find seven (7) legal concepts in the case that are not specifically named.

1. ______________________________

2. ______________________________

3. ______________________________

4. ______________________________

5. ______________________________

6. ______________________________

7. ______________________________

Mid-Term Practice Exam – Chapters 1–8

True-False Correction Determine if the statement is true or false; if false, insert the correct term in the blank below the question.

_____ 1. In civil cases defendants are found **guilty**.

____

_____ 2. A **prosecutor** represents the government and society.

____

_____ 3. The law enforcement official in a courtroom is a **master**.

____

_____ 4. A plaintiff's decision to withdraw a lawsuit is a **recusal**.

____

_____ 5. A case in controversy is **justicable**.

____

_____ 6. An **allegation** is the document heading for a pleading.

____

_____ 7. A prayer for relief seeking monetary damages is an **allegation**.

____

_____ 8. Leading questions can be used on **direct** examination.

____

_____ 9. When a judge agrees with an objection, he/she **overrules** the objections.

____

_____ 10. An **appellant** is sometimes called a defendant in error.

____

True-False Correction (continued)

_____ 11. The stage of the criminal process where the defendant enters a plea is the **indictment.**

____

_____ 12. A suspect who was elsewhere at the time of a crime has a **justification**.

____

_____ 13. To testify without fear of prosecution is to testify with **information**.

____

_____ 14. A **conspiracy** is a crime that failed.

____

_____ 15. Insanity is generally an **affirmative defense**.

____

_____ 16. Transferring a forged document for financial gain is **pilferage**.

____

_____ 17. Contract damages determined in advance are called **consequential** damages.

____

_____ 18. Food, clothing, and shelter for minors are **necessaries.**

____

_____ 19. Reducing damages due to a breach of contract is called **reformation.**

____

_____ 20. The property that benefits from an easement is the **servient** tenement.

____

True-False Correction (continued)

_____ 21. A legal description by lots and blocks is a **plat description**.

____

_____ 22. A remainder is a **present** interest in real estate.

____

_____ 23. Liability of two torfeasors is considered **vicarious** liability.

____

_____ 24. Duty under negligence concepts is determined by **forseeability**.

____

_____ 25. Acting despite knowledge of an obvious danger is **affirmative fraud**.

____

Proceed to next page

Definitions Insert the correct legal term in the blank above the definition.

1. ______________________________

A neutral third party who assists the parties in resolving a dispute

2. ______________________________

The penalty for violation of a judge's rules

3. ______________________________

The type of law made by legislatures

4. ______________________________

The court which hears legal issues of minors

5. ______________________________

A statement that one swears to tell the truth

6. ______________________________

The relocation of a trial to provide for fairness

7. ______________________________

A formal request of a court to appear and testify

8. ______________________________

Evidence that requires one to draw an inference

9. ______________________________

The act of a jury refusing to consider evidence and deciding a case on other reasons

10. ______________________________

A jury that is deadlocked and cannot reach a decision

11. ______________________________

A reasonable belief, along with reliable information, that a crime has been committed

Definitions (continued)

12. ______________________________

Two prison sentences that run at the same time

13. ______________________________

The term for representing ones self in a trial

14. ______________________________

Breaking and entering a dwelling at night to commit a felony therein

15. ______________________________

Conduct that gives rise to imminent fear of bodily harm

16. ______________________________

The theft of property by one in possession or custody of the property

17. ______________________________

The relationship between two parties to a contract

18. ______________________________

A contract clause that may allow for consequential damages due to untimely performance

19. ______________________________

A type of contract in which delegation of duties is generally not allowed

20. ______________________________

An item of personal property attached to land that materially affects the value of land

21. ______________________________

A lease tenancy that is month to month

22. ______________________________

The party who grants a security interest in real estate as collateral for a loan

Definitions (continued)

23. ______________________________

The person who commits a tort

24. ______________________________

"The thing speaks for itself"

25. ______________________________

The common law concept preventing lawsuits against a government

Proceed to next page

Matching/Word Association Match the term in the left column with the best corresponding term/phrase in the right column.

_____	1.	specialized federal court	A.	written argument on appeal
_____	2.	equitable remedy	B.	initial pleading in equity
_____	3.	standing	C.	constitutional crime
_____	4.	petition	D.	stop and frisk
_____	5.	garnishment	E.	supreme court judge
_____	6.	confidential	F.	tenancy at sufferance
_____	7.	burden of proof	G.	supreme law of the land
_____	8.	capital punishment	H.	printed defamation
_____	9.	misdemeanants	I.	illegal confinement
_____	10.	mens rea	J.	U.S. Tax Court
_____	11.	pornography	K.	aggrieved party
_____	12.	eviction	L.	death penalty
_____	13.	holdover tenant	M.	criminal knowledge
_____	14.	libel	N.	by a preponderance of the evidence
_____	15.	respondeat superior	O.	injunction
_____	16.	option contract	P.	criminal intent
_____	17.	scienter	Q.	master-servant
_____	18.	treason	R.	execution on wages
_____	19.	Terry stop	S.	unlawful detainer
_____	20.	habeas corpus	T.	obscenity
_____	21.	brief	U.	jurisdiction over the matter
_____	22.	ex parte	V.	lapse
_____	23.	in rem	W.	work product
_____	24.	justice	X.	county jail incarceration
_____	25.	U.S. Constitution	Y.	without an adversary

Proceed to next page

List/Fill in the Blank List the status of three parties who may be the plaintiff in a premises liability suit:

1. ____

2. ____

3. ____

List three types of recording statutes for real estate:

4. ____

5. ____

6. ____

List four equitable remedies for a breach of contract:

7. ____

8. ____

9. ____

10. ____

List the four mental states of culpability under the Model Penal Code:

11. ____

12. ____

13. ____

14. ____

List four pleas a criminal defendant may enter:

15. ______________________________

16. ______________________________

17. ______________________________

18. ______________________________

List the two adversaries in an equitable action:

19. ______________________________

20. ______________________________

List three types of clerks in the court system:

21. ______________________________

22. ______________________________

23. ______________________________

List two challenges to a juror:

24. ______________________________

25. ______________________________

Practice Final Exam – Chapters 1–16

True-False Correction Determine if the statement is true or false; if false, insert the proper term in the blank below the question for the term in bold to make the statement true.

_____ 1. Administrative law consists of **statutes**.

____

_____ 2. **Substantive** law includes notice and opportunity to be heard.

____

_____ 3. A small claims court has **amount in controversy** jurisdiction.

____

_____ 4. Commerce within one state is considered **interstate** commerce.

____

_____ 5. The President is elected by **popular vote**.

____

_____ 6. The branch of government responsible for enacting laws is the **judiciary**.

____

_____ 7. Eminent domain requires a payment of **just compensation**.

____

_____ 8. A reply is a responsive pleading to a **counterclaim**.

____

_____ 9. A more detailed statement of a complaint is a **writ**.

____

_____ 10. A party who files a **petition** is the moving party.

____

True-False Correction (continued)

_____ 11. Property not found in a decedents' estate or with the heir has adeemed by **satisfaction.**

____

_____ 12. A person caring for the day to day needs of a minor is the guardian of the **person**.

____

_____ 13. A legacy paid from a particular fund is a **specific** legacy.

____

_____ 14. A trustee is **appointed** under the terms of a will.

____

_____ 15. Specific performance is a **monetary damage** remedy.

____

_____ 16. A **rebuttal** occurs when the plaintiff calls witnesses to counter a defendant's case.

____

_____ 17. Citizens receive a **writ** to appear for jury duty.

____

_____ 18. A marriage ceremony is considered **consummation** of a marriage.

____

_____ 19. State regulation of marriage includes **licensure**.

____

_____ 20. A contract to bear a child for another is a **covenant** contract.

____

True-False Correction (continued)

_____ 21. Removing a minor's legal limitations is **child support**.

____

_____ 22. Evidence showing the innocence of a criminal defendant is considered **incompetent.**

____

_____ 23. To assemble a grand jury is said to **seat** a grand jury.

____

_____ 24. Separate charges for multiple crimes are called **counts.**

____

_____ 25. The Uniform Commercial Code is divided into **sections**.

____

_____ 26. Amounts still due on a note after sale of collateral are called a **default.**

____

_____ 27. A check drawn on a bank's checking account is called a **certified check**.

____

_____ 28. Delivery of goods under the UCC occurs at the **buyer's** place of business.

____

_____ 29. Having more than two spouses is considered **bigamy**.

____

_____ 30. An accessory after the fact could be charged with **aiding and abetting**.

____

True-False Correction (continued)

_____ 31. Sexual intercourse with a person under the age of consent is **rape**.

_____ 32. A corporation which complies with all statutory laws is a **de facto** corporation.

_____ 33. A financial disclosure document for sale of stock is a **proxy**.

_____ 34. The document evidencing a corporate officer's authority to act is a **security**.

_____ 35. Bondholders of a corporation receive **dividends** as earnings.

_____ 36. A party who lacks capacity to contract due to age is a **minor**.

_____ 37. The person who receives an offer is the **offeror**.

_____ 38. Taking back an offer is called **rejection**.

_____ 39. An **express** agency can be stated orally or in writing.

_____ 40. Entrusting goods to another for the sale of the goods is **reimbursement**.

True-False Correction (continued)

_____ 41. Authority necessary to carry out express authority of an agent is **apparent** authority.

_____

_____ 42. A corporation which is owned by another corporation is a **parent** corporation.

_____

_____ 43. A person who dies without a will is said to die **testate.**

_____

_____ 44. Default of payment on a mortgage note can result in **foreclosure**.

_____

_____ 45. A compilation of documents to reflect chain of title to land is a **land grant**.

_____

_____ 46. Intangible property from thought is **intellectual** property.

_____

_____ 47. Violation of a statute or ordinance is **gross negligence**.

_____

_____ 48. A solvent tortfeasor who seeks to recover from insolvent torfeasors is seeking **conversion**.

_____

_____ 49. Communication of a slanderous comment to a third party is **publication**.

_____

_____ 50. A customer who browses through a store is a **licensee.**

_____

Proceed to next page

Definitions Insert the correct term in the blank above the definition.

1. ______________________________

A type of legislature with only one chamber

2. ______________________________

The reason for which a government takes property under eminent domain

3. ______________________________

The doctrine of applying the Bill of Rights to the states through the 14th Amendment

4. ______________________________

The doctrine that makes yelling "fire" in a crowded theater unprotected speech

5. ______________________________

An attorney's fee calculated as a percentage of an award

6. ______________________________

The process of disclosing facts of your party to the adverse party in litigation

7. ______________________________

A proceeding without another party or adversary

8. ______________________________

The person within a court who prepares the transcript

9. ______________________________

The type of jurisdiction where two courts may hear the case

10. ______________________________

A secondary source of law containing definitions of legal terms

11. ______________________________

An heir who has been forgotten and omitted from a will

Definitions (continued)

12. ______________________________________

The primary residence that a surviving spouse may keep

13. ______________________________________

The interest possessed by a surviving wife in the separate property of the husband

14. ______________________________________

The legal relationship of a brother and a sister

15. ______________________________________

A trial with the judge as a trier of fact

16. ______________________________________

The term for a defendant that cannot pay the damages awarded a plaintiff

17. ______________________________________

The legal concept for a judge accepting a fact to be true without evidence

18. ______________________________________

The primary rule for determining child custody

19. ______________________________________

A joint tenancy with right of survivorship between husband and wife

20. ______________________________________

The claim for damages for loss of sexual ability

21. ______________________________________

The concept of failing to make child support payments

22. ______________________________________

A custodial detention by law enforcement

Definitions (continued)

23. ______________________________

An entry with the court of the prosecutor's decision not to proceed further

24. ______________________________

The process of completely erasing the criminal proceedings of a juvenile

25. ______________________________

The enclosed grounds and structures around a dwelling

26. ______________________________

The Latin term for a type of crime that violates a regulation

27. ______________________________

The sale of sexual services

28. ______________________________

A signature of a payee on a negotiable instrument

29. ______________________________

The party who orders a draft to be paid

30. ______________________________

A negotiable instrument containing a promise to pay by a bank

31. ______________________________

The term for all states' securities laws

32. ______________________________

A business organization formed for the economic benefit of the members

33. ______________________________

A document filed to terminate the existence of a corporation

Definitions (continued)

34. ______________________________

A business formed solely for the obtaining of financing

35. ______________________________

A contract that is yet to be performed

36. ______________________________

A contract with language that relieves a party from liability of their wrongful actions

37. ______________________________

Contract consideration derived from a waiver of a right

38. ______________________________

A document creating an agency which survives the disability of the principal

39. ______________________________

An agency created by a principal after the agent acts on behalf of the principal

40. ______________________________

Information known by an agent which is presumed to be known by the principal

41. ______________________________

The notice to terminate a tenancy at will

42. ______________________________

An index of real estate recordings that list transactions by parcel of land

43. ______________________________

The legal action against one who files a baseless criminal action which results in acquittal

44. ______________________________

Examples of this tort concept would be swimming pools and trampolines

Definitions (continued)

45. ______________________________

The legal concept for intentionally and wrongfully confining a person

46. ______________________________

A false oral statement injuring another's reputation

47. ______________________________

A general partnership for a single business activity

48. ______________________________

A negotiable instrument honored in advance by a bank

49. ______________________________

The introductory paragraph of a will identifying the testator

50. ______________________________

The doctrine allowing a charitable trust to continue if a specific charity ceases to exist

Proceed to next page

Matching/Word Association (1) Match the term in the left column on this page with the best corresponding term or phrase in the right column on this page.

_____	1.	abortion	A.	stare decisis
_____	2.	judicial restraint	B.	not guilty verdict
_____	3.	deposition	C.	constructive trust
_____	4.	general counsel	D.	digest
_____	5.	class action	E.	good faith
_____	6.	secondary source	F.	failure to answer or respond
_____	7.	sunshine laws	G.	testator signature
_____	8.	slayer statute	H.	unlawful burning
_____	9.	relevant	I.	in-house counsel
_____	10.	marriage	J.	jury selection
_____	11.	acquittal	K.	incorporator
_____	12.	arson	L.	legal encyclopedia
_____	13.	merchant	M.	multiple plaintiffs
_____	14.	unjust enrichment	N.	unprotected speech
_____	15.	promoter	O.	oral discovery
_____	16.	robbery	P.	forcible theft
_____	17.	burden of proof	Q.	wedlock
_____	18.	voir dire	R.	removal of judge
_____	19.	testimonium clause	S.	strict constructionist
_____	20.	promulgation	T.	rulemaking
_____	21.	precedent	U.	undue burden test
_____	22.	finding tool	V.	contract implied in law
_____	23.	recusal	W.	probative value of evidence
_____	24.	default judgment	X.	open meetings
_____	25.	obscenity	Y.	rulemaking

Matching/Word Association (1) (continued)

_____ 26. restraint of trade	A.	agent for service of process
_____ 27. frolic and detour	B.	unauthorized practice of law
_____ 28. sine qua non	C.	contract contrary to public policy
_____ 29. adverse possession	D.	first hand knowledge testimony
_____ 30. Secretary of State	E.	easement or license
_____ 31. ultra vires	F.	"as is"
_____ 32. priority creditor	G.	"but for"
_____ 33. possessory lien	H.	court calendar
_____ 34. cohabitation	I.	Chapter 11 Bankruptcy
_____ 35. lay witness	J.	spousal support
_____ 36. healthcare proxy	K.	cloud
_____ 37. document drafting	L.	common law marriage
_____ 38. docket	M.	secured creditor
_____ 39. religion	N.	advance directive
_____ 40. affirmative defense	O.	outside scope of authority
_____ 41. extradition	P.	prescriptive easement
_____ 42. alimony	Q.	assumption of risk
_____ 43. preliminary hearing	R.	bar
_____ 44. warranty disclaimer	S.	substantial factor
_____ 45. debtor in possession	T.	establishment clause
_____ 46. shareholder liability	U.	unauthorized corporate act
_____ 47. servitude	V.	probable cause determination
_____ 48. defect in title	W.	return of criminal to state
_____ 49. legal causation	X.	pierce the corporate veil
_____ 50. estoppel	Y.	garagemens' lien

Proceed to next page

List/Fill in the Blank List four types of endorsements of negotiable instruments

1. ______________________________

2. ______________________________

3. ______________________________

4. ______________________________

List two other legal terms for the term bankrupt

5. ______________________________

6. ______________________________

List three types of partners in a law firm

7. ______________________________

8. ______________________________

9. ______________________________

List the six sources of law

10. ______________________________

11. ______________________________

12. ______________________________

13. ______________________________

14. ______________________________

15. ______________________________

List four types of attorneys' fees

16. ______________________________

17. ______________________________

18. ______________________________

19. ______________________________

List four holdings an appeals court can issue

20. ______________________________

21. ______________________________

22. ______________________________

23. ______________________________

List the two primary elements of a crime

24. ______________________________

25. ______________________________

List three types of evictions

26. ______________________________

27. ______________________________

28. ______________________________

List four types of nuisances

29. ______________________________

30. ______________________________

31. ______________________________

32. ______________________________

List the four elements to form a common law contract

33. ______________________________

34. ______________________________

35. ______________________________

36. ______________________________

List the four elements to prove negligence in order

37. ______________________________

38. ______________________________

39. ______________________________

40. ______________________________

Fully identify the following abbreviations and acronyms

41. A.P.A.: ______________________________

42. C.F.R.: ______________________________

43. F.O.I.A: ______________________________

44. L.L.C.: ______________________________

45. U.P.A: ______________________________

46. U.S.C.A: ______________________________

List one synonym for each of the following terms

47. mutual will: ______________________________

48. forced share: ______________________________

49. living trust: ______________________________

50. legacy: ______________________________

Index

B

C

D

E

F

G

H

I

J

K

L

M

N

Q

T

U

V

W

Z